Mastering MongoDB 4.x
Second Edition

Expert techniques to run high-volume and fault-tolerant
database solutions using MongoDB 4.x

Alex Giamas

BIRMINGHAM - MUMBAI

Mastering MongoDB 4.x
Second Edition

Commissioning Editor: Amey Varangaonkar
Acquisition Editor: Porous Godhaa
Content Development Editor: Ronnel Mathew
Technical Editor: Suwarna Patil
Copy Editor: Safis Editing
Project Coordinator: Namrata Swetta
Proofreader: Safis Editing
Indexer: Rekha Nair
Graphics: Tom Scaria
Production Coordinator: Deepika Naik

First published: November 2017
Second edition: March 2019

Production reference: 1290319

Published by Packt Publishing Ltd.
Livery Place
35 Livery Street
Birmingham
B3 2PB, UK.

ISBN 978-1-78961-787-0

www.packtpub.com

`mapt.io`

Mapt is an online digital library that gives you full access to over 5,000 books and videos, as well as industry leading tools to help you plan your personal development and advance your career. For more information, please visit our website.

Why subscribe?

- Spend less time learning and more time coding with practical eBooks and Videos from over 4,000 industry professionals

- Improve your learning with Skill Plans built especially for you

- Get a free eBook or video every month

- Mapt is fully searchable

- Copy and paste, print, and bookmark content

Packt.com

Did you know that Packt offers eBook versions of every book published, with PDF and ePub files available? You can upgrade to the eBook version at `www.packt.com` and as a print book customer, you are entitled to a discount on the eBook copy. Get in touch with us at `customercare@packtpub.com` for more details.

At `www.packt.com`, you can also read a collection of free technical articles, sign up for a range of free newsletters, and receive exclusive discounts and offers on Packt books and eBooks.

Contributors

About the author

Alex Giamas is a consultant and a hands-on technical architect at the Department for International Trade in the UK Government. His experience spans software architecture and development using NoSQL and big data technologies. For more than 15 years, he has contributed to Fortune 15 companies and has worked as a start-up CTO.

He is the author of *Mastering MongoDB 3.x*, published by *Packt Publishing*, which is based on his use of MongoDB since 2009.

Alex has worked with a wide array of NoSQL and big data technologies, building scalable and highly available distributed software systems in Python, Java, and Ruby. He is a MongoDB Certified Developer, a Cloudera Certified Developer for Apache Hadoop and Data Science Essentials.

Writing a book is harder than I thought, but more rewarding than I could have ever imagined. I would like to thank my wife, Mary, for her love and constant support, day and night, and for being my editor and sounding board, my muse and my anchor in life.

Many thanks to my parents for all the support and the amazing chances they've given me over the years, without which I would never have been who I am today.

About the reviewers

Doug Bierer wrote his first program on a Digital Equipment Corporation PDP-8 in 1971. Since that time, he's written buckets of code in lots of different programming languages, including BASIC, C, Assembler, PL/I, FORTRAN, Prolog, FORTH, Java, PHP, Perl, and Python. He did networking for 10 years. The largest network he worked on was based in Brussels and had 35,000 nodes. Doug is certified in PHP 5.1, 5.3, 5.5, and 7.1, and Zend Framework 1 and 2. He has authored a bunch of books and videos for O'Reilly/Packt Publishing on PHP, security, and MongoDB. His most current authoring project is a book called *Learn MongoDB 4.0*, scheduled to be published by *Packt Publishing* in September 2019. He founded unlikelysource(dot)com in April 2008.

Sumit Sengupta has worked on several RDBMS and NoSQL databases, such as Oracle, SQL Server, Postgres, MongoDB, and Cassandra. A former employee of MongoDB, he has designed, architected, and managed many distributed and big data solutions, both on-premise and on AWS and Azure. Currently, he works on the Azure Data and AI Platform for Microsoft, helping partners to create innovative solutions based on data.

Packt is searching for authors like you

If you're interested in becoming an author for Packt, please visit `authors.packtpub.com` and apply today. We have worked with thousands of developers and tech professionals, just like you, to help them share their insight with the global tech community. You can make a general application, apply for a specific hot topic that we are recruiting an author for, or submit your own idea.

Table of Contents

Section 3: Administration and Data Management

Section 4: Scaling and High Availability

Preface

MongoDB has grown to become the de facto NoSQL database with millions of users, from small start-ups to Fortune 500 companies. Addressing the limitations of SQL schema-based databases, MongoDB pioneered a shift of focus for DevOps and offered sharding and replication that can be maintained by DevOps teams. This book is based on MongoDB 4.0 and covers topics ranging from database querying using the shell, built-in drivers, and popular ODM mappers, to more advanced topics such as sharding, high availability, and integration with big data sources.

You will get an overview of MongoDB and will learn how to play to its strengths, with relevant use cases. After that, you will learn how to query MongoDB effectively and make use of indexes as much as possible. The next part deals with the administration of MongoDB installations, whether on-premises or on the cloud. We deal with database internals in the following section, explaining storage systems and how they can affect performance. The last section of this book deals with replication and MongoDB scaling, along with integration with heterogeneous data sources. By the end this book, you will be equipped with all the required industry skills and knowledge to become a certified MongoDB developer and administrator.

Who this book is for

Mastering MongoDB 4.0 is a book for database developers, architects, and administrators who want to learn how to use MongoDB more effectively and productively. If you have experience with, and are interested in working with, NoSQL databases to build apps and websites, then this book is for you.

What this book covers

Chapter 1, *MongoDB – A Database for Modern Web*, takes us on a journey through web, SQL, and NoSQL technologies, from their inception to their current states.

Chapter 2, *Schema Design and Data Modeling*, teaches you schema design for relational databases and MongoDB, and how we can achieve the same goal from a different starting point.

Chapter 3, *MongoDB CRUD Operations*, provides a bird's-eye view of CRUD operations.

Chapter 4, *Advanced Querying*, covers advanced querying concepts using Ruby, Python, and PHP, using both the official drivers and an ODM.

Chapter 5, *Multi-Document ACID Transactions*, explores transactions following ACID characteristics, which is a new functionality introduced in MongoDB 4.0.

Chapter 6, *Aggregation*, dives deep into the aggregation framework. We also discuss when and why we should use aggregation, as opposed to MapReduce and querying the database.

Chapter 7, *Indexing*, explores one of the most important properties of every database, which is indexing.

Chapter 8, *Monitoring, Backup, and Security*, discusses the operational aspects of MongoDB. Monitoring, backup, and security should not be an afterthought, but rather are necessary processes that need to be taken care of before deploying MongoDB in a production environment.

Chapter 9, *Storage Engines*, teaches you about the different storage engines in MongoDB. We identify the pros and cons of each one, and the use cases for choosing each storage engine.

Chapter 10, *MongoDB Tooling*, covers all the different tools, both on-premises and in the cloud, that we can utilize in the MongoDB ecosystem.

Chapter 11, *Harnessing Big Data with MongoDB*, provides more detail on how MongoDB fits into the wider big data landscape and ecosystem.

Chapter 12, *Replication*, discusses replica sets and how to administer them. Starting from an architectural overview of replica sets and replica set internals around elections, we dive deep into setting up and configuring a replica set.

Chapter 13, *Sharding*, explores sharding, one of the most interesting features of MongoDB. We start with an architectural overview of sharding and move on to discuss how to design a shard, and especially, how to choose the right shard key.

Chapter 14, *Fault Tolerance and High Availability*, tries to fit in the information that we didn't manage to discuss in the previous chapters, and places emphasis on security and a series of checklists that developers and DBAs should keep into mind.

To get the most out of this book

You will need the following software to be able to smoothly sail through the chapters:

- MongoDB version 4+
- Apache Kafka version 1
- Apache Spark version 2+
- Apache Hadoop version 2+

Download the example code files

You can download the example code files for this book from your account at `www.packt.com`. If you purchased this book elsewhere, you can visit `www.packt.com/support` and register to have the files emailed directly to you.

You can download the code files by following these steps:

1. Log in or register at `www.packt.com`.
2. Select the **SUPPORT** tab.
3. Click on **Code Downloads & Errata**.
4. Enter the name of the book in the **Search** box and follow the onscreen instructions.

Once the file is downloaded, please make sure that you unzip or extract the folder using the latest version of:

- WinRAR/7-Zip for Windows
- Zipeg/iZip/UnRarX for Mac
- 7-Zip/PeaZip for Linux

The code bundle for the book is also hosted on GitHub at `https://github.com/PacktPublishing/Mastering-MongoDB-4.x-Second-Edition`. In case there's an update to the code, it will be updated on the existing GitHub repository.

We also have other code bundles from our rich catalog of books and videos available at `https://github.com/PacktPublishing/`. Check them out!

Conventions used

In this book, you will find a number of text styles that distinguish between different kinds of information. Here are some examples of these styles and an explanation of their meaning.

Code words in text, database table names, folder names, filenames, file extensions, pathnames, dummy URLs, user input, and Twitter handles are shown as follows: "In a sharded environment, each `mongod` applies its own locks, thus greatly improving concurrency."

A block of code is set as follows:

```
db.account.find( { "balance" : { $type : 16 } } );
db.account.find( { "balance" : { $type : "integer" } } );
```

Any command-line input or output is written as follows:

```
> db.types.insert({"a":4})
WriteResult({ "nInserted" : 1 })
```

Bold: Indicates a new term, an important word, or words that you see onscreen. For example, words in menus or dialog boxes appear in the text like this. Here is an example: "The following screenshot shows the **Zone configuration summary**:"

Warnings or important notes appear like this.

Tips and tricks appear like this.

Get in touch

Feedback from our readers is always welcome.

General feedback: If you have questions about any aspect of this book, mention the book title in the subject of your message and email us at customercare@packtpub.com.

Errata: Although we have taken every care to ensure the accuracy of our content, mistakes do happen. If you have found a mistake in this book, we would be grateful if you would report this to us. Please visit www.packt.com/submit-errata, selecting your book, clicking on the Errata Submission Form link, and entering the details.

Piracy: If you come across any illegal copies of our works in any form on the Internet, we would be grateful if you would provide us with the location address or website name. Please contact us at copyright@packt.com with a link to the material.

If you are interested in becoming an author: If there is a topic that you have expertise in and you are interested in either writing or contributing to a book, please visit authors.packtpub.com.

Reviews

Please leave a review. Once you have read and used this book, why not leave a review on the site that you purchased it from? Potential readers can then see and use your unbiased opinion to make purchase decisions, we at Packt can understand what you think about our products, and our authors can see your feedback on their book. Thank you!

For more information about Packt, please visit packt.com.

Section 1: Basic MongoDB – Design Goals and Architecture

In this section, we will go through the history of databases and how we arrived at the need for non-relational databases. We will also learn how to model our data so that storage and retrieval from MongoDB can be as efficient as possible. Even though MongoDB is schemaless, designing how data will be organized into documents can have a great effect in terms of performance.

This section consists of the following chapters:

- Chapter 1, *MongoDB – A Database for Modern Web*
- Chapter 2, *Schema Design and Data Modeling*

MongoDB – A Database for Modern Web

1

In this chapter, we will lay the foundations for understanding MongoDB, and how it claims to be a database that's designed for the modern web. Learning in the first place is as important as knowing how to learn. We will go through the references that have the most up-to-date information about MongoDB, for both new and experienced users. We will cover the following topics:

- SQL and MongoDB's history and evolution
- MongoDB from the perspective of SQL and other NoSQL technology users
- MongoDB's common use cases and why they matter
- MongoDB's configuration and best practices

Technical requirements

You will require MongoDB version 4+, Apache Kafka, Apache Spark and Apache Hadoop installed to smoothly sail through the chapter. The codes that have been used for all the chapters can be found
at: `https://github.com/PacktPublishing/Mastering-MongoDB-4.x-Second-Edition`.

The evolution of SQL and NoSQL

Structured Query Language (**SQL**) existed even before the WWW. Dr. E. F. Codd originally published the paper, *A Relational Model of Data for Large Shared Data Banks*, in June, 1970, in the **Association of Computer Machinery** (**ACM**) journal, **Communications of the ACM**. SQL was initially developed at IBM by Chamberlin and Boyce, in 1974. Relational Software (now Oracle Corporation) was the first to develop a commercially available implementation of SQL, targeted at United States governmental agencies.

The first **American National Standards Institute (ANSI)** SQL standard came out in 1986. Since then, there have been eight revisions, with the most recent being published in 2016 (SQL:2016).

SQL was not particularly popular at the start of the WWW. Static content could just be hardcoded into the HTML page without much fuss. However, as the functionality of websites grew, webmasters wanted to generate web page content driven by offline data sources, in order to generate content that could change over time without redeploying code.

Common Gateway Interface (CGI) scripts, developing Perl or Unix shells, were driving early database-driven websites in Web 1.0. With Web 2.0, the web evolved from directly injecting SQL results into the browser to using two-tier and three-tier architectures that separated views from the business and model logic, allowing for SQL queries to be modular and isolated from the rest of the web application.

On the other hand, **Not only SQL (NoSQL)** is much more modern and supervened web evolution, rising at the same time as Web 2.0 technologies. The term was first coined by Carlo Strozzi in 1998, for his open source database that did not follow the SQL standard, but was still relational.

This is not what we currently expect from a NoSQL database. Johan Oskarsson, a developer at Last.fm at the time, reintroduced the term in early 2009, in order to group a set of distributed, non-relational data stores that were being developed. Many of them were based on Google's **Bigtable** and **MapReduce** papers, or Amazon's **DynamoDB**, a highly available key-value based storage system.

NoSQL's foundations grew upon relaxed **atomicity, consistency, isolation, and durability (ACID)** properties, which guarantee the performance, scalability, flexibility, and reduced complexity. Most NoSQL databases have gone one way or another in providing as many of the previously mentioned qualities as possible, even offering adjustable guarantees to the developer. The following diagram describes the evolution of SQL and NoSQL:

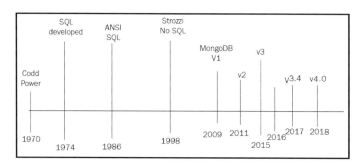

The evolution of MongoDB

10gen started to develop a cloud computing stack in 2007 and soon realized that the most important innovation was centered around the document-oriented database that they built to power it, which was MongoDB. MongoDB was initially released on August 27, 2009.

Version 1 of MongoDB was pretty basic in terms of features, authorization, and ACID guarantees but it made up for these shortcomings with performance and flexibility.

In the following sections, we will highlight the major features of MongoDB, along with the version numbers with which they were introduced.

Major feature set for versions 1.0 and 1.2

The different features of versions 1.0 and 1.2 are as follows:

- Document-based model
- Global lock (process level)
- Indexes on collections
- CRUD operations on documents
- No authentication (authentication was handled at the server level)
- Master and slave replication
- `MapReduce` (introduced in v1.2)
- Stored JavaScript functions (introduced in v1.2)

Version 2

The different features of version 2.0 are as follows:

- Background index creation (since v1.4)
- Sharding (since v1.6)
- More query operators (since v1.6)
- Journaling (since v1.8)
- Sparse and covered indexes (since v1.8)
- Compact commands to reduce disk usage
- Memory usage more efficient
- Concurrency improvements
- Index performance enhancements

- Replica sets are now more configurable and data center aware
- `MapReduce` improvements
- Authentication (since 2.0, for sharding and most database commands)
- Geospatial features introduced
- Aggregation framework (since v2.2) and enhancements (since v2.6)
- TTL collections (since v2.2)
- Concurrency improvements, among which is DB-level locking (since v2.2)
- Text searching (since v2.4) and integration (since v2.6)
- Hashed indexes (since v2.4)
- Security enhancements and role-based access (since v2.4)
- V8 JavaScript engine instead of SpiderMonkey (since v2.4)
- Query engine improvements (since v2.6)
- Pluggable storage engine API
- WiredTiger storage engine introduced, with document-level locking, while previous storage engine (now called **MMAPv1**) supports collection-level locking

Version 3

The different features of version 3.0 are as follows:

- Replication and sharding enhancements (since v3.2)
- Document validation (since v3.2)
- Aggregation framework enhanced operations (since v3.2)
- Multiple storage engines (since v3.2, only in Enterprise Edition)
- Query language and indexes collation (since v3.4)
- Read-only database views (since v3.4)
- Linearizable read concern (since v3.4)

Version 4

The different features of version 4.0 are as follows:

- Multi-document ACID transactions
- Change streams
- MongoDB tools (Stitch, Mobile, Sync, and Kubernetes Operator)

The following diagram shows MongoDB's evolution:

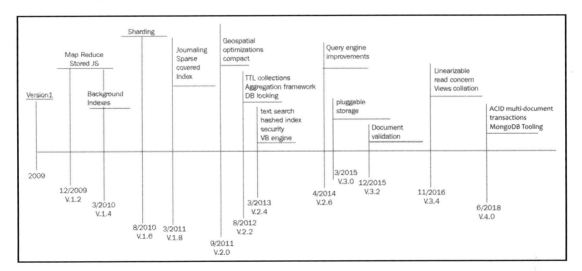

As we can observe, version 1 was pretty basic, whereas version 2 introduced most of the features present in the current version, such as sharding, usable and special indexes, geospatial features, and memory and concurrency improvements.

On the way from version 2 to version 3, the aggregation framework was introduced, mainly as a supplement to the ageing (and never up to par with dedicated frameworks, such as Hadoop) MapReduce framework. Then, text search was added, and slowly but surely, the framework was improving performance, stability, and security, to adapt to the increasing enterprise load of customers using MongoDB.

With WiredTiger's introduction in version 3, locking became much less of an issue for MongoDB, as it was brought down from the process (global lock) to the document level, almost the most granular level possible.

Version 4 marked a major transition, bridging the SQL and NoSQL world with the introduction of multi-document ACID transactions. This allowed for a wider range of applications to use MongoDB, especially applications that require a strong real-time consistency guarantee. Further, the introduction of change streams allowed for a faster time to market for real-time applications using MongoDB. A series of tools have also been introduced, to facilitate serverless, mobile, and **Internet of Things (IoT)** development.

In its current state, MongoDB is a database that can handle loads ranging from start up MVPs and POCs to enterprise applications with hundreds of servers.

MongoDB for SQL developers

MongoDB was developed in the Web 2.0 era. By then, most developers had been using SQL or **object-relational mapping (ORM)** tools from their language of choice to access RDBMS data. As such, these developers needed an easy way to get acquainted with MongoDB from their relational background.

Thankfully, there have been several attempts at making SQL to MongoDB cheat sheets that explain the MongoDB terminology in SQL terms.

On a higher level, we have the following:

- Databases and indexes (SQL databases)
- Collections (SQL tables)
- Documents (SQL rows)
- Fields (SQL columns)
- Embedded and linked documents (SQL joins)

Some more examples of common operations are shown in the following table:

SQL	MongoDB
Database	Database
Table	Collection
Index	Index
Row	Document
Column	Field
Joins	Embed in document or link via DBRef
CREATE TABLE employee (name VARCHAR(100))	db.createCollection("employee")
INSERT INTO employees VALUES (Alex, 36)	db.employees.insert({name: "Alex", age: 36})
SELECT * FROM employees	db.employees.find()
SELECT * FROM employees LIMIT 1	db.employees.findOne()
SELECT DISTINCT name FROM employees	db.employees.distinct("name")
UPDATE employees SET age = 37 WHERE name = 'Alex'	db.employees.update({name: "Alex"}, {$set: {age: 37}}, {multi: true})
DELETE FROM employees WHERE name = 'Alex'	db.employees.remove({name: "Alex"})

CREATE INDEX ON employees (name ASC)	db.employees.ensureIndex({name: 1})

Further examples of common operations can be seen at `http://s3.amazonaws.com/info-mongodb-com/sql_to_mongo.pdf`.

MongoDB for NoSQL developers

As MongoDB has grown from being a niche database solution to the Swiss Army knife of NoSQL technologies, more developers are coming to it from a NoSQL background, as well.

Putting the SQL to NoSQL differences aside, it is users from columnar-type databases that face the most challenges. With Cassandra and HBase being the most popular column-oriented database management systems, we will examine the differences and how a developer can migrate a system to MongoDB. The different features of MongoDB for NoSQL developers are as follows:

- **Flexibility**: MongoDB's notion of documents that can contain sub-documents nested in complex hierarchies is really expressive and flexible. This is similar to the comparison between MongoDB and SQL, with the added benefit that MongoDB can more easily map to plain old objects from any programming language, allowing for easy deployment and maintenance.
- **Flexible query model**: A user can selectively index some parts of each document; query based on attribute values, regular expressions, or ranges; and have as many properties per object as needed by the application layer. Primary and secondary indexes, as well as special types of indexes (such as sparse ones), can help greatly with query efficiency. Using a JavaScript shell with MapReduce makes it really easy for most developers (and many data analysts) to quickly take a look at data and get valuable insights.
- **Native aggregation**: The aggregation framework provides an **extract, transform, load** (ETL) pipeline for users to extract and transform data from MongoDB, and either load it in a new format or export it from MongoDB to other data sources. This can also help data analysts and scientists to get the slice of data they need in performing data wrangling along the way.
- **Schema-less model**: This is a result of MongoDB's design philosophy to give applications the power and responsibility to interpret the different properties found in a collection's documents. In contrast to Cassandra's or HBase's schema-based approach, in MongoDB, a developer can store and process dynamically generated attributes.

MongoDB's key characteristics and use cases

In this section, we will analyze MongoDB's characteristics as a database. Understanding the features that MongoDB provides can help developers and architects to evaluate the requirements at hand and how MongoDB can help to fulfill them. Also, we will go over some common use cases from the experience of MongoDB, Inc. that have delivered the best results for its users.

Key characteristics

MongoDB has grown to become a general purpose NoSQL database, offering the best of both the RDBMS and NoSQL worlds. Some of the key characteristics are as follows:

- **It is a general purpose database**: In contrast to other NoSQL databases that are built for specific purposes (for example, graph databases), MongoDB can serve heterogeneous loads and multiple purposes within an application. This became even more true after version 4.0 introduced multi-document ACID transactions, further expanding the use cases in which it can be effectively used.

- **Flexible schema design**: Document-oriented approaches with non-defined attributes that can be modified on the fly is a key contrast between MongoDB and relational databases.

- **It is built with high availability, from the ground up**: In our era of five nines in availability, this has to be a given. Coupled with automatic failover upon detection of a server failure, this can help to achieve high uptime.

- **Feature rich**: Offering the full range of SQL equivalent operators, along with features such as MapReduce, aggregation framework, Time to Live and capped collections, and secondary indexing, MongoDB can fit many use cases, no matter how diverse the requirements are.

- **Scalability and load balancing**: It is built to scale, both vertically and (mainly) horizontally. Using sharding, an architect can share a load between different instances and achieve both read and write scalability. Data balancing happens automatically (and transparently to the user) via the shard balancer.

- **Aggregation framework**: Having an ETL framework built in the database means that a developer can perform most of the ETL logic before the data leaves the database, eliminating, in many cases, the need for complex data pipelines.

- **Native replication**: Data will get replicated across a replica set without complicated setup.
- **Security features**: Both authentication and authorization are taken into account, so that an architect can secure their MongoDB instances.
- **JSON (BSON and Binary JSON) objects for storing and transmitting documents**: JSON is widely used across the web for frontend and API communication, and, as such, it is easier when the database is using the same protocol.
- **MapReduce**: Even though the MapReduce engine is not as advanced as it is in dedicated frameworks, it is nonetheless a great tool for building data pipelines.
- **Querying and geospatial information in 2D and 3D**: This may not be critical for many applications, but if it is for your use case, then it is really convenient to be able to use the same database for geospatial calculations and data storage.
- **Multi-document ACID transactions**: Starting from version 4.0, MongoDB supports ACID transactions across multiple documents.
- **Mature tooling**: The tooling for MongoDB has evolved to support from DBaaS to Sync, Mobile, and serverless (Stitch).

Use cases for MongoDB

Since MongoDB is a highly popular NoSQL database, there have been several use cases where it has succeeded in supporting quality applications, with a great delivery time to the market.

Many of its most successful use cases center around the following areas:

- Integration of siloed data, providing a single view of them
- IoT
- Mobile applications
- Real-time analytics
- Personalization
- Catalog management
- Content management

All of these success stories share some common characteristics. We will try to break them down in order of relative importance:

- Schema flexibility is probably the most important one. Being able to store documents inside of a collection that can have different properties can help during both the development phase and in ingesting data from heterogeneous sources that may or may not have the same properties. This is in contrast with an RDBMS, where columns need to be predefined and having sparse data can be penalized. In MongoDB, this is the norm, and it is a feature that most use cases share. Having the ability to deeply nest attributes into documents and add arrays of values into attributes while also being able to search and index these fields helps application developers to exploit the schema-less nature of MongoDB.

- Scaling and sharding are the most common patterns for MongoDB use cases. Easily scaling using built-in sharding and using replica sets for data replication and offloading primary servers from read load can help developers store data effectively.

- Many use cases also use MongoDB as a way of archiving data. Used as a pure data store (and not having the need to define schemas), it is fairly easy to dump data into MongoDB to be analyzed at a later date by business analysts, using either the shell or some of the numerous BI tools that can easily integrate with MongoDB. Breaking data down further, based on time caps or document counts, can help serve these datasets from RAM, the use case in which MongoDB is most effective.

- Keeping datasets in RAM helps performance, and that's why it is commonly used in practice. MongoDB uses MMAP storage (called **MMAPv1**) in most versions, up to the most recent, which delegates data mapping to the underlying operating system. This means that most GNU/Linux-based systems, working with collections that can be stored in RAM, will dramatically increase performance. This is less of an issue with the introduction of pluggable storage engines, such as WiredTiger (there will be more on that in `Chapter 8`, *Monitoring, Backup, and Security*).

- Capped collections are also a feature used in many use cases. Capped collections can restrict documents in a collection by count or by the overall size of the collection. In the latter case, we need to have an estimate of the size per document, in order to calculate how many documents will fit into our target size. Capped collections are a quick and dirty solution to answering requests such as *give me the last hour's overview of the logs* without the need for maintenance and running async background jobs to clean our collection. Oftentimes, these may be used to quickly build and operate a queuing system. Instead of deploying and maintaining a dedicated queuing system, such as ActiveMQ, a developer can use a collection to store messages, and then use the native tailable cursors provided by MongoDB to iterate through the results as they pile up and feed an external system.
- Low operational overhead is also a common pattern in many use cases. Developers working in agile teams can operate and maintain clusters of MongoDB servers without the need for a dedicated DBA. **MongoDB Management Service (MMS)** can greatly help in reducing administrative overhead, whereas MongoDB Atlas, the hosted solution by MongoDB, Inc., means that developers do not need to deal with operational headaches.
- In terms of business sectors using MongoDB, there is a huge variety coming from almost all industries. Where there seems to be a greater penetration, however, is in cases that have to deal with lots of data with a relatively low business value in each single data point. Fields such as IoT can benefit the most by exploiting the availability over consistency design, storing lots of data from sensors in a cost-efficient way. Financial services, on the other hand, have absolutely stringent consistency requirements, aligned with proper ACID characteristics that make MongoDB more of a challenge to adapt. A financial transaction may be small in size but big in impact, which means that we cannot afford to leave a single message without proper processing.
- Location-based data is also a field where MongoDB has thrived, with Foursquare being one of the most prominent early clients. MongoDB offers quite a rich set of features around two-dimensional and three-dimensional geolocation data, offering features such as searching by distance, geofencing, and intersections between geographical areas.
- Overall, the rich feature set is the common pattern across different use cases. By providing features that can be used in many different industries and applications, MongoDB can be a unified solution for all business needs, offering users the ability to minimize operational overhead and, at the same time, iterate quickly in product development.

MongoDB criticism

MongoDB's criticism is associated with the following points:

- MongoDB has had its fair share of criticism throughout the years. The web-scale proposition has been met with skepticism by many developers. The counter argument is that scale is not needed most of the time, and the focus should be on other design considerations. While this may occasionally be true, it is a false dichotomy, and in an ideal world, we would have both. MongoDB is as close as it can get to combining scalability with features, ease of use, and time to market.

- MongoDB's schema-less nature is also a big point of debate and argument. Schema-less can be really beneficial in many use cases, as it allows for heterogeneous data to be dumped into the database without complex cleansing and without ending up with lots of empty columns or blocks of text stuffed into a single column. On the other hand, this is a double-edged sword, as a developer may end up with many documents in a collection that have loose semantics in their fields, and it can become really hard to extract these semantics at the code level. If our schema design is not optimal, we may end up with a data store, rather than a database.

- A lack of proper ACID guarantees is a recurring complaint from the relational world. Indeed, if a developer needs access to more than one document at a time, it is not easy to guarantee RDBMS properties, as there are no transactions. Having no transactions, in the RDBMS sense, also means that complex writes will need to have application-level logic to roll back. If you need to update three documents in two collections to mark an application-level transaction complete, and the third document does not get updated for whatever reason, the application will need to undo the previous two writes, something that may not exactly be trivial.

- With the introduction of multi-document transactions in version 4.0, MongoDB can cope with ACID transactions at the expense of speed. While this is not ideal, and transactions are not meant to be used for every CRUD operation in MongoDB, it does address the main source of criticism.

- Defaults that favored setting up MongoDB but not operating it in a production environment are disapproved. For years, the default write behavior was **write and forget**; sending a write wouldn't wait for an acknowledgement before attempting the next write, resulting in insane write speeds with poor behaviors in cases of failure. Authentication is also an afterthought, leaving thousands of MongoDB databases on the public internet prey to whoever wants to read the stored data. Even though these were conscious design decisions, they are decisions that have affected developers' perceptions of MongoDB.

MongoDB configuration and best practices

In this section, we will present some of the best practice around operations, schema design, durability, replication, sharding, and security. Further information on when to implement these best practices will be presented in later chapters.

Operational best practices

As a database, MongoDB is built with developers in mind, and it was developed during the web era, so it does not require as much operational overhead as traditional RDBMS. That being said, there are some best practices that need to be followed to be proactive and achieve high availability goals.

In order of importance, the best practices are as follows:

- **Turn journaling on by default**: Journaling uses a write-ahead log to be able to recover if a MongoDB server gets shut down abruptly. With the MMAPv1 storage engine, journaling should always be on. With the WiredTiger storage engine, journaling and checkpointing are used together, to ensure data durability. In any case, it is a good practice to use journaling and fine-tune the size of journals and the frequency of checkpoints, to avoid the risk of data loss. In MMAPv1, the journal is flushed to the disk every 100 ms, by default. If MongoDB is waiting for the journal before acknowledging the write operation, the journal is flushed to the disk every 30 ms.
- **Your working set should fit in the memory**: Again, especially when using MMAPv1, the working set is best being less than the RAM of the underlying machine or VM. MMAPv1 uses memory mapped files from the underlying operating system, which can be a great benefit if there isn't much swap happening between the RAM and disk. WiredTiger, on the other hand, is much more efficient at using the memory, but still benefits greatly from the same principles. The working set is maximum the datasize and plus the index size as reported by db.stats().
- **Mind the location of your data files**: Data files can be mounted anywhere by using the --dbpath command-line option. It is really important to make sure that data files are stored in partitions with sufficient disk space, preferably XFS, or at least **Ext4**.

- **Keep yourself updated with versions**: Even major numbered versions are the stable ones. So, 3.2 is stable, whereas 3.3 is not. In this example, 3.3 is the developmental version that will eventually materialize into the stable version 3.4. It is a good practice to always update to the latest security updated version (4.0.2, at the time of writing this book) and to consider updating as soon as the next stable version comes out (4.2, in this example).
- **Use Mongo MMS to graphically monitor your service**: The free MongoDB, Inc. monitoring service is a great tool to get an overview of a MongoDB cluster, notifications, and alerts and to be proactive about potential issues.
- **Scale up if your metrics show heavy use**: Do not wait until it is too late. Utilizing more than 65% in CPU or RAM, or starting to notice disk swapping, should both be the threshold to start thinking about scaling, either vertically (by using bigger machines) or horizontally (by sharding).
- **Be careful when sharding**: Sharding is a strong commitment to your shard key. If you make the wrong decision, it may be really difficult to go back, from an operational perspective. When designing for sharding, architects need to take deep considerations of the current workloads (reads/writes) and what the current and expected data access patterns are.
- **Use an application driver maintained by the MongoDB team**: These drivers are supported and tend to get updated faster than drivers with no official support. If MongoDB does not support the language that you are using yet, please open a ticket in MongoDB's JIRA tracking system.
- **Schedule regular backups**: No matter whether you are using standalone servers, replica sets, or sharding, a regular backup policy should also be used as a second-level guard against data loss. XFS is a great choice as a filesystem, as it can perform snapshot backups.
- **Manual backups should be avoided**: Regular, automated backups should be used, when possible. If we need to resort to a manual backup, then we can use a hidden member in a replica set to take the backup from. We have to make sure that we are using `db.fsyncwithlock` at this member, to get the maximum consistency at this node, along with having journaling turned on. If this volume is on AWS, we can get away with taking an EBS snapshot straight away.
- **Enable database access control**: Never, ever put a database into a production system without access control. Access control should be implemented at a node level, by a proper firewall that only allows access to specific application servers to the database, and at a DB level, by using the built-in roles or defining custom defined ones. This has to be initialized at start up time by using the `--auth` command-line parameter and can be configured by using the `admin` collection.

- **Test your deployment using real data**: Since MongoDB is a schema-less, document-oriented database, you may have documents with varying fields. This means that it is even more important than with an RDBMS to test using data that resembles production data as closely as possible. A document with an extra field of an unexpected value can make the difference between an application working smoothly or crashing at runtime. Try to deploy a staging server using production-level data, or at least fake your production data in staging, by using an appropriate library, such as Faker for Ruby.

Schema design best practices

MongoDB is schema-less, and you have to design your collections and indexes to accommodate for this fact:

- **Index early and often**: Identify common query patterns, using MMS, Compass GUI, or logs, and index for these early, using as many indexes as possible at the beginning of a project.
- **Eliminate unnecessary indexes**: A bit counter-intuitive to the preceding suggestion, monitor your database for changing query patterns, and drop the indexes that are not being used. An index will consume RAM and I/O, as it needs to be stored and updated along with documents in the database. Using an aggregation pipeline and $indexStats, a developer can identify the indexes that are seldom being used and eliminate them.
- **Use a compound index, rather than index intersection**: Querying with multiple predicates (*A* and *B*, *C* or *D* and *E*, and so on) will work better with a single compound index than with multiple simple indexes, most of the time. Also, a compound index will have its data ordered by field, and we can use this to our advantage when querying. An index on fields *A*, *B*, and *C* will be used in queries for *A*, *(A,B)*, *(A,B,C)*, but not in querying for *(B,C)* or *(C)*.
- **Low selectivity indexes**: Indexing a field on gender, for example, will statistically return half of our documents back, whereas an index on last name will only return a handful of documents with the same last name.
- **Use regular expressions**: Again, since indexes are ordered by value, searching using a regular expression with leading wildcards (that is, / . *BASE/) won't be able to use the index. Searching with trailing wildcards (that is, /DATA . */) can be efficient, as long as there are enough case-sensitive characters in the expression.
- **Avoid negation in queries**: Indexes are indexing values, not the absence of them. Using NOT in queries can result in full table scans, instead of using the index.

- **Use partial indexes**: If we need to index a subset of the documents in a collection, partial indexes can help us to minimize the index set and improve performance. A partial index will include a condition on the filter that we use in the desired query.

- **Use document validation**: Use document validation to monitor for new attributes being inserted into your documents and decide what to do with them. With document validation set to warn, we can keep a log of documents that were inserted with arbitrary attributes that we did not expect during the design phase, and decide whether this is a bug or a feature of our design.

- **Use MongoDB Compass**: MongoDB's free visualization tool is great for getting a quick overview of our data and how it grows over time.

- **Respect the maximum document size of 16 MB**: The maximum document size for MongoDB is 16 MB. This is a fairly generous limit, but it is one that should not be violated under any circumstances. Allowing for documents to grow unbounded should not be an option, and, as efficient as it may be to embed documents, we should always keep in mind that this should be under control.

- **Use the appropriate storage engine**: MongoDB has introduced several new storage engines since version 3.2. The in-memory storage engine should be used for real-time workloads, whereas the encrypted storage engine should be the engine of choice when there are strict requirements around data security.

Best practices for write durability

Writing durability can be fine-tuned in MongoDB, and, according to our application design, it should be as strict as possible, without affecting our performance goals.

Fine-tune the data and flush it to the disk interval in the WiredTiger storage engine, the default is to flush data to the disk every 60 seconds after the last checkpoint, or after 2 GB of data has been written. This can be changed by using the `--wiredTigerCheckpointDelaySecs` command-line option.

In MMAPv1, data files are flushed to the disk every 60 seconds. This can be changed by using the `--syncDelay` command-line option. We can also perform various tasks, such as the following:

- With WiredTiger, we can use the XFS filesystem for multi-disk consistent snapshots

- We can turn off `atime` and `diratime` in data volumes

- You can make sure that you have enough swap space (usually double your memory size)

- You can use a NOOP scheduler if you are running in virtualization environments
- We can raise file descriptor limits to the tens of thousands
- We can disable transparent huge pages and enable standard 4-KVM pages instead
- Write safety should be journaled, at the very least
- SSD read ahead default should be set to 16 blocks; HDD should be 32 blocks
- We can turn NUMA off in BIOS
- We can use RAID 10
- You can synchronize the time between hosts by using NTP, especially in sharded environments
- Only use 64-bit builds for production; 32-bit builds are outdated and can only support up to 2 GB of memory

Best practices for replication

Replica sets are MongoDB's mechanism to provide redundancy, high availability, and higher read throughput, under the right conditions. In MongoDB, replication is easy to configure and focus in operational terms:

- **Always use replica sets**: Even if your dataset is small at the moment, and you don't expect it to grow exponentially, you never know when that might happen. Also, having a replica set of at least three servers helps to design for redundancy, separating the workloads between real time and analytics (using the secondary) and having data redundancy built from day one.
- **Use a replica set to your advantage**: A replica set is not just for data replication. We can (and should, in most cases) use the primary server for writes and preference reads from one of the secondary to offload the primary server. This can be done by setting read preferences for reads, along with the correct write concern, to ensure that writes propagate as needed.
- **Use an odd number of replicas in a MongoDB replica set**: If a server is down or loses connectivity with the rest of them (network partitioning), the rest have to vote as to which one will be elected as the primary server. If we have an odd number of replica set members, we can guarantee that each subset of servers knows if they belong to the majority or the minority of the replica set members. If we can not have an odd number of replicas, we need to have one extra host set as an arbiter, with the sole purpose of voting in the election process. Even a micro-instance in EC2 could serve this purpose.

Best practices for sharding

Sharding is MongoDB's solution for horizontal scaling. In Chapter 8, *Monitoring, Backup, and Security*, we will go over its usage in more detail, but the following are some best practices, based on the underlying data architecture:

- **Think about query routing**: Based on different shard keys and techniques, the mongos query router may direct the query to some (or all) of the members of a shard. It is important to take our queries into account when designing sharding, so that we don't end up with our queries hitting all of our shards.
- **Use tag-aware sharding**: Tags can provide more fine-grained distribution of data across our shards. Using the right set of tags for each shard, we can ensure that subsets of data get stored in a specific set of shards. This can be useful for data proximity between application servers, MongoDB shards, and the users.

Best practices for security

Security is always a multi-layered approach, and these few recommendations do not form an exhaustive list; they are just the bare basics that need to be done in any MongoDB database:

- The HTTP status interface should be disabled.
- The RESTful API should be disabled.
- The JSON API should be disabled.
- Connect to MongoDB using SSL.
- Audit the system activity.
- Use a dedicated system user to access MongoDB with appropriate system-level access.
- Disable server-side scripting if it is not needed. This will affect MapReduce, built-in db.group() commands, and $where operations. If these are not used in your codebase, it is better to disable server-side scripting at startup by using the --noscripting parameter.

Best practices for AWS

When we are using MongoDB, we can use our own servers in a data center, a MongoDB-hosted solution such as MongoDB Atlas, or we can get instances from Amazon by using EC2. EC2 instances are virtualized and share resources in a transparent way, with collocated VMs in the same physical host. So, there are some more considerations to take into account if you are going down that route, as follows:

- Use EBS-optimized EC2 instances.
- Get EBS volumes with provisioned **I/O operations per second (IOPS)** for consistent performance.
- Use EBS snapshotting for backup and restore.
- Use different availability zones for high availability and different regions for disaster recovery. Using different availability zones within each region that Amazon provides guarantees that our data will be highly available. Different regions should only be used for disaster recovery, in case a catastrophic event ever takes out an entire region. A region might be EU-West-2 (for London), whereas an availability zone is a subdivision within a region; currently, two availability zones are available for London.
- Deploy global; access local.
- For truly global applications with users from different time zones, we should have application servers in different regions access the data that is closest to them, using the right read preference configuration in each server.

Reference documentation

Reading a book is great (and reading this book is even greater), but continuous learning is the only way to keep up to date with MongoDB. In the following sections, we will highlight the places that you should go for updates and development/operational references.

MongoDB documentation

The online documentation available at `https://docs.mongodb.com/manual/` is the starting point for every developer, new or seasoned.

The JIRA tracker is a great place to take a look at fixed bugs and the features that are coming up next: `https://jira.mongodb.org/browse/SERVER/`.

Packt references

Some other great books on MongoDB are as follows:

- *MongoDB for Java Developers*, by Francesco Marchioni
- *MongoDB Data Modeling*, by Wilson da Rocha França
- Any book by Kristina Chodorow

Further reading

The MongoDB user group (`https://groups.google.com/forum/#!forum/mongodb-user`) has a great archive of user questions about features and long-standing bugs. It is a place to go when something doesn't work as expected.

Online forums (Stack Overflow and Reddit, among others) are always a source of knowledge, with the caveat that something may have been posted a few years ago and may not apply anymore. Always check before trying.

Finally, MongoDB University is a great place to keep your skills up to date and to learn about the latest features and additions: `https://university.mongodb.com/`.

Summary

In this chapter, we started our journey through web, SQL, and NoSQL technologies, from their inception to their current states. We identified how MongoDB has been shaping the world of NoSQL databases over the years, and how it is positioned against other SQL and NoSQL solutions.

We explored MongoDB's key characteristics and how MongoDB has been used in production deployments. We identified the best practices for designing, deploying, and operating MongoDB.

Initially, we identified how to learn by going through documentation and online resources that can be used to stay up-to-date with the latest features and developments.

In the next chapter, we will go deeper into schema design and data modeling, looking at how to connect to MongoDB by using both the official drivers and an **Object Document Mapper (ODM)**, a variation of object-relational mappers for NoSQL databases.

2
Schema Design and Data Modeling

This chapter will focus on schema design for schema less databases such as MongoDB. Although this may sound counter-intuitive, there are considerations that we should take into account when we develop for MongoDB. We will learn about the schema considerations and the data types supported by MongoDB. We will also learn about preparing data for text searches in MongoDB by connecting Ruby, Python, and PHP.

In this chapter, we will cover the following topics:

- Relational schema design
- Data modeling
- Modeling data for atomic operations
- Modeling relationships
- Connecting to MongoDB

Relational schema design

In relational databases, we design with the goal of avoiding anomalies and redundancy. Anomalies can happen when we have the same information stored in multiple columns; we update one of them but not the rest and so end up with conflicting information for the same column of information. An anomaly can also happen when we cannot delete a row without losing information that we need, possibly in other rows referenced by it. Data redundancy can happen when our data is not in a normal form, but has duplicate data across different tables. This can lead to data inconsistency and is difficult to maintain.

In relational databases, we use normal forms to normalize our data. Starting from the basic **First Normal Form** (**1NF**), onto the 2NF, 3NF, and BCNF, we model our data, taking functional dependencies into account and, if we follow the rules, we can end up with many more tables than domain model objects.

In practice, relational database modeling is often driven by the structure of the data that we have. In web applications following some sort of **Model-View-Controller** (**MVC**) model pattern, we will model our database according to our models, which are modeled after the **Unified Modeling Language** (**UML**) diagram conventions. Abstractions such as the ORM for **Django** or the **Active Record** for Rails help application developers abstract database structure to object models. Ultimately, many times, we end up designing our database based on the structure of the available data. Thus, we are designing around the answers that we can have.

MongoDB schema design

In contrast to relational databases, in MongoDB we have to base our modeling on our application-specific data access patterns. Finding out the questions that our users will have is paramount to designing our entities. In contrast to an RDBMS, data duplication and denormalization are used far more frequently and with solid reason.

The document model that MongoDB uses means that every document can hold substantially more or less information than the next one, even within the same collection. Coupled with rich and detailed queries being possible in MongoDB in the embedded document level, this means that we are free to design our documents in any way that we want. When we know our data access patterns, we can estimate which fields need to be embedded and which can be split out to different collections.

Read-write ratio

The read to write ratio is often an important design consideration for MongoDB modeling. When reading data, we want to avoid scatter/gather situations, where we have to hit several shards with random I/O requests to get the data our application needs.

When writing data, on the other hand, we want to spread out writes to as many servers as possible, to avoid overloading any single one of them. These goals appear to be conflicting on the surface, but they can be combined once we know our access patterns, coupled with application design considerations, such as using a replica set to read from secondary nodes.

Data modeling

In this section, we will discuss the different data types MongoDB uses, how they map to the data types that programming languages use, and how we can model data relationships in MongoDB using Ruby, Python, and PHP.

Data types

MongoDB uses BSON, a binary-encoded serialization for JSON documents. BSON extends the JSON data types, offering, for example, native data and binary data types.

BSON, compared to protocol buffers, allows for more flexible schemas that come at the cost of space efficiency. In general, BSON is space-efficient, easy to traverse, and time-efficient in encoding/decoding operations, as can be seen in the following table. (See the MongoDB documentation at `https://docs.mongodb.com/manual/reference/bson-types/`):

Type	Number	Alias	Notes
Double	1	`double`	
String	2	`string`	
Object	3	`object`	
Array	4	`array`	
Binary data	5	`binData`	
ObjectID	7	`objectId`	
Boolean	8	`bool`	
Date	9	`date`	
Null	10	`null`	
Regular expression	11	`regex`	
JavaScript	13	`javascript`	
JavaScript (with scope)	15	`javascriptWithScope`	
32-bit integer	16	`int`	
Timestamp	17	`timestamp`	
64-bit integer	18	`long`	
Decimal128	19	`decimal`	New in version 3.4
Min key	-1	`minKey`	
Max key	127	`maxKey`	
Undefined	6	`undefined`	Deprecated
DBPointer	12	`dbPointer`	Deprecated
Symbol	14	`symbol`	Deprecated

In MongoDB, we can have documents with different value types for a given field and we distinguish among them when querying using the `$type` operator.

For example, if we have a `balance` field in GBP with 32-bit integers and `double` data types, if `balance` has pennies in it or not, we can easily query for all accounts that have a rounded `balance` with any of the following queries shown in the example:

```
db.account.find( { "balance" : { $type : 16 } } );
db.account.find( { "balance" : { $type : "integer" } } );
```

We will compare the different data types in the following section.

Comparing different data types

Due to the nature of MongoDB, it's perfectly acceptable to have different data type objects in the same field. This may happen by accident or on purpose (that is, null and actual values in a field).

The sorting order of different types of data, from highest to lowest, is as follows:

1. Max key (internal type)
2. Regular expression
3. Timestamp
4. Date
5. Boolean
6. ObjectID
7. Binary data
8. Array
9. Object
10. Symbol, string
11. Numbers (`int`, `long`, `double`)
12. Null
13. Min key (internal type)

Non-existent fields get sorted as if they have `null` in the respective field. Comparing arrays is a bit more complex than fields. An ascending order of comparison (or <) will compare the smallest element of each array. A descending order of comparison (or >) will compare the largest element of each array.

For example, see the following scenario:

```
> db.types.find()
{ "_id" : ObjectId("5908d58455454e2de6519c49"), "a" : [ 1, 2, 3 ] }
{ "_id" : ObjectId("5908d59d55454e2de6519c4a"), "a" : [ 2, 5 ] }
```

In ascending order, this is as follows:

```
> db.types.find().sort({a:1})
{ "_id" : ObjectId("5908d58455454e2de6519c49"), "a" : [ 1, 2, 3 ] }
{ "_id" : ObjectId("5908d59d55454e2de6519c4a"), "a" : [ 2, 5 ] }
```

However, in descending order, it is as follows:

```
> db.types.find().sort({a:-1})
{ "_id" : ObjectId("5908d59d55454e2de6519c4a"), "a" : [ 2, 5 ] }
{ "_id" : ObjectId("5908d58455454e2de6519c49"), "a" : [ 1, 2, 3 ] }
```

The same applies when comparing an array with a single number value, as illustrated in the following example. Inserting a new document with an integer value of 4 is done as follows:

```
> db.types.insert({"a":4})
WriteResult({ "nInserted" : 1 })
```

The following example shows the code snippet for a descending sort:

```
> db.types.find().sort({a:-1})
{ "_id" : ObjectId("5908d59d55454e2de6519c4a"), "a" : [ 2, 5 ] }
{ "_id" : ObjectId("5908d73c55454e2de6519c4c"), "a" : 4 }
{ "_id" : ObjectId("5908d58455454e2de6519c49"), "a" : [ 1, 2, 3 ] }
```

And the following example is the code snippet for an ascending sort:

```
> db.types.find().sort({a:1})
{ "_id" : ObjectId("5908d58455454e2de6519c49"), "a" : [ 1, 2, 3 ] }
{ "_id" : ObjectId("5908d59d55454e2de6519c4a"), "a" : [ 2, 5 ] }
{ "_id" : ObjectId("5908d73c55454e2de6519c4c"), "a" : 4 }
```

In each case, we highlighted the values being compared in bold.

We will learn about the data type in the following section.

Date type

Dates are stored as milliseconds with effect from January 01, 1970 (epoch time). They are 64-bit signed integers, allowing for a range of 135 million years before and after 1970. A negative date value denotes a date before January 01, 1970. The BSON specification refers to the date type as UTC DateTime.

Dates in MongoDB are stored in UTC. There isn't timestamp with a timezone data type like in some relational databases. Applications that need to access and modify timestamps, based on local time, should store the timezone offset together with the date and offset dates on an application level.

In the MongoDB shell, this could be done using the following format with JavaScript:

```
var now = new Date();
db.page_views.save({date: now,
                    offset: now.getTimezoneOffset()});
```

Then you need to apply the saved offset to reconstruct the original local time, as in the following example:

```
var record = db.page_views.findOne();
var localNow = new Date( record.date.getTime() - ( record.offset * 60000 )
);
```

In the next section, we will cover ObjectId.

ObjectId

ObjectId is a special data type for MongoDB. Every document has an _id field from cradle to grave. It is the primary key for each document in a collection and has to be unique. If we omit this field in a create statement, it will be assigned automatically with an ObjectId.

Messing with ObjectId is not advisable but we can use it (with caution!) for our purposes.

ObjectId has the following distinctions:

- It has 12 bytes
- It is ordered
- Sorting by _id will sort by creation time for each document
- Storing the creation time can be accessed by .getTimeStamp() in the shell

The structure of an `ObjectId` has the following:

- A 4-byte value representing the seconds since the Unix epoch
- A 3-byte machine identifier
- A 2-byte process ID
- A 3-byte counter, starting with a random value

The following diagram shows the structure of an ObjectID:

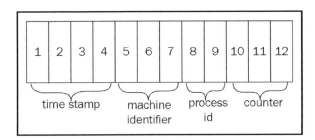

By its structure, `ObjectId` will be unique for all purposes; however, since this is generated on the client side, you should check the underlying library's source code to verify that implementation is according to specification.

In the next section, we will learn about modeling data for atomic operations.

Modeling data for atomic operations

MongoDB is relaxing many of the typical **Atomicity, Consistency, Isolation and Durability (ACID)** constraints found in RDBMS. In the absence of transactions, it can sometimes be difficult to keep the state consistent across operations, especially in the event of failures.

Luckily, some operations are atomic at the document level:

- `update()`
- `findandmodify()`
- `remove()`

These are all atomic (all or nothing) for a single document.

This means that, if we embed information in the same document, we can make sure they are always in sync.

An example would be an inventory application, with a document per item in our inventory, where we would need to total the available items left in stock how many have been placed in a shopping cart in sync, and use this data to sum up the total available items.

With `total_available = 5`, `available_now = 3`, `shopping_cart_count = 2`, this use case could look like the following: `{available_now : 3, Shopping_cart_by: ["userA", "userB"] }`

When someone places the item in their shopping cart, we can issue an atomic update, adding their user ID in the `shopping_cart_by` field and, at the same time, decreasing the `available_now` field by one.

This operation will be guaranteed to be atomic at the document level. If we need to update multiple documents within the same collection, the update operation may complete successfully without modifying all of the documents that we intended it to. This could happen because the operation is not guaranteed to be atomic across multiple document updates.

This pattern can help in some, but not all, cases. In many cases, we need multiple updates to be applied on all or nothing across documents, or even collections.

A typical example would be a bank transfer between two accounts. We want to subtract x GBP from user A, then add x to user B. If we fail to do either of the two steps, we would return to the original state for both balances.

The details of this pattern are outside the scope of this book, but roughly, the idea is to implement a hand-coded two phase **commit** protocol. This protocol should create a new transaction entry for each transfer with every possible state in this transaction: such as initial, pending, applied, done, cancelling, cancelled, and, based on the state that each transaction is left at, applying the appropriate rollback function to it.

If you find yourself having to implement transactions in a database that was built to avoid them, take a step back and rethink why you need to do that.

Write isolation

Sparingly, we could use `$isolated` to isolate writes to multiple documents from other writers or readers to these documents. In the previous example, we could use `$isolated` to update multiple documents and make sure that we update both balances before anyone else gets the chance to double-spend, draining the source account of its funds.

What this won't give us though, is atomicity, the all-or-nothing approach. So, if the update only partially modifies both accounts, we still need to detect and unroll any modifications made in the pending state.

`$isolated` uses an exclusive lock on the entire collection, no matter which storage engine is used. This means a severe speed penalty when using it, especially for WiredTiger document-level locking semantics.

`$isolated` does not work with sharded clusters, which may be an issue when we decide to go from replica sets to sharded deployment.

Read isolation and consistency

MongoDB read operations would be characterized as *read uncommitted* in a traditional RDBMS definition. What this means is that, by default, reads may get values that may not finally persist to the disk in the event of, for example, data loss or a replica set rollback operation.

In particular, when updating multiple documents with the default write behavior, lack of isolation may result in the following:

- Reads may miss documents that were updated during the update operations
- Non-serializable operations
- Read operations are not point-in-time

These can be resolved by using the `$isolated` operator with a heavy performance penalty.

Queries with cursors that don't use `.snapshot()` may also, in some cases, get inconsistent results. This can happen if the query's resultant cursor fetches a document, which receives an update while the query is still fetching results, and, because of insufficient padding, ends up in a different physical location on the disk, ahead of the query's result cursor position. `.snapshot()` is a solution for this edge case, with the following limitations:

- It doesn't work with sharding
- It doesn't work with `sort()` or `hint()` to force an index to be used
- It still won't provide point-in-time read behavior

If our collection has mostly static data, we can use a unique index in the query field to simulate `snapshot()` and still be able to apply `sort()` to it.

All in all, we need to apply safeguards at the application level to make sure that we won't end up with unexpected results.

Starting from version 3.4, MongoDB offers linearizable read concern. With linearizable read concern from the primary member of a replica set and a majority write concern, we can ensure that multiple threads can read and write a single document as if a single thread was performing these operations one after the other. This is considered a linearizable schedule in RDBMS, and MongoDB calls it the real-time order.

Modeling relationships

In the following sections, we will explain how we can translate relationships in RDBMS theory into MongoDB's document-collection hierarchy. We will also examine how we can model our data for text search in MongoDB.

One-to-one

Coming from the relational DB world, we identify objects by their relationships. A one-to-one relationship could be a person with an address. Modeling it in a relational database would most probably require two tables: a **Person** and an **Address** table with a foreign key `person_id` in the **Address** table, as shown in the following diagram:

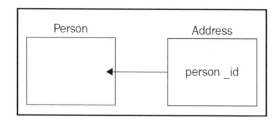

The perfect analogy in MongoDB would be two collections, `Person` and `Address`, as shown in the following code:

```
> db.Person.findOne()
{
"_id" : ObjectId("590a530e3e37d79acac26a41"), "name" : "alex"
}
> db.Address.findOne()
{
"_id" : ObjectId("590a537f3e37d79acac26a42"),
"person_id" : ObjectId("590a530e3e37d79acac26a41"),
"address" : "N29DD"
}
```

Now, we can use the same pattern as we do in a relational database to find `Person` from `address`, as shown in the following example:

```
> db.Person.find({"_id":
db.Address.findOne({"address":"N29DD"}).person_id})
{
"_id" : ObjectId("590a530e3e37d79acac26a41"), "name" : "alex"
}
```

This pattern is well known and works in the relational world.

In MongoDB, we don't have to follow this pattern, as there are more suitable ways to model these kinds of relationship.

One way in which we would typically model one-to-one or one-to-many relationships in MongoDB would be through embedding. If the person has two addresses, then the same example would then be shown in the following way:

```
{ "_id" : ObjectId("590a55863e37d79acac26a43"), "name" : "alex", "address"
: [ "N29DD", "SW1E5ND" ] }
```

Using an embedded array, we can have access to every `address` this user has. Embedding querying is rich and flexible so that we can store more information in each document, as shown in the following example:

```
{ "_id" : ObjectId("590a56743e37d79acac26a44"),
"name" : "alex",
"address" : [ { "description" : "home", "postcode" : "N29DD" },
{ "description" : "work", "postcode" : "SW1E5ND" } ] }
```

The advantages of this approach are as follows:

- No need for two queries across different collections
- It can exploit atomic updates to make sure that updates in the document will be all-or-nothing from the perspective of other readers of this document
- It can embed attributes in multiple nest levels creating complex structures

The most notable disadvantage is that the maximum size of the document is 16 MB so this approach cannot be used for an arbitrary, ever-growing number of attributes. Storing hundreds of elements in embedded arrays will also degrade performance.

One-to-many and many-to-many

When the number of elements in the *many* side of the relationship can grow unbounded, it's better to use references. References can come in two forms:

1. From the *one* side of the relationship, store an array of many-sided elements, as shown in the following example:

```
> db.Person.findOne()
{ "_id" : ObjectId("590a530e3e37d79acac26a41"), "name" : "alex",
addresses:
[ ObjectID('590a56743e37d79acac26a44'),
ObjectID('590a56743e37d79acac26a46'),
ObjectID('590a56743e37d79acac26a54') ] }
```

2. This way we can get the array of addresses from the one-side and then query with in to get all the documents from the many-side, as shown in the following example:

```
> person = db.Person.findOne({"name":"mary"})
> addresses = db.Addresses.find({_id: {$in: person.addresses} })
```

Turning this one-to-many to many-to-many is as easy as storing this array in both ends of the relationship (that is, in the Person and Address collections).

3. From the many-side of the relationship, store a reference to the one-side, as shown in the following example:

```
> db.Address.find()
{ "_id" : ObjectId("590a55863e37d79acac26a44"), "person":
ObjectId("590a530e3e37d79acac26a41"), "address" : [ "N29DD" ] }
{ "_id" : ObjectId("590a55863e37d79acac26a46"), "person":
ObjectId("590a530e3e37d79acac26a41"), "address" : [ "SW1E5ND" ] }
{ "_id" : ObjectId("590a55863e37d79acac26a54"), "person":
ObjectId("590a530e3e37d79acac26a41"), "address" : [ "N225QG" ] }
> person = db.Person.findOne({"name":"alex"})
> addresses = db.Addresses.find({"person": person._id})
```

As we can see, with both designs we need to make two queries to the database to fetch the information. The second approach has the advantage that it won't let any document grow unbounded, so it can be used in cases where one-to-many is one-to-millions.

Modeling data for keyword searches

Searching for keywords in a document is a common operation for many applications. If this is a core operation, it makes sense to use a specialized store for search, such as **Elasticsearch**; however, MongoDB can be used efficiently until scale dictates moving to a different solution.

The basic need for a keyword search is to be able to search the entire document for keywords. For example, with a document in the `products` collection, as shown in the following code:

```
{ name : "Macbook Pro late 2016 15in" ,
  manufacturer : "Apple" ,
  price: 2000 ,
  keywords : [ "Macbook Pro late 2016 15in", "2000", "Apple", "macbook",
"laptop", "computer" ]
 }
```

We can create a multi-key index in the `keywords` field, as shown in the following code:

```
> db.products.createIndex( { keywords: 1 } )
```

Now we can search in the `keywords` field for any name, manufacturer, price, and also any of the custom keywords that we set up. This is not an efficient or flexible approach, as we need to keep keywords lists in sync, we can't use stemming, and we can't rank results (it's more like filtering than searching). The only advantage of this method is that it is slightly quicker to implement.

Since version 2.4, MongoDB has had a special text index type. This can be declared in one or multiple fields and supports stemming, tokenization, exact phrase (" "), negation (−), and weighting results.

Index declaration on three fields with custom `weights` is shown in the following example:

```
db.products.createIndex({
    name: "text",
    manufacturer: "text",
  price: "text"
 },
 {
    weights: { name: 10,
      manufacturer: 5,
     price: 1 },
    name: "ProductIndex"
  })
```

In this example, `name` is 10 times more important than `price` but only two times from `manufacturer`.

A `text` index can also be declared with a wildcard, matching all the fields that match the pattern, as shown in the following example:

```
db.collection.createIndex( { "$**": "text" } )
```

This can be useful when we have unstructured data and we may not know all the fields that they will come with. We can drop the index by name, just like with any other index.

The greatest advantage though, other than all the features, is that all record keeping is done by the database.

In the next section, we will learn how to connect to MongoDB.

Connecting to MongoDB

There are two ways to connect to MongoDB. The first is by using the driver for your programming language. The second is by using an ODM layer to map your model objects to MongoDB in a transparent way. In this section, we will cover both ways, using three of the most popular languages for web application development: Ruby, Python, and PHP.

Connecting using Ruby

Ruby was one of the first languages to have support from MongoDB with an official driver. The official MongoDB Ruby driver on GitHub is the recommended way to connect to a MongoDB instance. Perform the following steps to connect MongoDB using Ruby:

1. Installation is as simple as adding it to the Gemfile, as shown in the following example:

    ```
    gem 'mongo', '~> 2.6'
    ```

     You need to install Ruby, then install RVM from `https://rvm.io/rvm/install`, and finally run `gem install bundler` for this.

2. Then, in our class, we can connect to a database, as shown in the following example:

```
require 'mongo'
client = Mongo::Client.new([ '127.0.0.1:27017' ], database: 'test')
```

3. This is the simplest example possible: connecting to a single database instance called `test` in our `localhost`. In most use cases, we would at least have a replica set to connect to, as shown in the following snippet:

```
client_host = ['server1_hostname:server1_ip,
server2_hostname:server2_ip']
 client_options = {
   database: 'YOUR_DATABASE_NAME',
   replica_set: 'REPLICA_SET_NAME',
   user: 'YOUR_USERNAME',
   password: 'YOUR_PASSWORD'
 }
client = Mongo::Client.new(client_host, client_options)
```

4. The `client_host` servers are seeding the client driver with servers to attempts to connect. Once connected, the driver will determine the server that it has to connect to according to the primary/secondary read or write configuration. The `replica_set` attribute needs to match `REPLICA_SET_NAME` to be able to connect.

5. `user` and `password` are optional, but highly recommended in any MongoDB instance. It's good practice to enable authentication by default in the `mongod.conf` file and we will learn more about this in Chapter 8, *Monitoring, Backup, and Security*.

6. Connecting to a sharded cluster is similar to a replica set, with the only difference being that, instead of supplying the server host/port, we need to connect to the MongoDB process that serves as the MongoDB router.

Mongoid ODM

Using a low-level driver to connect to the MongoDB database is often not the most efficient route. All the flexibility that a low-level driver provides is offset against longer development times and code to glue our models with the database.

An ODM can be the answer to these problems. Just like ORMs, ODMs bridge the gap between our models and the database. In Rails, the most widely-used MVC framework for Ruby—Mongoid—can be used to model our data in a similar way to Active Record.

Installing `gem` is similar to the Mongo Ruby driver, by adding a single file in the Gemfile, as shown in the following code:

```
gem 'mongoid', '~> 7.0'
```

Depending on the version of Rails, we may need to add the following to `application.rb` as well:

```
config.generators do |g|
  g.orm :mongoid
end
```

Connecting to the database is done through a config file, `mongoid.yml`. Configuration options are passed as key-value pairs with semantic indentation. Its structure is similar to `database.yml` used for relational databases.

Some of the options that we can pass through the `mongoid.yml` file are shown in the following table:

Option value	Description
`Database`	The database name.
`Hosts`	Our database hosts.
`Write/w`	The write concern (default is 1).
`Auth_mech`	Authentication mechanism. Valid options are: `:scram`, `:mongodb_cr`, `:mongodb_x509`, and `:plain`. The default option on 3.0 is `:scram`, whereas the default on 2.4 and 2.6 is `:plain`.
`Auth_source`	The authentication source for our authentication mechanism.
`Min_pool_size/max_pool_size`	Minimum and maximum pool size for connections.
`SSL`, `ssl_cert`, `ssl_key`, `ssl_key_pass_phrase`, `ssl_verify`	A set of options regarding SSL connections to the database.
`Include_root_in_json`	Includes the root model name in JSON serialization.
`Include_type_for_serialization`	Includes the _type field when serializing MongoDB objects.
`Use_activesupport_time_zone`	Uses active support's time zone when converting timestamps between server and client.

The next step is to modify our models to be stored in MongoDB. This is as simple as including one line of code in the model declaration, as shown in the following example:

```
class Person
  include Mongoid::Document
End
```

We can also use the following code:

```
include Mongoid::Timestamps
```

We use it to generate `created_at` and `updated_at` fields in a similar way to Active Record. Data fields do not need to be declared by type in our models, but it's good practice to do so. The supported data types are as follows:

- `Array`
- `BigDecimal`
- `Boolean`
- `Date`
- `DateTime`
- `Float`
- `Hash`
- `Integer`
- `BSON::ObjectId`
- `BSON::Binary`
- `Range`
- `Regexp`
- `String`
- `Symbol`
- `Time`
- `TimeWithZone`

If the types of fields are not defined, fields will be cast to the object and stored in the database. This is slightly faster, but doesn't support all types. If we try to use `BigDecimal`, `Date`, `DateTime`, or `Range`, we will get back an error.

Inheritance with Mongoid models

The following code is an example of inheritance using the Mongoid models:

```
class Canvas
  include Mongoid::Document
  field :name, type: String
  embeds_many :shapes
end
```

```
class Shape
  include Mongoid::Document
  field :x, type: Integer
  field :y, type: Integer
  embedded_in :canvas
end

class Circle < Shape
  field :radius, type: Float
end

class Rectangle < Shape
  field :width, type: Float
  field :height, type: Float
end
```

Now, we have a `Canvas` class with many `Shape` objects embedded in it. Mongoid will automatically create a field, which is `_type`, to distinguish between parent and child node fields. In scenarios where documents are inherited from their fields, relationships, validations, and scopes get copied down into their child documents, but not vice-versa.

`embeds_many` and `embedded_in` pairs will create embedded sub-documents to store the relationships. If we want to store these via referencing to `ObjectId`, we can do so by substituting these with `has_many` and `belongs_to`.

Connecting using Python

A strong contender to Ruby and Rails is Python with Django. Similar to Mongoid, there is MongoEngine and an official MongoDB low-level driver, PyMongo.

Installing PyMongo can be done using `pip` or `easy_install`, as shown in the following code:

```
python -m pip install pymongo
python -m easy_install pymongo
```

Then, in our class, we can connect to a database, as shown in the following example:

```
>>> from pymongo import MongoClient
>>> client = MongoClient()
```

Connecting to a replica set requires a set of seed servers for the client to find out what the primary, secondary, or arbiter nodes in the set are, as indicated in the following example:

```
client =
pymongo.MongoClient('mongodb://user:passwd@node1:p1,node2:p2/?replicaSet=rs
name')
```

Using the connection string URL, we can pass a username and password and the replicaSet name all in a single string. Some of the most interesting options for the connection string URL are present in the next section.

Connecting to a shard requires the server host and IP for the MongoDB router, which is the MongoDB process.

PyMODM ODM

Similar to Ruby's Mongoid, PyMODM is an ODM for Python that follows closely on Django's built-in ORM. Installing pymodm can be done via pip, as shown in the following code:

```
pip install pymodm
```

Then we need to edit settings.py and replace the database ENGINE with a dummy database, as shown in the following code:

```
DATABASES = {
    'default': {
        'ENGINE': 'django.db.backends.dummy'
    }
}
```

Then we add our connection string anywhere in settings.py, as shown in the following code:

```
from pymodm import connect
connect("mongodb://localhost:27017/myDatabase", alias="MyApplication")
```

Here, we have to use a connection string that has the following structure:

```
mongodb://[username:password@]host1[:port1][,host2[:port2],...[,hostN[:port
N]]][/[database][?options]]
```

Options have to be pairs of `name=value` with an `&` between each pair. Some interesting pairs are shown in the following table:

Name	Description
`minPoolSize`/`maxPoolSize`	Minimum and maximum pool size for connections.
`w`	Write concern option.
`wtimeoutMS`	Timeout for write concern operations.
`Journal`	Journal options.
`readPreference`	Read preference to be used for replica sets. Available options are: `primary`, `primaryPreferred`, `secondary`, `secondaryPreferred`, `nearest`.
`maxStalenessSeconds`	Specifies, in seconds, how stale (data lagging behind master) a secondary can be before the client stops using it for read operations.
`SSL`	Using SSL to connect to the database.
`authSource`	Used in conjunction with username, this specifies the database associated with the user's credentials. When we use external authentication mechanisms, this should be `$external` for LDAP or Kerberos.
`authMechanism`	Authentication mechanism can be used for connections. Available options for MongoDB are: **SCRAM-SHA-1, MONGODB-CR, MONGODB-X.509**. MongoDB enterprise (paid version) offers two more options: **GSSAPI** (Kerberos), **PLAIN (LDAP SASL)**

Model classes need to inherit from `MongoModel`. The following code shows what a sample class will look like:

```
from pymodm import MongoModel, fields
class User(MongoModel):
    email = fields.EmailField(primary_key=True)
    first_name = fields.CharField()
    last_name = fields.CharField()
```

This has a `User` class with `first_name`, `last_name`, and `email` fields, where `email` is the primary field.

Inheritance with PyMODM models

Handling one-to-one and one-to-many relationships in MongoDB can be done using references or embedding. The following example shows both ways, which are references for the model user and embedding for the comment model:

```
from pymodm import EmbeddedMongoModel, MongoModel, fields

class Comment(EmbeddedMongoModel):
    author = fields.ReferenceField(User)
    content = fields.CharField()

class Post(MongoModel):
    title = fields.CharField()
    author = fields.ReferenceField(User)
    revised_on = fields.DateTimeField()
    content = fields.CharField()
    comments = fields.EmbeddedDocumentListField(Comment)
```

Similar to Mongoid for Ruby, we can define relationships as being embedded or referenced, depending on our design decision.

Connecting using PHP

The MongoDB PHP driver was rewritten from scratch two years ago to support the PHP 5, PHP 7, and HHVM architectures. The current architecture is shown in the following diagram:

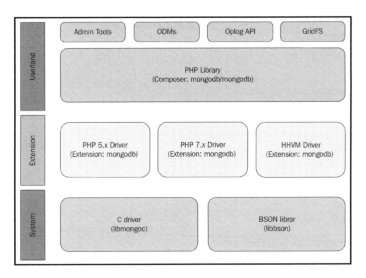

Currently, we have official drivers for all three architectures with full support for the underlying functionality.

Installation is a two-step process. First, we need to install the MongoDB extension. This extension is dependent on the version of PHP (or HHVM) that we have installed and can be done using `brew` in macOS. The following example is with PHP 7.0:

```
brew install php70-mongodb
```

Then, use `composer` (a widely-used dependency manager for PHP) as shown in the following example:

```
composer require mongodb/mongodb
```

Connecting to the database can be done by using the connection string URL or by passing an array of options.

Using the connection string URL, we have the following code:

```
$client = new MongoDB\Client($uri = 'mongodb://127.0.0.1/', array
$uriOptions = [], array $driverOptions = [])
```

For example, to connect to a replica set using SSL authentication, we use the following code:

```
$client = new
MongoDB\Client('mongodb://myUsername:myPassword@rs1.example.com,rs2.example
.com/?ssl=true&replicaSet=myReplicaSet&authSource=admin');
```

Or we can use the `$uriOptions` parameter to pass in parameters without using the connection string URL, as shown in the following code:

```
$client = new MongoDB\Client(
    'mongodb://rs1.example.com,rs2.example.com/'
    [
        'username' => 'myUsername',
        'password' => 'myPassword',
        'ssl' => true,
        'replicaSet' => 'myReplicaSet',
        'authSource' => 'admin',
    ],
);
```

The set of `$uriOptions` and the connection string URL options available are analogous to the ones used for Ruby and Python.

Doctrine ODM

Laravel is one of the most widely-used MVC frameworks for PHP, similar in architecture to Django and Rails from the Python and Ruby worlds respectively. We will follow through configuring our models using Laravel, Doctrine, and MongoDB. This section assumes that Doctrine is installed and working with Laravel 5.x.

Doctrine entities are **Plain Old PHP Objects (POPO)** that, unlike **Eloquent**, Laravel's default ORM doesn't need to inherit from the `Model` class. Doctrine uses the **Data Mapper Pattern**, whereas Eloquent uses Active Record. Skipping the `get()` and `set()` methods, a simple class would be shown in the following way:

```
use Doctrine\ORM\Mapping AS ORM;
use Doctrine\Common\Collections\ArrayCollection;
/**
 * @ORM\Entity
 * @ORM\Table(name="scientist")
 */
class Scientist
{
    /**
     * @ORM\Id
     * @ORM\GeneratedValue
     * @ORM\Column(type="integer")
     */
    protected $id;
    /**
     * @ORM\Column(type="string")
     */
    protected $firstname;
    /**
     * @ORM\Column(type="string")
     */
    protected $lastname;
    /**
     * @ORM\OneToMany(targetEntity="Theory", mappedBy="scientist",
cascade={"persist"})
     * @var ArrayCollection|Theory[]
     */
    protected $theories;
    /**
     * @param $firstname
     * @param $lastname
     */
    public function __construct($firstname, $lastname)
    {
        $this->firstname = $firstname;
```

```
        $this->lastname  = $lastname;
        $this->theories = new ArrayCollection;
    }
...
    public function addTheory(Theory $theory)
    {
        if(!$this->theories->contains($theory)) {
            $theory->setScientist($this);
            $this->theories->add($theory);
        }
    }
}
```

This POPO-based model uses annotations to define field types that need to be persisted in MongoDB. For example, @ORM\Column(type="string") defines a field in MongoDB with the string types firstname and lastname as the attribute names, in the respective lines.

There is a whole set of annotations available here: https://doctrine2.readthedocs.io/en/latest/reference/annotations-reference.html.

If we want to separate the POPO structure from annotations, we can also define them using YAML or XML instead of inlining them with annotations in our POPO model classes.

Inheritance with Doctrine

Modeling one-to-one and one-to-many relationships can be done via annotations, YAML, or XML. Using annotations, we can define multiple embedded sub-documents within our document, as shown in the following example:

```
/** @Document */
class User
{
    // ...
    /** @EmbedMany(targetDocument="Phonenumber") */
    private $phonenumbers = array();
    // ...
}
/** @EmbeddedDocument */
class Phonenumber
{
    // ...
}
```

Here, a User document embeds many phonenumbers. @EmbedOne() will embed one sub-document to be used for modeling one-to-one relationships.

Referencing is similar to embedding, as shown in the following example:

```
/** @Document */
class User
{
    // ...
    /**
     * @ReferenceMany(targetDocument="Account")
     */
    private $accounts = array();
    // ...
}
/** @Document */
class Account
{
    // ...
}
```

`@ReferenceMany()` and `@ReferenceOne()` are used to model one-to-many and one-to-one relationships via referencing into a separate collection.

Summary

In this chapter, we learned about schema design for relational databases and MongoDB and how we can achieve the same goal starting from a different starting point.

In MongoDB, we have to think about read and write ratios, the questions that our users will have in the most common cases, and cardinality among relationships.

We learnt about atomic operations and how we can construct our queries so that we can have ACID properties without the overhead of transactions.

We also learned about MongoDB data types, how they can be compared, and some special data types, such as the `ObjectId`, which can be used both by the database and to our own advantage.

Starting from modeling simple one-to-one relationships, we went through one-to-many and also many-to-many relationship modeling, without the need for an intermediate table, as we would do in a relational database, either using references or embedded documents.

We learned how to model data for keyword searches, one of the features that most applications need to support in a web context.

Finally, we explored different use cases for using MongoDB with three of the most popular web programming languages. We saw examples using Ruby with the official driver and Mongoid ODM. Then we explored how to connect using Python with the official driver and PyMODM ODM, and, lastly, we worked through an example using PHP with the official driver and Doctrine ODM.

With all these languages (and many others), there are both official drivers offering support and full access functionality to the underlying database operations and also **object data modeling** frameworks for ease of modeling our data and rapid development.

In the next chapter, we will dive deeper into the MongoDB shell and the operations we can achieve using it. We will also master using the drivers for CRUD operations on our documents.

Section 2: Querying Effectively
2

In this section, we will cover more advanced MongoDB operations. We will start with CRUD operations, which are the most commonly used operations. Then, we will move on to more advanced querying concepts, followed by multi-document ACID transactions, which were introduced in version 4.0. The next topic to be covered is the aggregation framework, which can help users process big data in a structured and efficient way. Finally, we will learn how to index our data such that reads are way faster, but without impacting write performance.

This section consists of the following chapters:

- Chapter 3, *MongoDB CRUD Operations*
- Chapter 4, *Advanced Querying*
- Chapter 5, *Multi-Document ACID Transactions*
- Chapter 6, *Aggregation*
- Chapter 7, *Indexing*

3
MongoDB CRUD Operations

In this chapter, we will learn how to use the mongo shell for database administration operations. Starting with simple **create, read, update, and delete (CRUD)** operations, we will master scripting from the shell. We will also learn how to write MapReduce scripts from the shell and contrast them to the aggregation framework, into which we will dive deeper in `Chapter 6`, *Aggregation*. Finally, we will explore authentication and authorization using the MongoDB community and its paid counterpart, the Enterprise Edition.

In this chapter we will cover the following topics:

- CRUD using the shell
- Administration
- Aggregation framework
- Securing the shell
- Authentication with MongoDB

CRUD using the shell

The mongo shell is equivalent to the administration console used by relational databases. Connecting to the mongo shell is as easy as typing the following code:

```
$ mongo
```

Type this on the command line for standalone servers or replica sets. Inside the shell, you can view available databases simply by typing the following code:

```
$ db
```

Then, you can connect to a database by typing the following code:

```
> use <database_name>
```

The mongo shell can be used to query and update data into our databases. Inserting this document in the `books` collection can be done as follows:

```
> db.books.insert({title: 'mastering mongoDB', isbn: '101'})
WriteResult({ "nInserted" : 1 })
```

We can then find documents from a collection named `books` by typing the following:

```
> db.books.find()
{ "_id" : ObjectId("592033f6141daf984112d07c"), "title" : "mastering
mongoDB", "isbn" : "101" }
```

The result we get back from MongoDB informs us that the write succeeded and inserted one new document in the database.

Deleting this document has a similar syntax and results in the following code:

```
> db.books.remove({isbn: '101'})
WriteResult({ "nRemoved" : 1 })
```

You can try to update this same document as shown in the following code block:

```
> db.books.update({isbn:'101'}, {price: 30})
WriteResult({ "nMatched" : 1, "nUpserted" : 0, "nModified" : 1 })
> db.books.find()
{ "_id" : ObjectId("592034c7141daf984112d07d"), "price" : 30 }
```

Here, we notice a couple of things:

- The JSON-like formatted field in the `update` command is our query for searching for documents to update
- The `WriteResult` object notifies us that the query matched one document and modified one document
- Most importantly, the contents of this document were entirely replaced by the contents of the second JSON-like formatted field but we have lost information on `title` and `isbn`

By default, the `update` command in MongoDB will replace the contents of our document with the document we specify in the second argument. If we want to update the document and add new fields to it, we need to use the `$set` operator, as follows:

```
> db.books.update({isbn:'101'}, {$set: {price: 30}})
WriteResult({ "nMatched" : 1, "nUpserted" : 0, "nModified" : 1 })
```

Now, our document matches what we would expect:

```
> db.books.find()
{ "_id" : ObjectId("592035f6141daf984112d07f"), "title" : "mastering
mongoDB", "isbn" : "101", "price" : 30 }
```

However, deleting a document can be done in several ways, the most simple way is through its unique `ObjectId`:

```
> db.books.remove("592035f6141daf984112d07f")
WriteResult({ "nRemoved" : 1 })
> db.books.find()
>
```

You can see here that when there are no results, the mongo shell will not return anything other than the shell prompt itself: >.

Scripting for the mongo shell

Administering the database using built-in commands is helpful, but it's not the main reason for using the shell. The true power of the mongo shell comes from the fact that it is a JavaScript shell.

We can declare and assign variables in the shell as follows:

```
> var title = 'MongoDB in a nutshell'
> title
MongoDB in a nutshell
> db.books.insert({title: title, isbn: 102})
WriteResult({ "nInserted" : 1 })
> db.books.find()
{ "_id" : ObjectId("59203874141daf984112d080"), "title" : "MongoDB in a
nutshell", "isbn" : 102 }
```

In the previous example, we declared a new `title` variable as MongoDB in a nutshell and used the variable to insert a new document into our books collection, as shown in the following code.

As it's a JavaScript shell, we can use it for functions and scripts that generate complex results from our database:

```
> queryBooksByIsbn = function(isbn) { return db.books.find({isbn: isbn})}
```

With this one-liner, we are creating a new function named `queryBooksByIsbn` that takes a single argument, which is the `isbn` value. With the data that we have in our collection, we can use our new function and fetch books by `isbn`, as shown in the following code:

```
> queryBooksByIsbn("101")
{ "_id" : ObjectId("592035f6141daf984112d07f"), "title" : "mastering
mongoDB", "isbn" : "101", "price" : 30 }
```

Using the shell, we can write and test these scripts. Once we are satisfied, we can store them in the `.js` file and invoke them directly from the command line:

```
$ mongo <script_name>.js
```

Here are some useful notes about the default behavior of these scripts:

- Write operations will use a default write concern of 1, which is global for MongoDB as of the current version. As write concern of 1 will request an acknowledgement that the write operation has propagated to the standalone `mongod` server or the primary server in a replica set.
- To get results from operations from a script back to standard output, we must use either JavaScript's built-in `print()` function or the mongo-specific `printjson()` function, which prints out results formatted in JSON.

The differences between scripting for the mongo shell and using it directly

When writing scripts for the mongo shell, we cannot use the shell helpers. MongoDB's commands, such as `use <database_name>`, `show collections`, and other helpers are built into the shell and so are not available from the JavaScript context where our scripts will get executed. Fortunately, there are equivalents to them that are available from the JavaScript execution context, as shown in the following table:

Shell helpers	JavaScript equivalents
`show dbs, show databases`	`db.adminCommand('listDatabases')`
`use <database_name>`	`db = db.getSiblingDB('<database_name>')`
`show collections`	`db.getCollectionNames()`

show users	db.getUsers()
show roles	db.getRoles({showBuiltinRoles: true})
show log <logname>	db.adminCommand({ 'getLog' : '<logname>' })
show logs	db.adminCommand({ 'getLog' : '*' })

it	cursor = db.collection.find()
	if (cursor.hasNext()){
	  cursor.next();
	}

In the previous table, `it` is the iteration cursor that the mongo shell returns when we query and get back too many results to show in one batch.

Using the mongo shell, we can script almost anything that we would from a client, meaning that we have a really powerful tool for prototyping and getting quick insights into our data.

Batch inserts using the shell

When using the shell, there will be many times we want to insert a large number of documents programmatically. The most straightforward implementation since we have a JavaScript shell, is to iterate through a loop, generating each document along the way, and performing a write operation in every iteration in the loop, as follows:

```
> authorMongoFactory = function() {for(loop=0;loop<1000;loop++)
{db.books.insert({name: "MongoDB factory book" + loop})}}
function () {for(loop=0;loop<1000;loop++) {db.books.insert({name: "MongoDB
factory book" + loop})}}
```

In this simple example, we create an `authorMongoFactory()` method for an author who writes 1000 books on MongoDB with a slightly different name for each one:

```
> authorMongoFactory()
```

This will result in 1000 writes being issued to the database. While it is simple from a development point of view, this method will put a strain on the database.

Instead, using a `bulk` write, we can issue a single database `insert` command with the 1000 documents that we have prepared beforehand, as follows:

```
> fastAuthorMongoFactory = function() {
var bulk = db.books.initializeUnorderedBulkOp();
for(loop=0;loop<1000;loop++) {bulk.insert({name: "MongoDB factory book" +
loop})}
bulk.execute();
}
```

The end result is the same as before, with the 1000 documents being inserted with the following structure in our `books` collection:

```
> db.books.find()
{ "_id" : ObjectId("59204251141daf984112d851"), "name" : "MongoDB factory
book0" }
{ "_id" : ObjectId("59204251141daf984112d852"), "name" : "MongoDB factory
book1" }
{ "_id" : ObjectId("59204251141daf984112d853"), "name" : "MongoDB factory
book2" }
...
{ "_id" : ObjectId("59204251141daf984112d853"), "name" : "MongoDB factory
book999" }
```

The difference from the user's perspective lies in the speed of execution and reduced strain on the database.

In the preceding example, we used `initializeUnorderedBulkOp()` for the `bulk` operation builder setup. The reason we did this is because we don't care about the order of insertions being the same as the order in which we add them to our `bulk` variable with the `bulk.insert()` command.

This makes sense when we can make sure that all operations are unrelated to each other or idempotent.

If we care about having the same order of insertions, we can use `initializeOrderedBulkOp()`; by changing the second line of our function, we get the following code snippet:

```
var bulk = db.books.initializeOrderedBulkOp();
```

Batch operations using the mongo shell

In the case of inserts, we can generally expect that the order of operations doesn't matter.

`bulk`, however, can be used with many more operations than just inserts. In the following example, we have a single book with `isbn : 101` and the `name` of `Mastering MongoDB` in a `bookOrders` collection with the number of available copies to purchase in the `available` field, with the `99` books available for purchase:

```
> db.bookOrders.find()
{ "_id" : ObjectId("59204793141daf984112dc3c"), "isbn" : 101, "name" :
"Mastering MongoDB", "available" : 99 }
```

With the following series of operations in a single `bulk` operation, we are adding one book to the inventory and then ordering `100` books, for a final total of zero copies available:

```
> var bulk = db.bookOrders.initializeOrderedBulkOp();
> bulk.find({isbn: 101}).updateOne({$inc: {available : 1}});
> bulk.find({isbn: 101}).updateOne({$inc: {available : -100}});
> bulk.execute();
```

With the code, we will get the following output:

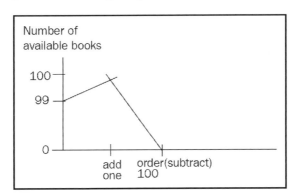

Using `initializeOrderedBulkOp()`, we can make sure that we are adding one book before ordering `100` so that we are never out of stock. On the contrary, if we were using `initializeUnorderedBulkOp()`, we won't have such a guarantee and we might end up with the 100-book order coming in before the addition of the new book, resulting in an application error as we don't have that many books to fulfill the order.

When executing through an ordered list of operations, MongoDB will split the operations into batches of 1000 and group these by operation. For example, if we have 1002 inserts, 998 updates, 1004 deletes, and finally, 5 inserts, we will end up with the following:

```
[1000 inserts]
[2 inserts]
[998 updates]
[1000 deletes]
[4 deletes]
[5 inserts]
```

The previous code can be explained as follows:

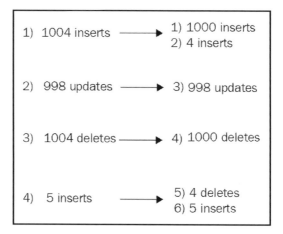

This doesn't affect the series of operations, but it implicitly means that our operations will leave the database in batches of 1000. This behavior is not guaranteed to stay in future versions.

If we want to inspect the execution of a bulk.execute() command, we can issue bulk.getOperations() right after we type execute().

 Since version 3.2, MongoDB has offered an alternative command for bulk writes, bulkWrite().

`bulkWrite` arguments are the series of operations we want to execute. `WriteConcern` (the default is again 1), and if the series of write operations should get applied in the order that they appear in the array (they will be ordered by default):

```
> db.collection.bulkWrite(
  [ <operation 1>, <operation 2>, ... ],
  {
  writeConcern : <document>,
  ordered : <boolean>
  }
)
```

The following operations are the same ones supported by `bulk`:

- `insertOne`
- `updateOne`
- `updateMany`
- `deleteOne`
- `deleteMany`
- `replaceOne`

`updateOne`, `deleteOne`, and `replaceOne` have matching filters; if they match more than one document, they will only operate on the first one. It's important to design these queries so that they don't match more than one document, otherwise, the behavior will be undefined.

Administration

Using MongoDB should, for the most part, be as transparent as possible to the developer. Since there are no schemas, there is no need for migrations, and generally, developers find themselves spending less time on administrative tasks in the database world.

That said, there are several tasks that an experienced MongoDB developer or architect can perform to keep up the speed and performance of MongoDB.

Administration is generally performed in three different levels, ranging from more generic to more specific: **process**, **collection**, and **index**.

At the process level, there is the `shutDown` command to shut down the MongoDB server.

At the database level, we have the following commands:

- `dropDatabase`
- `listCollections`
- `copyDB` or `clone` to clone a remote database locally
- `repairDatabase` for when our database is not in a consistent state due to an unclean shutdown

In comparison, at the collection level, the following commands are used:

- `drop`: To drop a collection
- `create`: To create a collection
- `renameCollection`: To rename a collection
- `cloneCollection`: To clone a remote collection to our local DB
- `cloneCollectionAsCapped`: To clone a collection into a new capped collection
- `convertToCapped`: To convert a collection to a capped one

At the index level, we can use the following commands:

- `createIndexes`
- `listIndexes`
- `dropIndexes`
- `reIndex`

We will also go through a few other commands that are more important from an administration standpoint.

fsync

MongoDB normally writes all operations to the disk every 60 seconds. fsync will force data to persist to the disk immediately and synchronously.

If we want to take a backup of our databases, we need to apply a lock as well. Locking will block all writes and some reads while fsync is operating.

In almost all cases, it's better to use journaling and refer to our techniques for backup and restore, which will be covered in Chapter 8, *Monitoring, Backup, and Security*, for maximum availability and performance.

compact

MongoDB documents take up a specified amount of space on a disk. If we perform an update that increases the size of a document, this may end up being moved out of sequence to the end of the storage block, creating a hole in storage, resulting in increased execution times for this update, and possibly missing it from running queries. The compact operation will defragment space and result in less space being used.

We can update a document by adding an extra 10 bytes, showing how it will be moved to the end of the storage block, and creating an empty space in the physical storage:

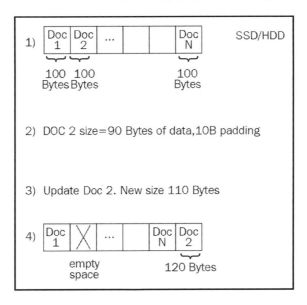

compact can also take a paddingFactor argument as follows:

```
> db.runCommand ( { compact: '<collection>', paddingFactor: 2.0 } )
```

paddingFactor is the preallocated space in each document that ranges from 1.0 (that is, no padding, which is the default value) to 4.0 for calculating the padding of 300 bytes for each 100 bytes of document space that is needed when we initially insert it.

Adding padding can help alleviate the problem of updates moving documents around, at the expense of more disk space being needed for each document when created. By padding each document, we are allocating more space for it that will prevent it from being moved to the end of the storage block if our updated document can still fit in the preallocated storage space.

currentOp and killOp

`db.currentOp()` will show us the currently-running operation in the database and will attempt to kill it. We need to run the `use admin` command before running `killOp()`. Needless to say, using `killOp()` against internal MongoDB operations is not recommended or advised, as the database may end up in an undefined state. The `killOp()` command can be used as follows:

```
> db.runCommand( { "killOp": 1, "op": <operationId> } )
```

collMod

`collMod` is used to pass flags to a collection by modifying the underlying database's behavior.

Since version 3.2, the most interesting set of flags that we can pass to a collection is document validation.

Document validation can specify a set of rules to be applied to new updates and inserts into a collection. This means that current documents will be checked if they get modified.

We can only apply validations to documents that are already valid if we set `validationLevel` to `moderate`. By specifying `validationAction`, we can log documents that are invalid by setting it to `warn` or prevent updates from happening altogether by setting it to `error`.

For example, with the previous example of `bookOrders` we can set `validator` on the `isbn` and `name` fields being present for every insert or update, as demonstrated in the following code:

```
> db.runCommand( { collMod: "bookOrders",
"validator" : {
        "$and" : [
            {
                "isbn" : {
                    "$exists" : true
                }
            },
            {
                "name" : {
                    "$exists" : true
                }
            }
        ]
```

```
            }
  })
```

Here, we get back the following code:

```
  { "ok" : 1 }
```

Then, if we try to insert a new document with only the isbn field being present, we get an error:

```
  > db.bookOrders.insert({isbn: 102})
  WriteResult({
  "nInserted" : 0,
  "writeError" : {
  "code" : 121,
  "errmsg" : "Document failed validation"
  }
  })
  >
```

We get an error because our validation has failed. Managing validation from the shell is really useful as we can write scripts to manage it, and also make sure that everything is in place.

touch

The touch command will load data and/or index data from storage to memory. This is typically useful if our script will subsequently use this data, speeding up the execution:

```
  > db.runCommand({ touch: "bookOrders", data: true/false, index: true/false
  })
```

This command should be used with caution in production systems, as loading data and indexes into memory will displace existing data from it.

MapReduce in the mongo shell

One of the most interesting features that has been underappreciated and not widely supported throughout MongoDB history, is the ability to write MapReduce natively using the shell.

MapReduce is a data processing method for getting aggregation results from large sets of data. The main advantage of this is that it is inherently parallelizable as evidence by frameworks such as Hadoop.

MapReduce is really useful when used to implement a data pipeline. Multiple MapReduce commands can be chained to produce different results. An example of this is aggregating data by using different reporting periods (such as hour, day, week, month, and year) where we use the output of each more granular reporting period to produce a less granular report.

A simple example of MapReduce in our examples given that our input books collection is as follows:

```
> db.books.find()
{ "_id" : ObjectId("592149c4aabac953a3a1e31e"), "isbn" : "101", "name" :
"Mastering MongoDB", "price" : 30 }
{ "_id" : ObjectId("59214bc1aabac954263b24e0"), "isbn" : "102", "name" :
"MongoDB in 7 years", "price" : 50 }
{ "_id" : ObjectId("59214bc1aabac954263b24e1"), "isbn" : "103", "name" :
"MongoDB for experts", "price" : 40 }
```

Our map and reduce functions are defined as follows:

```
> var mapper = function() {
                    emit(this.id, 1);
            };
```

In this `mapper`, we simply output a key of `id` of each document with a value of 1:

```
> var reducer = function(id, count) {
                    return Array.sum(count);
            };
```

In `reducer`, we sum across all values (where each one has a value of 1):

```
> db.books.mapReduce(mapper, reducer, { out:"books_count" });
{
"result" : "books_count",
"timeMillis" : 16613,
"counts" : {
"input" : 3,
"emit" : 3,
"reduce" : 1,
"output" : 1
},
"ok" : 1
}
> db.books_count.find()
```

```
{ "_id" : null, "value" : 3 }
>
```

Our final output will be a document with no ID, since we didn't output any value for ID, and a value of six, since there are six documents in the input dataset.

Using MapReduce, MongoDB will apply a map to each input document, emitting key-value pairs at the end of the map phase. Then each reducer will get key-value pairs with the same key as input, processing all multiple values. The reducer's output will be a single key-value pair for each key.

Optionally, we can use a `finalize` function to further process the results of `mapper` and `reducer`. MapReduce functions use JavaScript and run within the `mongod` process. MapReduce can output inline as a single document, subject to the 16 MB document size limit, or as multiple documents in an output collection. Input and output collections can be sharded.

MapReduce concurrency

MapReduce operations will place several short-lived locks that should not affect operations. However, at the end of the `reduce` phase, if we output the data to an existing collection, then output actions such as `merge`, `reduce`, and `replace` will take an exclusive global write lock for the whole server, blocking all other writes to the `db` instance. If we want to avoid this, then we should invoke `mapReduce` in the following way:

```
> db.collection.mapReduce(
                     mapper,
                     reducer,
                     {
                        out: { merge/reduce: bookOrders, nonAtomic: true
}
                     })
```

We can apply `nonAtomic` only to `merge` or `reduce` actions. `replace` will just replace the contents of documents in `bookOrders`, which will not take much time anyway.

With the `merge` action, the new result is merged with the existing result if the output collection already exists. If an existing document has the same key as the new result, then it will overwrite the existing document.

With the `reduce` action, the new result is processed together with the existing result if the output collection already exists. If an existing document has the same key as the new result, it will apply the `reduce` function to both the new and the existing documents, and will overwrite the existing document with the result.

Although MapReduce has been present since the early versions of MongoDB, it hasn't evolved as much as the rest of the database, resulting in its usage being less than that of specialized MapReduce frameworks such as Hadoop, which we will learn more about in `Chapter 11`, *Harnessing Big Data with MongoDB*.

Incremental MapReduce

Incremental MapReduce is a pattern where we use MapReduce to aggregate to previously calculated values. An example of this could be counting non-distinct users in a collection for different reporting periods (that is, by hour, day, or month) without the need to recalculate the result every hour.

To set up our data for incremental MapReduce, we need to do the following:

- Output our reduce data to a different collection
- At the end of every hour, query only for the data that got into the collection in the last hour
- With the output of our reduce data, merge our results with the calculated results from the previous hour

Continuing with the previous example, let's assume that we have a `published` field in each of the documents with our input dataset, as shown in the following code:

```
> db.books.find()
{ "_id" : ObjectId("592149c4aabac953a3a1e31e"), "isbn" : "101", "name" :
"Mastering MongoDB", "price" : 30, "published" :
ISODate("2017-06-25T00:00:00Z") }
{ "_id" : ObjectId("59214bc1aabac954263b24e0"), "isbn" : "102", "name" :
"MongoDB in 7 years", "price" : 50, "published" :
ISODate("2017-06-26T00:00:00Z") }
```

Using our previous example of counting books, we will get the following code:

```
var mapper = function() {
                    emit(this.id, 1);
              };
var reducer = function(id, count) {
                    return Array.sum(count);
              };
> db.books.mapReduce(mapper, reducer, { out: "books_count" })
{
"result" : "books_count",
"timeMillis" : 16700,
"counts" : {
"input" : 2,
"emit" : 2,
"reduce" : 1,
"output" : 1
},
"ok" : 1
}
> db.books_count.find()
{ "_id" : null, "value" : 2 }
```

Now we get a third book in our `mongo_book` collection with a document, as follows:

```
{ "_id" : ObjectId("59214bc1aabac954263b24e1"), "isbn" : "103", "name" :
"MongoDB for experts", "price" : 40, "published" :
ISODate("2017-07-01T00:00:00Z") }
> db.books.mapReduce( mapper, reducer, { query: { published: { $gte:
ISODate('2017-07-01 00:00:00') } }, out: { reduce: "books_count" } } )
> db.books_count.find()
{ "_id" : null, "value" : 3 }
```

What happened in the preceding code is that by querying for documents in July, 2017, we only got the new document out of the query and then used its value to reduce the value with the already-calculated value of 2 in our `books_count` document, adding 1 to the final sum of 3 documents.

This example, as contrived as it is, shows a powerful attribute of MapReduce: the ability to re-reduce results to incrementally calculate aggregations over time.

Troubleshooting MapReduce

Over the years, one of the major shortcomings of MapReduce frameworks has been the inherent difficulty in troubleshooting, as opposed to simpler non-distributed patterns. Most of the time, the most effective tool is debugging using `log` statements to verify that output values match our expected values. In the mongo shell, which is a JavaScript shell, it is as simple as providing the output using the `console.log()` function.

Diving deeper into MapReduce in MongoDB, we can debug both in the map and the reduce phase by overloading the output values.

By debugging the `mapper` phase, we can overload the `emit()` function to test what the output key values will be, as follows:

```
> var emit = function(key, value) {
  print("debugging mapper's emit");
  print("key: " + key + "  value: " + tojson(value));
}
```

We can then call it manually on a single document to verify that we get back the key-value pair that we expect:

```
> var myDoc = db.orders.findOne( { _id:
ObjectId("50a8240b927d5d8b5891743c") } );
> mapper.apply(myDoc);
```

The `reducer` function is somewhat more complicated. A MapReduce `reducer` function must meet the following criteria:

- It must be idempotent
- It must be commutative
- The order of values coming from the `mapper` function should not matter for the reducer's result
- The `reducer` function must return the same type of result as the `mapper` function

We will dissect each of these following requirements to understand what they really mean:

- **It must be idempotent**: MapReduce, by design, may call the `reducer` function multiple times for the same key with multiple values from the `mapper` phase. It also doesn't need to reduce single instances of a key as it's just added to the set. The final value should be the same no matter the order of execution. This can be verified by writing our own `verifier` function and forcing `reducer` to re-reduce, or by executing `reducer` many times as shown in the following code snippet:

    ```
    reduce( key, [ reduce(key, valuesArray) ] ) == reduce( key,
    valuesArray )
    ```

- **It must be commutative**: As multiple invocations of the `reducer` function may happen for the same `key`, if it has multiple values, the following code should hold:

    ```
    reduce(key, [ C, reduce(key, [ A, B ]) ] ) == reduce( key, [ C,
    A, B ] )
    ```

- **The order of values coming from the mapper function should not matter for the reducer's result**: We can test that the order of values from `mapper` doesn't change the output for `reducer`, by passing in documents to `mapper` in a different order and verifying that we get the same results out:

    ```
    reduce( key, [ A, B ] ) == reduce( key, [ B, A ] )
    ```

- **The reduce function must return the same type of result as the mapper function**: Hand-in-hand with the first requirement, the type of object that the `reduce` function returns should be the same as the output of the `mapper` function.

Aggregation framework

Since version 2.2, MongoDB has provided a better way to work with aggregation, one that has been supported, adopted, and enhanced regularly ever since. The aggregation framework is modeled after data processing pipelines.

In data processing pipelines, there are three main operations: filters that operate like queries, filtering documents, and document transformations that transform documents to get them ready for the next stage.

SQL to aggregation

An aggregation pipeline can replace and augment querying operations in the shell. A common pattern for development is as follows:

- To verify that we have the correct data structures and get quick results using a series of queries in the shell
- To prototype pipeline results using the aggregation framework
- To refine and refactor if/when needed, either by ETL processes to get data into a dedicated data warehouse, or by more extensive usage of the application layer to get the insights that we need

In the following table, we can see how SQL commands map to the aggregation framework operators:

SQL	Aggregation framework
WHERE/HAVING	$match
GROUP BY	$group
SELECT	$project
ORDER BY	$sort
LIMIT	$limit
sum()/count()	$sum
join	$lookup

Aggregation versus MapReduce

In MongoDB, we can essentially get data out of our database by using three methods: querying, the aggregation framework, and MapReduce. All three of them can be chained to each other and many times it is useful to do so; however, it's important to understand when we should use aggregation and when MapReduce may be a better alternative.

 We can use both aggregation and MapReduce with sharded databases.

Aggregation is based on the concept of a pipeline. As such, it's important to be able to model our data from the input to the final output, in a series of transformations and processing that can get us there. It's also mostly useful when our intermediate results can be used on their own, or feed parallel pipelines. Our operations are limited by the operators that we have available from MongoDB, so it's important to make sure that we can calculate all the results we need by using the available commands.

MapReduce, on the other hand, can be used to construct pipelines by chaining the output of one MapReduce job to the input of the next one via an intermediate collection, but this is not its primary purpose.

MapReduce's most common use case is to periodically calculate aggregations for large datasets. Having MongoDB's querying in place, we can incrementally calculate these aggregations without the need to scan through the whole input table every time. In addition, its power comes from its flexibility as we can define mappers and reducers in JavaScript with the full flexibility of the language when calculating intermediate results. Not having the operators that the aggregation framework provides us with, we have to implement them on our own.

In many cases, the answer is not either/or. We can (and should) use the aggregation framework to construct our ETL pipeline and resort to MapReduce for the parts that are not yet supported sufficiently by it.

A complete use case with aggregation and MapReduce is provided in Chapter 6, *Aggregation*.

Securing the shell

MongoDB is a database developed with the ease of development in mind. As such, security at the database level was not baked in from the beginning and it was up to the developers and administrators to secure the MongoDB host from accessing outside the application server.

Unfortunately, this means that as far as back as 2015, there were 39,890 databases found open to the internet, with no security access configured. Many of them were production databases, one belonging to a French telecom operator and containing more than eight million records from its customers.

Nowadays, there is no excuse for leaving any MongoDB server with the default authentication off settings at any stage of development, from local server deployment to production.

Authentication and authorization

Authentication and authorization are closely connected and sometimes confused. Authentication is about verifying the identity of a user to the database. An example of authentication is **Secure Sockets Layer (SSL)**, where the web server verifies its identity—that it is who it claims to be—to the user.

Authorization is about determining what actions a user can take on a resource. In the next sections, we will discuss authentication and authorization with these definitions in mind.

Authorization with MongoDB

MongoDB's most basic authorization relies on the username/password method. By default, MongoDB will not start with authorization enabled. To enable it, we need to start our server with the `--auth` parameter:

```
$ mongod --auth
```

To set up authorization, we need to start our server without authorization to set up a user. Setting up an admin user is simple:

```
> use admin
> db.createUser(
  {
    user: <adminUser>,
    pwd: <password>,
    roles: [ { role: <adminRole>, db: "admin" } ]
  }
)
```

Here, `<adminUser>` is the name of the user we want to create, `<password>` is the password, and `<adminRole>` can be any of the following values ordered from the most powerful to the least powerful, as shown in the following list:

- root
- dbAdminAnyDatabase
- userAdminAnyDatabase
- readWriteAnyDatabase

- readAnyDatabase
- dbOwner
- dbAdmin
- userAdmin
- readWrite
- read

Of these roles, root is the superuser that allows access to everything. This is not recommended to be used, except for special circumstances.

All the AnyDatabase roles provide access to all databases, of which dbAdminAnyDatabase combines the userAdminAnyDatabase and readWriteAnyDatabase scopes being an admin again in all databases.

The rest of the roles are defined in the database that we want them to apply, by changing the roles subdocument of the preceding db.createUser(); for example, to create a dbAdmin for our mongo_book database, we would use the following code:

```
> db.createUser(
 {
 user: <adminUser>,
 pwd: <password>,
 roles: [ { role: "dbAdmin", db: "mongo_book" } ]
 }
)
```

Cluster administration has even more roles, which we will cover in more depth in Chapter 12, *Replication*.

Finally, when we restart our database with the --auth flag set, we can use either the command line or the connection string (from any driver) to connect as admin and create new users with predefined or custom-defined roles:

```
mongodb://[username:password@]host1[:port1][,host2[:port2],...[,hostN[:port
N]]][/[database][?options]]
```

Security tips for MongoDB

Common software system security precautions apply with MongoDB. We will outline some of them here and learn how to enable them.

Encrypting communication using TLS/SSL

Communication between the `mongod` or `mongos` server and the client mongo shell or applications should be encrypted. This is supported in most MongoDB distributions from version 3.0 onward; however, we need to take care that we download the proper version with SSL support.

After this, we need to get a signed certificate from a trusted certificate authority or sign our own. Using self-signed certificates is fine for preproduction systems, but in production it will mean that MongoDB servers won't be able to verify our identity, leaving us susceptible to man-in-the-middle attacks; thus using a proper certificate is highly recommended.

To start our MongoDB server with SSL, we need the following code:

```
$ mongod --sslMode requireSSL --sslPEMKeyFile <pem> --sslCAFile <ca>
```

Here, `<pem>` is our `.pem` signed certificate file and `<ca>` is the `.pem` root certificate from the certificate authority that contains the root certificate chain.

These options can also be defined in our configuration file, `mongod.conf` or `mongos.conf`, in YAML file format, as follows:

```
net:
  ssl:
    mode: requireSSL
    PEMKeyFile: /etc/ssl/mongodb.pem
    CAFile: /etc/ssl/ca.pem
    disabledProtocols: TLS1_0,TLS1_1,TLS1_2
```

Here, we specified a `PEMKeyFile`, a `CAFile`, and also that we won't allow the server to start with certificates that follow the `TLS1_0`, `TLS1_1` or `TLS1_2` versions. These are the available versions for `disabledProtocols` at this time.

Encrypting data

Using WiredTiger is highly recommended for encrypting data at rest, as it supports it natively from version 3.2.

For users of the Community Edition version, this can be achieved in the storage selection of their choice; for example, in **Amazon Web Services** (**AWS**) using **Elastic Block Store** (**EBS**) encrypted storage volumes.

This feature is available only for MongoDB Enterprise Edition.

Limiting network exposure

The oldest security method to secure any server is to disallow it from accepting connections from unknown sources. In MongoDB, this is done in a configuration file with a simple line as follows:

```
net:
    bindIp: <string>
```

Here, `<string>` is a comma-separated list of IPs that the MongoDB server will accept connections from.

Firewalls and VPNs

Together with limiting network exposure on the server side, we can use firewalls to prevent access to our network from the outside internet. VPNs can also provide tunneled traffic between our servers, but regardless, they shouldn't be used as our sole security mechanism.

Auditing

No matter how secure any system is, we need to keep a close eye on the system from an auditing perspective to make sure that we detect possible breaches and stop them as soon as possible.

 This feature is available only for MongoDB Enterprise Edition.

For users of the Community Edition version, we have to set up auditing manually by logging changes to documents and collections in the application layer, possibly in a different database altogether. This will be addressed in the next chapter, which covers advanced querying using client drivers.

Using secure configuration options

It goes without saying that the same configuration options should be used. We must use one of the following:

- MapReduce
- The mongo shell group operation or a group operation from our client driver
- `$where` JavaScript server evaluation

If we don't, we should disable server-side scripting by using the `--noscripting` option on the command line when we start our server.

The mongo shell group operation, as mentioned in the previous list, can be a tricky one as many drivers may use MongoDB's `group()` command when we issue group commands in the driver. However, given the limitations that `group()` has in terms of performance and output documents, we should rethink our design to use the aggregation framework or application-side aggregations.

The web interface also has to be disabled by not using any of the following commands:

- `net.http.enabled`
- `net.http.JSONPEnabled`
- `net.http.RESTInterfaceEnabled`

On the contrary, `wireObjectCheck` needs to remain enabled as it is by default, and ensures that all documents stored by the `mongod` instance are valid BSON.

Authentication with MongoDB

By default, MongoDB uses SCRAM-SHA-1 as the default challenge and response authentication mechanism. This is an SHA-1 username/password-based mechanism for authentication. All drivers and the mongo shell itself have built-in methods to support it.

 The authentication protocol in MongoDB has changed since version 3.0. In older versions, the less secure MONGODB-CR was used.

Enterprise Edition

MongoDB's Enterprise Edition is a paid subscription product offering more features around security and administration.

Kerberos authentication

MongoDB Enterprise Edition also offers Kerberos authentication. Kerberos, named after the character Kerberos (or Cerberus) from Greek mythology—which is the ferocious three-headed guard-dog of the god of the underworld, Hades—focuses on mutual authentication between client and server, protecting against eavesdropping and replay attacks.

Kerberos is widely used in Windows systems through integration with Microsoft's Active Directory. To install Kerberos, we need to start `mongod` without Kerberos set up, then connect to the `$external` database (not the admin that we normally use for admin authorization), and create a user with a Kerberos role and permissions:

```
use $external
db.createUser(
  {
    user: "mongo_book_user@packt.net",
    roles: [ { role: "read", db: "mongo_book" } ]
  }
)
```

In the preceding example, we authorize the `mongo_book_user@packt.net` user to read our `mongo_book` database, just like we would do with a user using our admin system.

After that, we need to start our server with Kerberos support by passing in the `authenticationMechanisms` parameter, as follows:

```
--setParameter authenticationMechanisms=GSSAPI
```

Now we can connect from our server or command line, as follows:

```
$ mongo.exe --host <mongoserver> --authenticationMechanism=GSSAPI --
authenticationDatabase='$external' --username mongo_book_user@packt.net
```

LDAP authentication

Similar to Kerberos authentication, we can also use **Lightweight Directory Access Protocol (LDAP)** in MongoDB Enterprise Edition only. The user setup needs to be done in the `$external` database and must match the name of the authentication LDAP name. The name may need to pass through a transformation and this may cause a mismatch between the LDAP name and the user entry in the `$external` database.

Setting up LDAP authentication is beyond the scope of this book, but the important thing to consider is that any changes in the LDAP server may need changes in the MongoDB server, which won't happen automatically.

Summary

In this chapter, we scratched the tip of the iceberg of CRUD operations. Starting from the mongo shell, we learned how to insert, delete, read, and modify documents. We also discussed the differences between one-off inserts and inserting in batches for performance.

Following that, we discussed administration tasks and how to perform them in the mongo shell. MapReduce and its successor, aggregation framework, were also discussed in this chapter, including how they compare, how to use them, and how we can translate SQL queries to aggregation framework pipeline commands.

Finally, we discussed security and authentication with MongoDB. Securing our database is of paramount importance; we will learn more about this in Chapter 8, *Monitoring, Backup, and Security*.

In the next chapter, we will dive deeper into CRUD using three of the most popular languages for web development: Ruby, Python, and **PHP: Hypertext Preprocessor (PHP)**.

Advanced Querying

4

In the previous chapter, we learned how to use the mongo shell for scripting, administration, and developing in a secure way. In this chapter, we will dive deeper into using MongoDB with drivers and popular frameworks from Ruby, Python, and PHP: **Hypertext Preprocessor (PHP)**.

We will also show the best practices for using these languages and the variety of comparison and update operators that MongoDB supports on a database level, which are accessible through Ruby, Python, and PHP.

In this chapter we will learn the following topics:

- MongoDB operations
- CRUD using Ruby, Mongoid, Python, PyMODM, PHP and Doctrine
- Comparison operators
- Change streams

MongoDB CRUD operations

In this section, we will cover CRUD operations using Ruby, Python, and PHP with the official MongoDB driver and some popular frameworks for each language, respectively.

CRUD using the Ruby driver

In Chapter 3, *MongoDB CRUD Operations*, we covered how to connect to MongoDB from Ruby, Python, and PHP using the drivers and ODM. In this chapter, we will explore create, read, update, and delete operations using the official drivers and the most commonly used ODM frameworks.

Creating documents

Using the process described in Chapter 2, *Schema Design and Data Modeling,* we assume that we have an @collection instance variable pointing to our books collection in a mongo_book database in the 127.0.0.1:27017 default database:

```
@collection = Mongo::Client.new([ '127.0.0.1:27017' ], :database =>
'mongo_book').database[:books]
```

We insert a single document with our definition, as follows:

```
document = { isbn: '101', name: 'Mastering MongoDB', price: 30}
```

This can be performed with a single line of code as follows:

```
result = @collection.insert_one(document)
```

The resulting object is a Mongo::Operation::Result class with content that is similar to what we had in the shell, as shown in the following code:

```
{"n"=>1, "ok"=>1.0}
```

Here, n is the number of affected documents; 1 means we inserted one object and ok means 1 (true).

Creating multiple documents in one step is similar to this. For two documents with isbn 102 and 103, and using insert_many instead of insert_one, we have the following code:

```
documents = [ { isbn: '102', name: 'MongoDB in 7 years', price: 50 },
              { isbn: '103', name: 'MongoDB for experts', price: 40 } ]
result = @collection.insert_many(documents)
```

The resulting object is now a Mongo::BulkWrite::Result class, meaning that the BulkWrite interface was used for improved performance.

The main difference is that we now have an attribute, inserted_ids,, which will return ObjectId of the inserted objects from the BSON::ObjectId class.

Read

Finding documents work in the same way as creating them, that is, at the collection level:

```
@collection.find( { isbn: '101' } )
```

Multiple search criteria can be chained and are equivalent to an AND operator in SQL:

```
@collection.find( { isbn: '101', name: 'Mastering MongoDB' } )
```

The mongo-ruby-driver API provides several query options to enhance queries; the most widely used query options are listed in the following table:

Option	Description
allow_partial_results	This is for use with sharded clusters. If a shard is down, it allows the query to return results from the shards that are up, potentially getting only a portion of the results.
batch_size (Integer)	This can change the batch size that the cursor will fetch from MongoDB. This is done on each GETMORE operation (for example, by typing it on the mongo shell).
comment (String)	With this command we can add a comment in our query for documentation reasons.
hint (Hash)	We can force usage of an index using hint().
limit (Integer)	We can limit the result set to the number of documents specified by Integer.
max_scan (Integer)	We can limit the number of documents that will be scanned. This will return incomplete results and is useful if we are performing operations where we want to guarantee that they won't take a long time, such as when we connect to our production database.
no_cursor_timeout	If we don't specify this parameter, MongoDB will close any inactive cursor after 600 seconds. With this parameter our cursor will never be closed.
projection (Hash)	We can use this parameter to fetch or exclude specific attributes from our results. This will reduce data transfer over the wire. An example of this can be client[:books].find.projection(:price => 1).
read (Hash)	We can specify a read preference to be applied only for this query: client[:books].find.read(:mode => :secondary_preferred).
show_disk_loc (Boolean)	We should use this option if we want to find the actual location of our results on a disk.
skip (Integer)	This can be used to skip the specified number of documents. It's useful for the pagination of results.

snapshot	This can be used to execute our query in snapshot mode. This is useful for when we want a more stringent consistency.
sort (Hash)	We can use this to sort our results, for example, `client[:books].find.sort(:name => -1)`.

On top of the query options, mongo-ruby-driver provides some helper functions that can be chained at the method call level, as follows:

- `.count`: The total count for the preceding query
- `.distinct(:field_name)`: To distinguish between the results of the preceding query by `:field_name`

`Find()` returns a cursor containing the result set that we can iterate using `.each` in Ruby like every other object:

```
result = @collection.find({ isbn: '101' })
result.each do |doc|
  puts doc.inspect
end
```

The output for our `books` collection is as follows:

```
{"_id"=>BSON::ObjectId('592149c4aabac953a3a1e31e'), "isbn"=>"101",
"name"=>"Mastering MongoDB", "price"=>30.0, "published"=>2017-06-25
00:00:00 UTC}
```

Chaining operations in find()

`find()`, by default, uses an AND operator to match multiple fields. If we want to use an OR operator, our query needs to be as follows:

```
result = @collection.find('$or' => [{ isbn: '101' }, { isbn: '102' }]).to_a
puts result
```

The output of the preceding code is as follows:

```
{"_id"=>BSON::ObjectId('592149c4aabac953a3a1e31e'), "isbn"=>"101",
"name"=>"Mastering MongoDB", "price"=>30.0, "published"=>2017-06-25
00:00:00 UTC}{"_id"=>BSON::ObjectId('59214bc1aabac954263b24e0'),
"isbn"=>"102", "name"=>"MongoDB in 7 years", "price"=>50.0,
"published"=>2017-06-26 00:00:00 UTC}
```

We can also use `$and` instead of `$or` in the previous example:

```
result = @collection.find('$and' => [{ isbn: '101' }, { isbn: '102'
}]).to_a
puts result
```

This, of course, will return no results since no document can have both isbn 101 and 102.

An interesting and hard bug to find is if we define the same key multiple times, such as in the following code:

```
result = @collection.find({ isbn: '101', isbn: '102' })
puts result

{"_id"=>BSON::ObjectId('59214bc1aabac954263b24e0'), "isbn"=>"102",
"name"=>"MongoDB in 7 years", "price"=>50.0, "published"=>2017-06-26
00:00:00 UTC}
```

In comparison, the opposite order will cause the document with isbn 101 to be returned:

```
result = @collection.find({ isbn: '102', isbn: '101' })
puts result

{"_id"=>BSON::ObjectId('592149c4aabac953a3a1e31e'), "isbn"=>"101",
"name"=>"Mastering MongoDB", "price"=>30.0, "published"=>2017-06-25
00:00:00 UTC}
```

 This is because in Ruby hashes, by default, all duplicated keys except for the last one are silently ignored. This may not happen in the simplistic form shown in the preceding example, but it is prone to happen if we create keys programmatically.

Nested operations

Accessing embedded documents in mongo-ruby-driver is as simple as using the dot notation:

```
result = @collection.find({'meta.authors': 'alex giamas'}).to_a
puts result

"_id"=>BSON::ObjectId('593c24443c8ca55b969c4c54'), "isbn"=>"201",
"name"=>"Mastering MongoDB, 2nd Edition", "meta"=>{"authors"=>"alex
giamas"}}
```

We need to enclose the key name in quotes (' ') to access the embedded object just as we need it for operations starting with $, such as '$set'.

Update

Updating documents using mongo-ruby-driver is chained to finding them. Using our example `books` collection, we can do the following:

```
@collection.update_one( { 'isbn': 101}, { '$set' => { name: 'Mastering
MongoDB, 2nd Edition' } } )
```

This finds the document with `isbn 101` and changes its name to `Mastering MongoDB, 2nd Edition`.

In a similar way to `update_one`, we can use `update_many` to update multiple documents retrieved via the first parameter of the method.

If we don't use the `$set` operator, the contents of the document will be replaced by the new document.

Assuming Ruby version >=2.2, keys can be either quoted or unquoted; however, keys that start with $ need to be quoted as follows:

```
@collection.update( { isbn: '101'}, { "$set": { name: "Mastering MongoDB,
2nd edition" } } )
```

The resulting object of an update will contain information about the operation, including these methods:

- `ok?`: A Boolean value that shows whether the operation was successful or not
- `matched_count`: The number of documents matching the query
- `modified_count`: The number of documents affected (updated)
- `upserted_count`: The number of documents upserted if the operation includes `$set`
- `upserted_id`: The unique `ObjectId` of the upserted document if there is one

Updates that modify fields of a constant data size will be *in place*; this means that they won't move the document from its physical location on the disk. This includes operations such as `$inc` and `$set` on the `Integer` and `Date` fields.

Updates that can increase the size of a document may result in the document being moved from its physical location on the disk to a new location at the end of the file. In this case, queries may miss or return the document multiple times. To avoid this, we can use `$snapshot: true` while querying.

Delete

Deleting documents work in a similar way to finding documents. We need to find documents and then apply the delete operation.

For example, with our `books` collection used before, we can issue the following code:

```
@collection.find( { isbn: '101' } ).delete_one
```

This will delete a single document. In our case, since `isbn` is unique for every document, this is expected. If our `find()` clause had matched multiple documents, then `delete_one` would have deleted just the first one that `find()` returned, which may or may not have been what we wanted.

> If we use `delete_one` with a query matching multiple documents, the results may be unexpected.

If we want to delete all documents matching our `find()` query, we have to use `delete_many`, as follows:

```
@collection.find( { price: { $gte: 30 } ).delete_many
```

In the preceding example, we are deleting all books that have a price greater than or equal to 30.

Batch operations

We can use the `BulkWrite` API for batch operations. In our previous insert many documents example, this would be as follows:

```
@collection.bulk_write([ { insertMany: documents
                          }],
                        ordered: true)
```

The `BulkWrite` API can take the following parameters:

- `insertOne`
- `updateOne`
- `updateMany`
- `replaceOne`
- `deleteOne`
- `deleteMany`

One version of these commands will `insert/update/replace/delete` a single document even if the filter that we specify matches more than one document. In this case, it's important to have a filter that matches a single document to avoid unexpected behaviors.

It's also possible, and a perfectly valid use case, to include several operations in the first argument of the `bulk_write` command. This allows us to issue commands in a sequence when we have operations that depend on each other and we want to batch them in a logical order according to our business logic. Any error will stop `ordered:true` batch writes and we will need to manually roll back our operations. A notable exception is `writeConcern` errors, for example, requesting a majority of our replica set members to acknowledge our write. In this case, batch writes will go through and we can observe the errors in the `writeConcernErrors` result field:

```
old_book = @collection.findOne(name: 'MongoDB for experts')
new_book = { isbn: 201, name: 'MongoDB for experts, 2nd Edition', price: 55
}
@collection.bulk_write([ {deleteOne: old_book}, { insertOne: new_book
                        }],
                        ordered: true)
```

In the previous example, we made sure that we deleted the original book before adding the new (and more expensive) edition of our `MongoDB for experts` book.

BulkWrite can batch up to 1,000 operations. If we have more than 1,000 underlying operations in our commands, these will be split into chunks of thousands. It is good practice to try to keep our write operations to a single batch if we can to avoid unexpected behavior.

CRUD in Mongoid

In this section, we will use Mongoid to perform create, read, update, and delete operations. All of this code is also available on GitHub at https://github.com/agiamas/mastering-mongodb/tree/master/chapter_4.

Read

Back in Chapter 2, *Schema Design and Data Modeling*, we described how to install, connect, and set up models, including an inheritance to Mongoid. Here, we will go through the most common use cases of CRUD.

Finding documents is done using a DSL similar to **Active Record** (**AR**). As with AR using a relational database, Mongoid assigns a class to a MongoDB collection (table) and any object instance to a document (row from a relational database):

```
Book.find('592149c4aabac953a3a1e31e')
```

This will find the document by ObjectId and return the document with isbn 101, as will the query by a name attribute:

```
Book.where(name: 'Mastering MongoDB')
```

In a similar fashion to the dynamically generated AR queries by an attribute, we can use the helper method:

```
Book.find_by(name: 'Mastering MongoDB')
```

This queries by attribute name, equivalent to the previous query.

We should enable QueryCache to avoid hitting the database for the same query multiple times, as follows:

```
Mongoid::QueryCache.enabled = true
```

This can be added in any code block that we want to enable, or in the initializer for Mongoid.

Scoping queries

We can scope queries in Mongoid using class methods, as follows:

```
Class Book
...
  def self.premium
     where(price: {'$gt': 20'})
   end
End
```

Then we will use this query:

```
Book.premium
```

It will query for books with a price greater than 20.

Create, update, and delete

The Ruby interface for creating documents is similar to active record:

```
Book.where(isbn: 202, name: 'Mastering MongoDB, 3rd Edition').create
```

This will return an error if the creation fails.

We can use the bang version to force an exception to be raised if saving the document fails:

```
Book.where(isbn: 202, name: 'Mastering MongoDB, 3rd Edition').create!
```

The BulkWrite API is not supported as of Mongoid version 6.x. The workaround is to use the mongo-ruby-driver API, which will not use the mongoid.yml configuration or custom validations. Otherwise, you can use insert_many([array_of_documents]), which will insert the documents one by one.

To update documents, we can use update or update_all. Using update will update only the first document retrieved by the query part, whereas update_all will update all of them:

```
Book.where(isbn: 202).update(name: 'Mastering MongoDB, THIRD Edition')
Book.where(price: { '$gt': 20 }).update_all(price_range: 'premium')
```

Deleting a document is similar to creating it, providing delete to skip callbacks, and destroy if we want to execute any available callbacks in the affected document.

delete_all and destroy_all are convenient methods for multiple documents.

> destroy_all should be avoided if possible, as it will load all documents into the memory to execute callbacks and thus can be memory-intensive.

CRUD using the Python driver

PyMongo is the officially supported driver for Python by MongoDB. In this section, we will use PyMongo to `create`, `read`, `update`, and `delete` documents in MongoDB.

Creating and deleting

The Python driver provides methods for CRUD just like Ruby and PHP. Following on from Chapter 2, *Schema Design and Data Modeling,* and the `books` variable that points to our `books` collection, we will write the following code block:

```
from pymongo import MongoClient
from pprint import pprint

>>> book = {
 'isbn': '301',
 'name': 'Python and MongoDB',
 'price': 60
}
>>> insert_result = books.insert_one(book)
>>> pprint(insert_result)

<pymongo.results.InsertOneResult object at 0x104bf3370>

>>> result = list(books.find())
>>> pprint(result)

[{u'_id': ObjectId('592149c4aabac953a3a1e31e'),
 u'isbn': u'101',
 u'name': u'Mastering MongoDB',
 u'price': 30.0,
 u'published': datetime.datetime(2017, 6, 25, 0, 0)},
 {u'_id': ObjectId('59214bc1aabac954263b24e0'),
 u'isbn': u'102',
 u'name': u'MongoDB in 7 years',
 u'price': 50.0,
 u'published': datetime.datetime(2017, 6, 26, 0, 0)},
 {u'_id': ObjectId('593c24443c8ca55b969c4c54'),
 u'isbn': u'201',
```

```
     u'meta': {u'authors': u'alex giamas'},
     u'name': u'Mastering MongoDB, 2nd Edition'},
    {u'_id': ObjectId('594061a9aabac94b7c858d3d'),
     u'isbn': u'301',
     u'name': u'Python and MongoDB',
     u'price': 60}]
```

In the previous example, we used insert_one() to insert a single document, which we can define using the Python dictionary notation; we can then query it for all documents in the collection.

The resulting object for insert_one and insert_many has two fields of interest:

- Acknowledged: A Boolean that is true if the insert has succeeded and false if it hasn't, or if write concern is 0 (fire and forget write).
- inserted_id for insert_one: The ObjectId of the written document and inserted_ids for insert_many. The array of ObjectIds of the written documents.

We used the pprint library to pretty-print the find() results. The built-in way to iterate through the result set is by using the following code:

```
for document in results:
    print(document)
```

Deleting documents work in a similar to creating them. We can use delete_one to delete the first instance or delete_many to delete all instances of the matched query:

```
>>> result = books.delete_many({ "isbn": "101" })
>>> print(result.deleted_count)
1
```

The deleted_count instance tells us how many documents were deleted; in our case, it is 1, even though we used the delete_many method.

To delete all documents from a collection, we can pass in the empty document { }.

To drop a collection, we can use drop():

```
>>> books.delete_many({})
>>> books.drop()
```

Finding documents

To find documents based on top-level attributes, we can simply use a dictionary:

```
>>> books.find({"name": "Mastering MongoDB"})

[{u'_id': ObjectId('592149c4aabac953a3a1e31e'),
  u'isbn': u'101',
  u'name': u'Mastering MongoDB',
  u'price': 30.0,
  u'published': datetime.datetime(2017, 6, 25, 0, 0)}]
```

To find documents in an embedded document, we can use the dot notation. In the following example, we use `meta.authors` to access the `authors` embedded document inside the `meta` document:

```
>>> result = list(books.find({"meta.authors": {"$regex": "aLEx",
"$options": "i"}}))
>>> pprint(result)

[{u'_id': ObjectId('593c24443c8ca55b969c4c54'),
  u'isbn': u'201',
  u'meta': {u'authors': u'alex giamas'},
  u'name': u'Mastering MongoDB, 2nd Edition'}]
```

In this example, we used a regular expression to match aLEx, which is case insensitive, in every document that the string is mentioned in the `meta.authors` embedded document. PyMongo uses this notation for regular expression queries, called the `$regex` notation in MongoDB documentation. The second parameter is the options parameter for `$regex`, which we will explain in detail in the *Using regular expressions* section later in this chapter.

Comparison operators are also supported, and a full list of these are given in the *Comparison operators* section, which can be seen later in this chapter:

```
>>> result = list(books.find({ "price": {  "$gt":40 } }))
>>> pprint(result)

[{u'_id': ObjectId('594061a9aabac94b7c858d3d'),
  u'isbn': u'301',
  u'name': u'Python and MongoDB',
  u'price': 60}]
```

Adding multiple dictionaries in our query results in a logical AND query:

```
>>> result = list(books.find({"name": "Mastering MongoDB", "isbn": "101"}))
>>> pprint(result)

[{u'_id': ObjectId('592149c4aabac953a3a1e31e'),
  u'isbn': u'101',
  u'name': u'Mastering MongoDB',
  u'price': 30.0,
  u'published': datetime.datetime(2017, 6, 25, 0, 0)}]
```

For books having both isbn=101 and name=Mastering MongoDB, to use logical operators such as $or and $and, we have to use the following syntax:

```
>>> result = list(books.find({"$or": [{"isbn": "101"}, {"isbn": "102"}]}))
>>> pprint(result)

[{u'_id': ObjectId('592149c4aabac953a3a1e31e'),
  u'isbn': u'101',
  u'name': u'Mastering MongoDB',
  u'price': 30.0,
  u'published': datetime.datetime(2017, 6, 25, 0, 0)},
 {u'_id': ObjectId('59214bc1aabac954263b24e0'),
  u'isbn': u'102',
  u'name': u'MongoDB in 7 years',
  u'price': 50.0,
  u'published': datetime.datetime(2017, 6, 26, 0, 0)}]
```

For books having an isbn of 101 or 102, if we want to combine AND and OR operators, we have to use the $and operator, as follows:

```
>>> result = list(books.find({"$or": [{"$and": [{"name": "Mastering
MongoDB", "isbn": "101"}]}, {"$and": [{"name": "MongoDB in 7 years",
"isbn": "102"}]}]}))
>>> pprint(result)
[{u'_id': ObjectId('592149c4aabac953a3a1e31e'),
  u'isbn': u'101',
  u'name': u'Mastering MongoDB',
  u'price': 30.0,
  u'published': datetime.datetime(2017, 6, 25, 0, 0)},
 {u'_id': ObjectId('59214bc1aabac954263b24e0'),
  u'isbn': u'102',
  u'name': u'MongoDB in 7 years',
  u'price': 50.0,
  u'published': datetime.datetime(2017, 6, 26, 0, 0)}]
```

For a result of OR between two queries, consider the following:

- The first query is asking for documents that have isbn=101 AND name=Mastering MongoDB
- The second query is asking for documents that have isbn=102 AND name=MongoDB in 7 years.
- The result is the union of these two datasets

Updating documents

In the following code block, you can see an example of updating a single document using the update_one helper method.

This operation matches one document in the search phase and modifies one document based on the operation to be applied to the matched documents:

```
>>> result = books.update_one({"isbn": "101"}, {"$set": {"price": 100}})
>>> print(result.matched_count)
1
>>> print(result.modified_count)
1
```

In a similar way to inserting documents, when updating documents, we can use update_one or update_many:

- The first argument here is the filter document for matching the documents that will be updated
- The second argument is the operation to be applied to the matched documents
- The third (optional) argument is to use upsert=false (the default) or true, which is used to create a new document if it's not found

Another interesting argument is bypass_document_validation=false (the default) or true, which is optional. This will ignore validations (if there are any) for the documents in the collection.

The resulting object will have matched_count for the number of documents that matched the filter query, and modified_count for the number of documents that were affected by the update part of the query.

In our example, we are setting `price=100` for the first book with `isbn=101` through the `$set` update operator. A list of all update operators is displayed in the *Update operators* section later in this chapter.

> If we don't use an update operator as the second argument, the contents of the matched document will be entirely replaced by the new document.

CRUD using PyMODM

PyMODM is a core ODM that provides simple and extensible functionality. It is developed and maintained by MongoDB's engineers who get fast updates and support for the latest stable version of MongoDB available.

In Chapter 2, *Schema Design and Data Modeling*, we explored how to define different models and connect to MongoDB. CRUD when using PyMODM, as with every ODM, is simpler than when using low-level drivers.

Creating documents

A new `user` object, as defined in Chapter 2, *Schema Design and Data Modeling*, can be created with a single line:

```
>>> user = User('alexgiamas@packt.com', 'Alex', 'Giamas').save()
```

In this example, we used positional arguments in the same order that they were defined in the `user` model to assign values to the `user` model attributes.

We can also use keyword arguments or a mix of both, as follows:

```
>>> user = User(email='alexgiamas@packt.com', 'Alex',
last_name='Giamas').save()
```

Bulk saving can be done by passing in an array of users to `bulk_create()`:

```
>>> users = [ user1, user2,...,userN]
>>>  User.bulk_create(users)
```

Updating documents

We can modify a document by directly accessing the attributes and calling `save()` again:

```
>>> user.first_name = 'Alexandros'
>>> user.save()
```

If we want to update one or more documents, we have to use `raw()` to filter out the documents that will be affected and chain `update()` to set the new values:

```
>>> User.objects.raw({'first_name': {'$exists': True}})
            .update({'$set': {'updated_at': datetime.datetime.now()}})
```

In the preceding example, we search for all `User` documents that have a first name and set a new field, `updated_at`, to the current timestamp. The result of the `raw()` method is `QuerySet`, a class used in PyMODM to handle queries and work with documents in bulk.

Deleting documents

Deleting an API is similar to updating it – by using `QuerySet` to find the affected documents and then chaining on a `.delete()` method to delete them:

```
>>> User.objects.raw({'first_name': {'$exists': True}}).delete()
```

The `BulkWrite` API is still not supported at the time of writing this book (December, 2018) and the relevant ticket, PYMODM-43, is open. Methods such as `bulk_create()` will, under the hood, issue multiple commands to the database.

Querying documents

Querying is done using `QuerySet`, as described before the `update` and `delete` operations.

Some convenience methods available include the following:

- `all()`
- `count()`
- `first()`
- `exclude(*fields)` to exclude some fields from the result
- `only(*fields)` to include only some fields in the result (this can be chained for a union of fields)
- `limit(limit)`

- order_by(ordering)
- reverse() if we want to reverse the order_by() order
- skip(number)
- values() to return Python dict instances instead of model instances

By using raw(), we can use the same queries that we described in the previous PyMongo section for querying and still exploit the flexibility and convenience methods provided by the ODM layer.

CRUD using the PHP driver

In PHP, there is a new driver called mongo-php-library that should be used instead of the deprecated MongoClient. The overall architecture was explained in Chapter 2, *Schema Design and Data Modeling*. Here, we will cover more details of the API and how we can perform CRUD operations using it.

Creating and deleting

The following command will insert a single $document that contains an array of two key/value pairs, with the key names of isbn and name:

```
$document = array( "isbn" => "401", "name" => "MongoDB and PHP" );
$result = $collection->insertOne($document);
var_dump($result);
```

The output from the var_dump($result) command is shown as follows:

```
MongoDB\InsertOneResult Object
(
    [writeResult:MongoDB\InsertOneResult:private] =>
MongoDB\Driver\WriteResult Object
        (
            [nInserted] => 1
            [nMatched] => 0
            [nModified] => 0
            [nRemoved] => 0
            [nUpserted] => 0
            [upsertedIds] => Array
                (
                )

            [writeErrors] => Array
```

```
                        (
                        )

            [writeConcernError] =>
            [writeConcern] => MongoDB\Driver\WriteConcern Object
                        (
                        )

                )

        [insertedId:MongoDB\InsertOneResult:private] => MongoDB\BSON\ObjectID
    Object
            (
                [oid] => 5941ac50aabac9d16f6da142
            )

        [isAcknowledged:MongoDB\InsertOneResult:private] => 1
    )
```

This rather lengthy output contains all the information that we may need. We can get the ObjectId of the document inserted; the number of inserted, matched, modified, removed, and upserted documents by fields prefixed with n; and information about writeError or writeConcernError.

There are also convenience methods in the $result object if we want to get the information:

- $result->getInsertedCount(): To get the number of inserted objects
- $result->getInsertedId(): To get the ObjectId of the inserted document

We can also use the ->insertMany() method to insert many documents at once, as follows:

```
$documentAlpha = array( "isbn" => "402", "name" => "MongoDB and PHP, 2nd
Edition" );
$documentBeta  = array( "isbn" => "403", "name" => "MongoDB and PHP,
revisited" );
$result = $collection->insertMany([$documentAlpha, $documentBeta]);

print_r($result);
```

The result can be seen as follows:

```
(
    [writeResult:MongoDB\InsertManyResult:private] =>
MongoDB\Driver\WriteResult Object
        (
```

```
                    [nInserted] => 2
                    [nMatched] => 0
                    [nModified] => 0
                    [nRemoved] => 0
                    [nUpserted] => 0
                    [upsertedIds] => Array
                        (
                        )

                    [writeErrors] => Array
                        (
                        )

                    [writeConcernError] =>
                    [writeConcern] => MongoDB\Driver\WriteConcern Object
                        (
                        )

                )

        [insertedIds:MongoDB\InsertManyResult:private] => Array
            (
                [0] => MongoDB\BSON\ObjectID Object
                    (
                        [oid] => 5941ae85aabac9d1d16c63a2
                    )

                [1] => MongoDB\BSON\ObjectID Object
                    (
                        [oid] => 5941ae85aabac9d1d16c63a3
                    )

            )

        [isAcknowledged:MongoDB\InsertManyResult:private] => 1
    )
```

Again, `$result->getInsertedCount()` will return 2, whereas `$result->getInsertedIds()` will return an array with the two newly-created ObjectIds:

```
array(2) {
  [0]=>
  object(MongoDB\BSON\ObjectID)#13 (1) {
    ["oid"]=>
    string(24) "5941ae85aabac9d1d16c63a2"
  }
  [1]=>
```

```
object(MongoDB\BSON\ObjectID)#14 (1) {
  ["oid"]=>
  string(24) "5941ae85aabac9d1d16c63a3"
 }
}
```

Deleting documents is a similar process to inserting documents, but uses the deleteOne()
and deleteMany() methods instead; an example of deleteMany() is shown as follows:

```
$deleteQuery = array( "isbn" => "401");
$deleteResult = $collection->deleteMany($deleteQuery);
print($deleteResult->getDeletedCount());
```

The following code block shows the output:

```
MongoDB\DeleteResult Object
(
    [writeResult:MongoDB\DeleteResult:private] => MongoDB\Driver\WriteResult
Object
        (
            [nInserted] => 0
            [nMatched] => 0
            [nModified] => 0
            [nRemoved] => 2
            [nUpserted] => 0
            [upsertedIds] => Array
                (
                )

            [writeErrors] => Array
                (
                )

            [writeConcernError] =>
            [writeConcern] => MongoDB\Driver\WriteConcern Object
                (
                )

        )

    [isAcknowledged:MongoDB\DeleteResult:private] => 1
)
2
```

In this example, we used ->getDeletedCount() to get the number of affected documents,
which is printed in the last line of the output.

BulkWrite

The new PHP driver supports the `BulkWrite` interface to minimize network calls to MongoDB:

```
$manager = new MongoDB\Driver\Manager('mongodb://localhost:27017');
$bulk = new MongoDB\Driver\BulkWrite(array("ordered" => true));
$bulk->insert(array( "isbn" => "401", "name" => "MongoDB and PHP" ));
$bulk->insert(array( "isbn" => "402", "name" => "MongoDB and PHP, 2nd
Edition" ));
$bulk->update(array("isbn" => "402"), array('$set' => array("price" =>
15)));
$bulk->insert(array( "isbn" => "403", "name" => "MongoDB and PHP,
revisited" ));


$result = $manager->executeBulkWrite('mongo_book.books', $bulk);
print_r($result);
```

The result can be seen as follows:

```
MongoDB\Driver\WriteResult Object
(
    [nInserted] => 3
    [nMatched] => 1
    [nModified] => 1
    [nRemoved] => 0
    [nUpserted] => 0
    [upsertedIds] => Array
        (
        )

    [writeErrors] => Array
        (
        )

    [writeConcernError] =>
    [writeConcern] => MongoDB\Driver\WriteConcern Object
        (
        )

)
```

In the preceding example, we executed two inserts, one `update`, and a third `insert` in an ordered fashion. The `WriteResult` object contains a total of three inserted documents and one modified document.

The main difference compared to simple create/delete queries is that `executeBulkWrite()` is a method of the `MongoDB\Driver\Manager` class, which we instantiate on the first line.

Read

Querying an interface is similar to inserting and deleting, with the `findOne()` and `find()` methods used to retrieve the first result or all results of a query:

```
$document = $collection->findOne( array("isbn" => "401") );
$cursor = $collection->find( array( "name" => new
MongoDB\BSON\Regex("mongo", "i") ) );
```

In the second example, we are using a regular expression to search for a key name with the value, `mongo` (which is case insensitive).

Embedded documents can be queried using the `.` notation, as with the other languages that we examined earlier in this chapter:

```
$cursor = $collection->find( array('meta.price' => 50) );
```

We do this to query for a `price` embedded document inside the meta key field.

Similarly to Ruby and Python, in PHP, we can query using comparison operators, as shown in the following code:

```
$cursor = $collection->find( array( 'price' => array('$gte'=> 60) ) );
```

A complete list of comparison operators supported in the PHP driver is available at the end of this chapter.

Querying with multiple key-value pairs is an implicit AND, whereas queries using `$or`, `$in`, `$nin`, or AND (`$and`) combined with `$or` can be achieved with nested queries:

```
$cursor = $collection->find( array( '$or' => array(
                                      array("price" => array( '$gte'
=> 60)),
                                      array("price" => array( '$lte'
=> 20))
                               )));
```

This finds documents that have `price>=60 OR price<=20`.

Updating documents

Updating documents has a similar interface with the `->updateOne()` OR `->updateMany()` method.

The first parameter is the query used to find documents and the second one will update our documents.

We can use any of the update operators explained at the end of this chapter to update in place, or specify a new document to completely replace the document in the query:

```
$result = $collection->updateOne(
  array( "isbn" => "401"),
    array( '$set' => array( "price" => 39 ) )
);
```

 We can use single quotes or double quotes for key names, but if we have special operators starting with $, we need to use single quotes. We can use `array( "key" => "value" )` or `["key" => "value"]`. We prefer the more explicit `array()` notation in this book.

The `->getMatchedCount()` and `->getModifiedCount()` methods will return the number of documents matched in the query part or the ones modified from the query. If the new value is the same as the existing value of a document, it will not be counted as modified.

CRUD using Doctrine

Following on from our Doctrine example in Chapter 2, *Schema Design and Data Modeling*, we will work on these models for CRUD operations.

Creating, updating, and deleting

Creating documents is a two-step process. First, we create our document and set the attribute values:

```
$book = new Book();
$book->setName('MongoDB with Doctrine');
$book->setPrice(45);
```

Following this, we ask Doctrine to save $book in the next flush() call:

```
$dm->persist($book);
```

We can force saving by manually calling flush(), as follows:

```
$dm->flush();
```

In this example, $dm is a DocumentManager object that we use to connect to our MongoDB instance, as follows:

```
$dm = DocumentManager::create(new Connection(), $config);
```

Updating a document is as easy as assigning values to the attributes:

```
$book->price = 39;
$book->persist($book);
```

This will save our MongoDB with Doctrine book with the new price of 39.

Updating documents in place uses the QueryBuilder interface.

Doctrine provides several helper methods around atomic updates, listed as follows:

- set($name, $value, $atomic = true)
- setNewObj($newObj)
- inc($name, $value)
- unsetField($field)
- push($field, $value)
- pushAll($field, array $valueArray)
- addToSet($field, $value)
- addManyToSet($field, array $values)
- popFirst($field)
- popLast($field)
- pull($field, $value)
- pullAll($field, array $valueArray)

update will, by default, update the first document found by the query. If we want to change multiple documents, we need to use ->updateMany():

```
$dm->createQueryBuilder('Book')
    ->updateMany()
    ->field('price')->set(69)
```

```
    ->field('name')->equals('MongoDB with Doctrine')
    ->getQuery()
    ->execute();
```

In the preceding example, we are setting the price of the book with `name='MongoDB with Doctrine'` to be `69`. The list of comparison operators in Doctrine is available in the following *Read* section.

We can chain multiple comparison operators, resulting in an AND query and also multiple helper methods, resulting in updates to several fields.

Deleting a document is similar to creating it, as demonstrated in the following code block:

```
$dm->remove($book);
```

Removing multiple documents is best done using the `QueryBuilder` interface, which we will explore further in the following section:

```
$qb = $dm->createQueryBuilder('Book');
$qb->remove()
    ->field('price')->equals(50)
    ->getQuery()
    ->execute();
```

Read

Doctrine provides a `QueryBuilder` interface to build queries for MongoDB. Given that we have defined our models as described in Chapter 2, *Schema Design and Data Modeling*, we can do this to obtain an instance of a `QueryBuilder` interface named $db, get a default find-all query, and execute it, as follows:

```
$qb = $dm->createQueryBuilder('Book');
$query = $qb->getQuery();
$books = $query->execute();
```

The $books variable now contains an iterable lazy data-loading cursor over our result set.

Using `$qb->eagerCursor(true);` over the `QueryBuilder` object will return an eager cursor, fetching all data from MongoDB as soon as we start iterating our results.

Some helper methods for querying are listed here:

- `->getSingleResult()`: This is equivalent to `findOne()`.
- `->select('name')`: This returns only the values for the `'key'` attribute from our `books` collection. `ObjectId` will always be returned.

- ->hint('book_name_idx'): This forces the query to use this index. We'll see more about indexes in Chapter 7, *Indexing*.
- ->distinct('name'): This returns distinct results by name.
- ->limit(10): This returns the first 10 results.
- ->sort('name', 'desc'): This sorts by name (such as desc or asc).

Doctrine uses the concept of hydration when fetching documents from MongoDB. Hydration defines the query's result schema. We can, for example, configure hydration to return a collection of objects, a single scalar value, or an array of arrays representing different records. Using an identity map, it will cache MongoDB results in memory and consult this map before hitting the database. Disabling hydration can be done per query by using ->hydration(false), or globally using the configuration as explained in Chapter 2, *Schema Design and Data Modeling*.

We can also force Doctrine to refresh data in the identity map for a query from MongoDB using ->refresh() on $qb.

The comparison operators that we can use with Doctrine are as follows:

- where($javascript)
- in($values)
- notIn($values)
- equals($value)
- notEqual($value)
- gt($value)
- gte($value)
- lt($value)
- lte($value)
- range($start, $end)
- size($size)
- exists($bool)
- type($type)
- all($values)
- mod($mod)
- addOr($expr)
- addAnd($expr)
- references($document)

- `includesReferenceTo($document)`

Consider the following query as an example:

```
$qb = $dm->createQueryBuilder('Book')
                ->field('price')->lt(30);
```

This will return all books whose price is less than 30.

`addAnd()` may seem redundant since chaining multiple query expressions in Doctrine is implicitly `AND`, but it is useful if we want to do `AND ( (A OR B), (C OR D) )` where `A`, `B`, `C`, and `D` are standalone expressions.

To nest multiple `OR` operators with an external `AND` query, and in other equally complex cases, the nested `OR`s need to be evaluated as expressions using `->expr()`:

```
$expression = $qb->expr()->field('name')->equals('MongoDB with Doctrine')
```

`$expression` is a standalone expression that can be used with `$qb->addOr($expression)` and similarly with `addAnd()`.

Best practices

Some best practices for using Doctrine with MongoDB are as follows:

- Don't use unnecessary cascading.
- Don't use unnecessary life cycle events.
- Don't use special characters such as non-ASCII ones in class, field, table, or column names, as Doctrine is not Unicode-safe yet.
- Initialize collection references in the model's constructor.
- Constrain relationships between objects as much as possible. Avoid bidirectional associations between models and eliminate the ones that are not needed. This helps with performance, loose coupling, and produces simpler and more easily maintainable code.

Comparison operators

The following is a list of all comparison operators that MongoDB supports:

Name	Description
$eq	Matches values that are equal to a specified value
$gt	Matches values that are greater than a specified value
$gte	Matches values that are greater than or equal to the specified value
$lt	Matches values that are less than the specified value
$lte	Matches values that are less than or equal to the specified value
$ne	Matches all values that are not equal to the specified value
$in	Matches any of the values specified in an array
$nin	Matches none of the values specified in an array

Update operators

The following is a list of all update operators that MongoDB supports:

Name	Description
$inc	This increments the value of the field by the specified amount.
$mul	This multiplies the value of the field by the specified amount.
$rename	This renames a field.
$setOnInsert	This sets the value of a field if an update results in an insert of a document. It has no effect on update operations and modifying existing documents.
$set	This sets the value of a field in a document.
$unset	This removes the specified field from a document.
$min	This only updates the field if the specified value is less than the existing field value.
$max	This only updates the field if the specified value is greater than the existing field value.
$currentDate	This sets the value of a field to the current date, either as a date or as a timestamp.

Smart querying

There are several considerations when querying in MongoDB that we have to take into account. Here are some best practices for using regular expressions, query results, cursors, and when deleting documents.

Using regular expressions

MongoDB offers a rich interface for querying using regular expressions. In its simplest form, we can use regular expressions in queries by modifying the query string:

```
> db.books.find({"name": /mongo/})
```

This is done to search for books in our `books` collection that contain the `mongo` name. It is the equivalent of a SQL `LIKE` query.

 MongoDB uses **Perl Compatible Regular Expression (PCRE)** version 8.39 with UTF-8 support.

We can also use some options when querying:

Option	Description
i	This option queries case insensitivity.
m	For patterns that include anchors (that is, ^ for the start and $ for the end), this option matches at the beginning or end of each line for strings with multiline values. Without this option, these anchors match at the beginning or end of the string. If the pattern contains no anchors, or if the string value has no newline characters (for example, \n), the m option has no effect.

In our previous example, if we wanted to search for mongo, Mongo, MONGO, and any other case-insensitive variation, we would need to use the i option, as follows:

```
> db.books.find({"name": /mongo/i})
```

Alternatively, we can use the $regex operator, which provides more flexibility.

The same queries using $regex will be written as follows:

```
> db.books.find({'name': { '$regex': /mongo/ } })
> db.books.find({'name': { '$regex': /mongo/i } })
```

By using the `$regex` operator, we can also use the following two options:

Option	Description
x	Extended capability to ignore all whitespace characters in the `$regex` pattern, unless they have escaped or are included in a character class. Additionally, it ignores characters in between (and including) an unescaped hash/pound (#, £) character and the next newline so that you may include comments in complicated patterns. This only applies to data characters; whitespace characters may never appear within special character sequences in a pattern. The x option does not affect the handling of the VT character.
s	This option allows the dot character (that is, .) to match all characters, including newline characters.

Expanding matching documents using regex makes our queries slower to execute.

Indexes using regular expressions can only be used if our regular expression does queries for the beginning of a string that is indexed; that is, regular expressions starting with ^ or \A. If we want to query only using a `starts with` regular expression, we should avoid writing lengthier regular expressions, even if they will match the same strings.

Take the following code block as an example:

```
> db.books.find({'name': { '$regex': /mongo/ } })
> db.books.find({'name': { '$regex': /^mongo.*/ } })
```

Both queries will match name values starting with `mongo` (case-sensitive), but the first one will be faster as it will stop matching as soon as it hits the sixth character in every name value.

Querying results and cursors

MongoDB's lack of support for transactions means that several semantics that we take for granted in RDBMS work differently.

As explained previously, updates can modify the size of a document. Modifying the size can result in MongoDB moving the document on the disk to a new slot toward the end of the storage file.

When we have multiple threads querying and updating a single collection, we can end up with a document appearing multiple times in the result set.

This will happen in the following scenario:

- Thread A starts querying the collection and matches document A1.
- Thread B updates document A1, increasing its size and forcing MongoDB to move it to a different physical location toward the end of the storage file.
- Thread A is still querying the collection. It reaches the end of the collection and finds document A1 again with its new value, as shown in the following diagram:

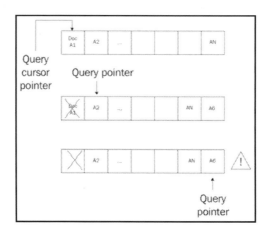

This is rare, but it can happen in production; if we can't safeguard from such a case in the application layer, we can use snapshot() to prevent it.

snapshot() is supported by official drivers and the shell by appending it into an operation that returns a cursor:

```
> db.books.find().snapshot()
```

$snapshot cannot be used with sharded collections. $snapshot has to be applied before the query returns the first document. Snapshot cannot be used together with the hint() or sort() operators.

We can simulate the snapshot() behavior by querying using hint({id :1}), thus forcing the query engine to use the id index just like the $snapshot operator.

If our query runs on a unique index of a field whose values won't get modified during the duration of the query, we should use this query to get the same query behavior. Even then, snapshot() cannot protect us from insertions or deletions happening in the middle of a query. The $snapshot operator will traverse the built-in index that every collection has on the id field, making it inherently slow. This should only be used as a last resort.

If we want to `update`, `insert`, or `delete` multiple documents without other threads seeing the results of our operation while it's happening, we can use the `$isolated` operator:

```
> db.books.remove( { price: { $gt: 30 }, $isolated: 1 } )
```

In this example, threads querying the `books` collection will see either all books with a price greater than 30 or no books at all. The isolated operator will acquire an exclusive write lock in the collection for the whole duration of the query, no matter what the storage engine can support, contributing to the contention in this collection.

Isolated operations are still not transactions; they don't provide `atomicity ( "all-or-nothing")`. So, if they fail midway, we need to manually roll back the operation to get our database into a consistent state.

Again, this should be a last resort and only used in cases where it's mission-critical to avoid multiple threads seeing inconsistent information at any time.

Storage considerations for the delete operation

Deleting documents in MongoDB does not reclaim the disk space used by it. If we have 10 GB of disk space used by MongoDB and we delete all documents, we will still be using 10 GB. What happens under the hood is that MongoDB will mark these documents as deleted and may use the space to store new documents.

This results in our disk having space that is not used, but is not freed up for the operating system. If we want to claim it back, we can use `compact ()` to reclaim any unused space:

```
> db.books.compact ()
```

Alternatively, we can start the `mongod` server with the `--repair` option.

A better option is to enable compression, which is available from version 3.0 and only with the WiredTiger storage engine. We can use the snappy or zlib algorithms to compress our document size. This will, again, not prevent storage holes, but if we are tight on disk space, it is preferable to the heavy operational route of repair and compact.

Storage compression uses less disk space at the expense of CPU usage, but this trade-off is mostly worth it.

Always take a backup before running operations that can result in a catastrophic loss of data. Repair or compact will run in a single thread, blocking the entire database from other operations. In production systems, always perform these on the slave first; then switch the master-slave roles, and compact the ex-master, now-slave instance.

Change streams

Change streams functionality was introduced in version 3.6 and augmented in version 4.0, making it a safe and efficient way to listen for database changes.

Introduction

The fundamental problem that change streams solve is the need for applications to react immediately to changes in the underlying data. Modern web applications need to be reactive to data changes and refresh the page view without reloading the entire page. This is one of the problems that frontend frameworks (such as Angular, React, and Vue.js) are solving. When a user performs an action, the frontend framework will submit the request to the server asynchronously and refresh the relevant fragment of the page based on the response from the server.

Thinking of a multiuser web application, there are cases where a database change may have occurred as a result of another user's action. For example, in a project management Kanban board, user A may be viewing the Kanban board, while another user, B, may be changing the status of a ticket from "To do" to "In progress".

User A's view needs to be updated with the change that user B has performed in real time, without refreshing the page. There are already three approaches to this problem, as follows:

- The most simple approach is to poll the database every X number of seconds and determine if there has been a change. Usually this code will need to use some kind of status, timestamp, or version number to avoid fetching the same change multiple times. This is simple, yet inefficient, as it cannot scale with a great number of users. Having thousands of users polling the database at the same time will result in a high database-locking rate.

- To overcome the problems imposed by the first approach, database-and application-level triggers have been implemented. A database trigger relies on the underlying database executing some code in response to a database change. However, the main downside is again similar to the first approach in that the more triggers that we add to a database, the slower our database will become. It is also coupled to the database, instead of being a part of the application code base.

- Finally, we can use the database transaction or replication log to query for the latest changes and react to them. This is the most efficient and scalable approach of the three previously mentioned as it doesn't put a strain on the database. The database writes to this log anyway, it is usually append only and our background task serially reads entries as they come into the log. The downside of this method is that it is the most complicated one to implement and one that can lead to nasty bugs if it's not implemented properly.

Change streams provide a way to solve this problem that is developer-friendly and easy to implement and maintain. It is based on the oplog, which is essentially MongoDB's operations log, containing each and every operation happening server-wide across all databases in the server. This way the developer does not have to deal with the server-wide oplog or tailable cursors, which are often not exposed or easy to deal with from MongoDB language-specific drivers. Also, the developer does not have to decipher and understand any of the internal oplog data structures that are designed and built for MongoDB's benefit, and not for an application developer.

Change streams have other advantages in which they are secure: users can only create change streams on collections, databases, or deployments to those for which they have read access.

Change streams are also idempotent by design. Even in the case that the application cannot fetch the absolute latest change stream event notification ID, it can resume applying from an earlier known one and it will eventually reach the same state.

Finally, change streams are resumable. Every change stream response document includes a resume token. If the application gets out of sync with the database, it can send the latest resume token back to the database and continue processing from there. This token needs to be persisted in the application, as the MongoDB driver won't keep application failures and restarts. It will only keep state and retry in case of transient network failures and MongoDB replica set elections.

Setup

A change stream can be opened against a collection, a database, or an entire deployment (such as a replica set or sharded cluster). A change stream will not react to changes in any system collection or any collection in the admin, config, and local databases.

A change stream requires a WiredTiger storage engine and replica set protocol version 1 (pv1). pv1 is the only supported version starting from MongoDB 4.0. Change streams are compatible with deployments that use encryption-at-rest.

Using change streams

To use a change stream, we need to connect to our replica set. A replica set is a prerequisite to using change streams. As change streams internally use the oplog, it's not possible to work without it. Change streams will also output documents that won't be rolled back in a replica set setting, so they need to follow a majority read concern. Either way, it's a good practice to develop and test locally using a replica set, as this is the recommended deployment for production. As an example, we are going to use a `signals` collection within our database named `streams`.

We will use the following sample Python code:

```python
from pymongo import MongoClient

class MongoExamples:
    def __init__(self):
        self.client = MongoClient('localhost', 27017)
        db = self.client.streams
        self.signals = db.signals
    # a basic watch on signals collection
    def change_books(self):
        with self.client.watch() as stream:
            for change in stream:
                print(change)
def main():
    MongoExamples().change_books()
if __name__ == '__main__':
    main()
```

We can open one Terminal and run it using `python change_streams.py`.

Then, in another Terminal, we connect to our MongoDB replica set using the following code:

```
> mongo
> use streams
> db.signals.insert({value: 114.3, signal:1})
```

Going back to our first Terminal window, we can now observe that the output is similar to the following code block:

```
{'_id': {'_data':
'825BB7A25E0000000129295A1004A34408FB07864F8F960BF14453DFB98546645F69640064
5BB7A25EE10ED33145BCF7A70004'}, 'operationType': 'insert', 'clusterTime':
Timestamp(1538761310, 1), 'fullDocument': {'_id':
ObjectId('5bb7a25ee10ed33145bcf7a7'), 'value': 114.3, 'signal': 1.0}, 'ns':
{'db': 'streams', 'coll': 'signals'}, 'documentKey': {'_id':
ObjectId('5bb7a25ee10ed33145bcf7a7')}}
```

What has happened here is that we have opened a cursor watching the entire streams database for changes. Every data update in our database will be logged and outputted in the console.

For example, if we go back to the mongo shell, we can issue the following code:

```
> db.a_random_collection.insert({test: 'bar'})
```

The Python code output should then be similar to the following code:

```
{'_id': {'_data':
'825BB7A3770000000229295A10044AB37F707D104634B646CC5810A40EF246645F69640064
5BB7A377E10ED33145BCF7A80004'}, 'operationType': 'insert', 'clusterTime':
Timestamp(1538761591, 2), 'fullDocument': {'_id':
ObjectId('5bb7a377e10ed33145bcf7a8'), 'test': 'bar'}, 'ns': {'db':
'streams', 'coll': 'a_random_collection'}, 'documentKey': {'_id':
ObjectId('5bb7a377e10ed33145bcf7a8')}}
```

This means that we are getting notifications for each and every data update across all collections in our database.

We can then change line 11 of our code to the following:

```
> with self.signals.watch() as stream:
```

This will result in only watching the signals collection, as should be the most common use case.

PyMongo's `watch` command can take several parameters, as follows:

```
watch(pipeline=None, full_document='default', resume_after=None,
max_await_time_ms=None, batch_size=None, collation=None,
start_at_operation_time=None, session=None)
```

The most important parameters are as follows:

- `Pipeline`: This is an optional parameter that we can use to define an aggregation pipeline to be executed on each document that matches `watch()`. Because the change stream itself uses the aggregation pipeline, we can attach events to it. The aggregation pipeline events we can use are as follows:

  ```
  $match
  $project
  $addFields
  $replaceRoot
  $redact
  ```

- `Full_document`: This is an optional parameter that we can use by setting it to `'updateLookup'` to make change streams return both a delta describing the changes to the document, and a copy of the entire document that was changed from some time after the change occurred in the case of a partial update.
- `Start_at_operation_time`: This is an optional parameter that we can use to only watch for changes that occurred at, or after, the specified timestamp.
- `Session`: This is an optional parameter in case our driver supports passing a `ClientSession` object to watch for updates.

Change streams response documents have to be under 16 MB in size. This is a global limit in MongoDB for BSON documents and the change stream has to follow this rule.

Specification

The following document shows all of the possible fields that a change event response may or may not include, depending on the actual change that happened:

```
{  _id : { <BSON Object> },
   "operationType" : "<operation>",
   "fullDocument" : { <document> },
   "ns" : {
      "db" : "<database>",
      "coll" : "<collection"
```

```
    },
    "documentKey" : { "_id" : <ObjectId> },
    "updateDescription" : {
        "updatedFields" : { <document> },
        "removedFields" : [ "<field>", ... ]
    }
    "clusterTime" : <Timestamp>,
    "txnNumber" : <NumberLong>,
    "lsid" : {
        "id" : <UUID>,
        "uid" : <BinData>
    }
}
```

The most important fields are as follows:

fullDocument	This is the new state of the document, which can include the following: • If it's a delete operation, this field is omitted as the document no longer exists. • If it's an insert or replace operation, this will be the new value of the document. • If it's an update operation and we have enabled 'updateLookup', then it will have the most recently major-committed version of the document modified by the update operation.
operationType	This is the type of operation; it can be either of insert, delete, replace, update, or invalidate.
documentKey	This is ObjectID of the document that was affected by the operation.
updateDescription.updatedFields / removedFields	This is a document or an array of keys respectively, showing the data that was updated or removed by the update or remove operation.
txnNumber	This is the transaction number. It is only applicable if the operation is part of a multi-document **ACID (atomicity, consistency, isolation, durability)** transaction.
lsid	This is the session identifier of the transaction. It is only applicable if the operation is part of a multi-document ACID transaction.

Important notes

When using a sharded database, change streams need to be opened against a MongoDB server. When using replica sets, a change stream can only be opened against a data-bearing instance. Each change stream will open a new connection, as of 4.0.2. If we want to have lots of change streams in parallel, we need to increase the connection pool (as per the SERVER-32946 JIRA MongoDB ticket) to avoid severe performance degradation.

Production recommendations

Change streams are a fairly recent addition to the MongoDB database. As such, the following recommendations for production deployments may change in later versions. These are the guidelines as recommended by MongoDB and expert architects at the time of writing this chapter.

Replica sets

A change stream will only process an event that has been written to the majority of members processing data. It will pause if we lose the majority of data-storing servers, or if we rely on arbiters to establish a majority.

Invalidating events, such as dropping or renaming a collection, will close the change stream. We cannot resume a change stream after an invalidate event closes it.

As the change stream relies on the oplog size, we need to make sure that the oplog size is large enough to hold events until they are processed by the application.

Sharded clusters

On top of the considerations for replica sets, there are a few more to keep in mind for sharded clusters. They are as follows:

- The change stream is executed against every shard in a cluster and will be as fast as the slowest shard.
- To avoid creating change stream events for orphaned documents, we need to use the new feature of ACID compliant transactions if we have multi-document updates under sharding.

While sharding an unsharded collection (that is, migrating from replica sets to sharding), `documentKey` of the change stream notification document will include `_id` until the change stream catches up to the first chunk migration.

Summary

In this chapter, we went through advanced querying concepts using Ruby, Python, and PHP by both using the official drivers and an ODM.

Using Ruby and the Mongoid ODM, Python and the PyMODM ODM, and PHP and the Doctrine ODM, we went through code samples exploring how to `create`, `read`, `update`, and `delete` documents.

We also discussed batching operations for performance and best practices. We presented an exhaustive list of comparison and update operators that MongoDB uses.

Finally, we discussed smart querying, how cursors in querying work, what our storage performance considerations should be on delete, and how to use regular expressions.

In the next chapter, we will learn about the aggregation framework, using a complete use case that involves processing transaction data from the Ethereum blockchain.

5
Multi-Document ACID Transactions

MongoDB introduced multi-document **atomicity**, **consistency**, **isolation**, and **durability** (**ACID**) transactions in version 4.0, which was released in July 2018. Transactions are an integral part of relational databases. Every **relational database management system** (**RDBMS**) from the very early days relied on transactions to achieve ACID. Getting these in a non-relational database is a breakthrough that can fundamentally change the way developers and database architects design software systems.

In the previous chapter, we learned how to query MongoDB using Ruby, Python, and PHP drivers and frameworks. In this chapter, we will learn about the following topics:

- Multi-document ACID transactions
- Using transactions with Ruby and Python

Background

MongoDB is a non-relational database and provides few guarantees around ACID. Data modeling in MongoDB is not focused around BCNF, 2NF, and 3NF normalization, but rather, quite the opposite direction.

In MongoDB, many times, the best approach is to embed our data into subdocuments, resulting in more self-contained documents than a single row of data in an RDBMS. This means that a logical transaction can affect a single document many times. Single-document transactions are ACID-compliant in MongoDB, meaning that multi-document ACID transactions have not been essential for MongoDB development.

However, there are a few reasons why getting multi-document transactions is a good idea. Over the years, MongoDB has grown from being a niche database to a multi-purpose database that is used everywhere – from startups to major Fortune 500 companies. Across many different use cases, there are inevitably a few corner cases where data modeling can't, or shouldn't, fit data in subdocuments and arrays. Also, even when the best solution for a data architect today is to embed data, they can't be sure this will always be the case. This makes choosing the right database layer difficult.

RDBMS data modeling has been around for over 40 years and is a well-known and understood data modeling process. Helping data architects work in a familiar way is always an added bonus.

Before multi-document transactions were introduced, the only workaround was implementing them in a customized way in the application layer. This was both time consuming and prone to error. Implementing a 2-phase commit process in the application layer could also be slower and lead to increased database locks.

In this chapter, we will focus on using the native MongoDB transactions, as it is now strongly recommended by MongoDB Inc.

ACID

ACID stands for atomicity, consistency, isolation, and durability. In the following sections, we will explain what each of these means for our database design and architecture.

Atomicity

Atomicity refers to the concept that transactions need to be atomic. Either it succeeds and its results are visible to every subsequent user reading them, or it fails and every change is rolled back to the point it was at before it started. Either all actions in a transaction occur, or none at all.

A simple example to understand atomicity is by transferring money from account A to account B. Money needs to be credited from account A and then debited into account B. If the operation fails midway, then both accounts A and B need to be reverted to their state before the operation started.

In MongoDB, operations in a single document are always atomic even if the operation spans multiple subdocuments or arrays within the document.

Operations spanning multiple documents need to use MongoDB transactions to be made atomic.

Consistency

Consistency refers to the database always being in a consistent state. Every database operation may complete successfully, fail, or abort; however, in the end, our database must be in a state where its data is consistent.

Database constraints must be respected at all times. Any future transaction must also be able to view data updated by past transactions. The consistency model most commonly used in practice for distributed data systems is eventual consistency.

Eventual consistency guarantees that once we stop updating our data, all future reads will eventually read the latest committed write value. In distributed systems, this is the only acceptable model in terms of performance, as data needs to be replicated over the network across different servers.

In contrast, the least popular model of strong consistency guarantees that every future read will always read the write value that was committed last. This implies that every update is propagated and committed to every server before the next read comes in, which will cause a huge strain on performance for these systems.

MongoDB falls somewhere in between eventual and strict consistency. In fact, MongoDB adopts a causal consistency model. With causal consistency, any transaction execution sequence is the same as if all causally-related read/write ops were executed in an order that reflects their causality.

What this means in practice is that concurrent operations may be seen in different orders, and reads correspond to the latest value written with regard to the writes that they are causally dependent on.

Eventually, it's a trade-off between how many concurrent operations can happen at once and the consistency of data being read by the application.

Isolation

Isolation refers to the visibility of transaction operations to other operations happening in parallel.

An example of why isolation levels are essential is described in the following scenario:

- Transaction *A* updates user 1's account balance from 50 to 100, but does not commit the transaction.
- Transaction *B* reads user 1's account balance as 100.
- Transaction *A* is rolled back, reverting user 1's account balance to 50.
- Transaction *B* thinks that user 1 has 100 pounds, whereas they only have 50.
- Transaction *B* updates user 2's value, by adding 100 pounds. User 2 receives 100 pounds out of thin air from user 1, since user 1 only has 50 pounds in their account. Our imaginary bank is in trouble.

Isolation typically has four levels, with the most to the least strict, as follows:

- Serializable
- Repeatable read
- Read committed
- Read uncommitted

The problems we can run into from the least to the most serious, and depending on the isolation level, are as follows:

- Phantom reads
- Non-repeatable reads
- Dirty reads
- Lost updates

Losing data about an operational update is the worst thing that can happen in any database, because this would render our database unusable and make it a store of data that cannot be trusted. That's why, in every isolation level, even read uncommitted isolation will not lose data.

However, the other three issues may also arise. We will briefly explain what these are in the following sections.

Phantom reads

A phantom read occurs when, during the course of a transaction, another transaction modifies its result set by adding or deleting rows that belong to its result set. An example of this would be the following:

- Transaction *A* queries for all users. 1,000 users are returned but the transaction does not commit.
- Transaction *B* adds another user; 1,001 users are now in our database.
- Transaction *A* queries for all users for a second time. 1,001 users are now returned. Transaction *A* now commits.

Under a strict serializable isolation level, transaction *B* should be blocked from adding the new user until transaction *A* commits its transaction. This can, of course, cause huge contention in the database and contention in the database and lead to performance degradation, as every update operation needs to wait for reads to commit their transactions. This is why, typically, serializable is rarely used in practice.

Non-repeatable reads

A non-repeatable read occurs when, during a transaction, a row is retrieved twice and the row's values are different with every read operation.

Following the previous money transfer example, we can illustrate a non-repeatable read in a similar way:

- Transaction *B* reads user 1's account balance as 50.
- Transaction *A* updates user 1's account balance from 50 to 100, and commits the transaction.
- Transaction *B* reads user 1's account balance again and gets the new value, 100, and then commits the transaction.

The problem here is that transaction *B* has got a different value in the course of its transaction because it was affected by transaction *A*'s update. This is a problem because transaction *B* is getting different values within its own transaction. However, in practice, it solves the issue of transferring money between users when they don't exist.

This is why a read committed isolation level, which does not prevent non-repeatable reads but does prevent dirty reads, is the most commonly-used isolation level in practice.

Dirty reads

The previous example, where we made money out of thin air and ended up transferring 100 pounds out of an account that only had 50 pounds in balance, is a classic example of dirty reads.

A read uncommitted isolation level does not protect us from dirty reads and that is why it is rarely used in production level systems.

The following is the isolation levels versus potential issues:

Isolation level	Lost updates	Dirty reads	Non-repeatable reads	Phantoms
Read uncommitted	Don't occur	May occur	May occur	May occur
Read committed	Don't occur	Don't occur	May occur	May occur
Repeatable read	Don't occur	Don't occur	Don't occur	May occur
Serializable	Don't occur	Don't occur	Don't occur	Don't occur

PostgreSQL uses a default (and configurable) isolation level of read committed. As MongoDB is not inherently an RDBMS, using transactions for every operation makes the situation is more complicated.

The equivalent isolation level in these terms is read uncommitted. This may look scary based on the examples previously given, but on the other hand, in MongoDB, there is (again, in general) no concept of transactions or rolling them back. Read uncommitted refers to the fact that changes will be made visible before they are made durable. More details on the made durable part are provided in the following section on durability.

Durability

Durability in relational database systems refers to the property that every transaction that has successfully committed will survive in the face of failure. This usually refers to writing the contents of the committed transaction in persistent storage (such as a hard disk or SDD). RDBMSes are always following the durability concept by writing every committed transaction to a transaction log or **write-ahead log** (**WAL**). MongoDB, using the WiredTiger storage engine, is committing writes using WAL to its persistent storage-based journal every 60 msec and is, for all practical purposes, durable. As durability is important, every database system prefers relaxing other aspects of ACID first, and durability usually gets relaxed last.

When do we need ACID in MongoDB ?

Existing atomicity guarantees, for single-document operations, that MongoDB can meet the integrity needs for most real-world applications. However, there are some use cases that have traditionally benefited from ACID transactions; modeling them in MongoDB could be significantly more difficult than using the well-known ACID paradigm.

Unsurprisingly, many of these cases come from the financial industry. Dealing with money and stringent regulation frameworks means that each and every operation needs to be stored, sometimes in strict execution order, logged, verified, and be able to be audited if requested. Building a digital bank requires interaction between multiple accounts that could be represented as documents in MongoDB.

Managing high volumes of financial transactions, either by users or algorithms executing high-frequency trading, also requires verifying each and every single one of them. These transactions may span multiple documents, as they would again refer to multiple accounts.

The general pattern for using multi-document ACID transactions is when we can have an unbounded number of entities, sometimes to the millions. In this case, modeling entities in subdocuments and arrays cannot work, as the document would eventually outgrow the built-in 16 MB document size limit present in MongoDB.

Building a digital bank using MongoDB

The most common use cases for multi-document ACID transactions come from the financial sector. In this section, we will model a digital bank using transactions and go through progressively more complicated examples of how we can use transactions for our benefit.

The basic functionality that a bank must provide is accounts and transferring monetary amounts between them. Before transactions were introduced, MongoDB developers had two options. The first option – the MongoDB way of doing it – is to embed data in a document, either as a subdocument or as an array of values. In the case of accounts, this could result in a data structure like the following code block:

```
{accounts: [ {account_id: 1, account_name: 'alex', balance: 100},
{account_id: 2, account_name: 'bob', balance: 50}]}
```

However, even in this simple format, it will quickly outgrow the fixed 16 MB document limit in MongoDB. The advantage of this approach is that since we have to deal with a single document, all operations will be atomic, resulting in strong consistency guarantees when we transfer money from one account to another.

The only viable alternative, except for using a relational database, is to implement guarantees in the application level that will simulate a transaction with the appropriate code in place to undo parts, or the whole, of a transaction in case of an error. This can work, but will result in a longer time to market and is more prone to error.

MongoDB's multi-document ACID transactions approach is similar to how we would work with transactions in a relational database. Taking the most simple example from MongoDB Inc.'s white paper, *MongoDB Multi-Document ACID Transactions*, published in June, 2018, the generic transaction in MongoDB will look like the following code block:

```
s.start_transaction()
orders.insert_one(order, session=s)
stock.update_one(item, stockUpdate, session=s)
s.commit_transaction()
```

However, the same transaction in MySQL will be as follows:

```
db.start_transaction()
cursor.execute(orderInsert, orderData)
cursor.execute(stockUpdate, stockData)
db.commit()
```

That said, in modern web application frameworks, most of the time transactions are hidden in the **object-relational mapping (ORM)** layer and not immediately visible to the application developer. The framework ensures that web requests are wrapped in transactions to the underlying database layer. This is not yet the case for ODM frameworks, but you would expect that this could now change.

Setting up our data

We are going to use a sample `init_data.json` file with two accounts. Alex has 100 of the hypnotons imaginary currency, whereas Mary has 50 of them:

```
{"collection": "accounts", "account_id": "1", "account_name": "Alex",
"account_balance":100}{"collection": "accounts", "account_id": "2",
"account_name": "Mary", "account_balance":50}
```

Using the following Python code, we can insert these values into our database as follows:

```
import json
class InitData:
    def __init__(self):
        self.client = MongoClient('localhost', 27017)
        self.db = self.client.mongo_bank
        self.accounts = self.db.accounts
```

```
        # drop data from accounts collection every time to start from a
clean slate
        self.accounts.drop()
        # load data from json and insert them into our database
        init_data = InitData.load_data(self)
        self.insert_data(init_data)
    @staticmethod
    def load_data(self):
        ret = []
        with open('init_data.json', 'r') as f:
            for line in f:
                ret.append(json.loads(line))
        return ret
    def insert_data(self, data):
        for document in data:
            collection_name = document['collection']
            account_id = document['account_id']
            account_name = document['account_name']
            account_balance = document['account_balance']
            self.db[collection_name].insert_one({'account_id': account_id,
'name': account_name, 'balance': account_balance})
```

This results in our `mongo_bank` database having the following documents in our `accounts` collection:

```
> db.accounts.find()
{ "_id" : ObjectId("5bc1fa7ef8d89f2209d4afac"), "account_id" : "1", "name"
: "Alex", "balance" : 100 }
{ "_id" : ObjectId("5bc1fa7ef8d89f2209d4afad"), "account_id" : "2", "name"
: "Mary", "balance" : 50 }
```

Transferring between accounts – part 1

As a MongoDB developer, the most familiar approach to model a transaction is to implement basic checks in the code. With our sample account documents, you may be tempted to implement an account transfer as follows:

```
    def transfer(self, source_account, target_account, value):
        print(f'transferring {value} Hypnotons from {source_account} to
{target_account}')
        with self.client.start_session() as ses:
            ses.start_transaction()
            self.accounts.update_one({'account_id': source_account},
{'$inc': {'balance': value*(-1)} })
            self.accounts.update_one({'account_id': target_account},
{'$inc': {'balance': value} })
```

```
            updated_source_balance = self.accounts.find_one({'account_id':
    source_account})['balance']
            updated_target_balance = self.accounts.find_one({'account_id':
    target_account})['balance']
            if updated_source_balance < 0 or updated_target_balance < 0:
                ses.abort_transaction()
            else:
                ses.commit_transaction()
```

Calling this method in Python will transfer 300 hypnotons from account 1 to account 2:

```
>>> obj = InitData.new
>>> obj.transfer('1', '2', 300)
```

This will result in the following:

```
> db.accounts.find()
{ "_id" : ObjectId("5bc1fe25f8d89f2337ae40cf"), "account_id" : "1", "name"
: "Alex", "balance" : -200 }
{ "_id" : ObjectId("5bc1fe26f8d89f2337ae40d0"), "account_id" : "2", "name"
: "Mary", "balance" : 350 }
```

The problem here isn't the checks on `updated_source_balance` and `updated_target_balance`. Both of these values reflect the new values of −200 and 350, respectively. The problem isn't the `abort_transaction()` operation either. Instead, the problem is that we are not using the session.

The single most important thing to learn about transactions in MongoDB is that we need to use the session object to wrap operations in a transaction; but, all the while, we can still perform operations outside the transaction scope within a transaction code block.

What happened here is that we initiated a transaction session, as follows:

```
        with self.client.start_session() as ses:
```

And then completely ignored it by doing all of our updates in a non-transactional way. Then we invoked `abort_transaction`, as follows:

```
            ses.abort_transaction()
```

The transaction to be aborted was essentially void and didn't have anything to roll back.

Transferring between accounts – part 2

The correct way to implement a transaction is to use the session object in each and every operation that we want to either commit or roll back at the end of it, as you can see from the following code:

```
def tx_transfer_err(self, source_account, target_account, value):
    print(f'transferring {value} Hypnotons from {source_account} to
{target_account}')
    with self.client.start_session() as ses:
        ses.start_transaction()
        res = self.accounts.update_one({'account_id': source_account},
{'$inc': {'balance': value*(-1)} }, session=ses)
        res2 = self.accounts.update_one({'account_id': target_account},
{'$inc': {'balance': value} }, session=ses)
        error_tx = self.__validate_transfer(source_account,
target_account)

        if error_tx['status'] == True:
            print(f"cant transfer {value} Hypnotons from
{source_account} ({error_tx['s_bal']}) to {target_account}
({error_tx['t_bal']})")
            ses.abort_transaction()
        else:
            ses.commit_transaction()
```

The only difference now is that we are passing `session=ses` in both of our update statements. In order to validate whether we have enough funds to actually make the transfer, we wrote a helper method, `__validate_transfer`, with its arguments being the source and target account IDs:

```
def __validate_transfer(self, source_account, target_account):
    source_balance = self.accounts.find_one({'account_id':
source_account})['balance']
    target_balance = self.accounts.find_one({'account_id':
target_account})['balance']

    if source_balance < 0 or target_balance < 0:
        return {'status': True, 's_bal': source_balance, 't_bal':
target_balance}
    else:
        return {'status': False}
```

Unfortunately, this attempt will also *fail*. The reason is the same as before. When we are inside a transaction, we make changes to the database that follow the ACID principles. Changes inside a transaction are not visible to any queries outside of it, until they are committed.

Transferring between accounts – part 3

The correct implementation to the transfer problem will look like the following code (the full code sample is attached with the code bundle):

```python
from pymongo import MongoClient
import json

class InitData:
    def __init__(self):
        self.client = MongoClient('localhost', 27017, w='majority')
        self.db = self.client.mongo_bank
        self.accounts = self.db.accounts

        # drop data from accounts collection every time to start from a
clean slate
        self.accounts.drop()

        init_data = InitData.load_data(self)
        self.insert_data(init_data)
        self.transfer('1', '2', 300)

    @staticmethod
    def load_data(self):
        ret = []
        with open('init_data.json', 'r') as f:
            for line in f:
                ret.append(json.loads(line))
        return ret

    def insert_data(self, data):
        for document in data:
            collection_name = document['collection']
            account_id = document['account_id']
            account_name = document['account_name']
            account_balance = document['account_balance']

            self.db[collection_name].insert_one({'account_id': account_id,
'name': account_name, 'balance': account_balance})

    # validating errors, using the tx session
    def tx_transfer_err_ses(self, source_account, target_account, value):
        print(f'transferring {value} Hypnotons from {source_account} to
{target_account}')
        with self.client.start_session() as ses:
            ses.start_transaction()
            res = self.accounts.update_one({'account_id': source_account},
{'$inc': {'balance': value * (-1)}}, session=ses)
```

```
            res2 = self.accounts.update_one({'account_id': target_account},
{'$inc': {'balance': value}}, session=ses)
            error_tx = self.__validate_transfer_ses(source_account,
target_account, ses)

            if error_tx['status'] == True:
                print(f"cant transfer {value} Hypnotons from
{source_account} ({error_tx['s_bal']}) to {target_account}
({error_tx['t_bal']})")
                ses.abort_transaction()
            else:
                ses.commit_transaction()

    # we are passing the session value so that we can view the updated
values
    def __validate_transfer_ses(self, source_account, target_account, ses):
        source_balance = self.accounts.find_one({'account_id':
source_account}, session=ses)['balance']
        target_balance = self.accounts.find_one({'account_id':
target_account}, session=ses)['balance']
        if source_balance < 0 or target_balance < 0:
            return {'status': True, 's_bal': source_balance, 't_bal':
target_balance}
        else:
            return {'status': False}

def main():
    InitData()

if __name__ == '__main__':
    main()
```

In this case, by passing the session object's `ses` value, we ensure that we can both make changes in our database using `update_one()` and also view these changes using `find_one()`, before doing either an `abort_transaction()` operation or a `commit_transaction()` operation.

Transactions cannot perform **data definition language (DDL)** operations, so `drop()`, `create_collection()`, and other operations that can affect MongoDB's DDL will fail inside a transaction. This is why we are setting `w='majority'` in our `MongoClient` object, to make sure that, when we drop a collection right before we start our transaction, this change will be visible to the transaction.

Even if we explicitly take care not to create or remove collections during a transaction, there are operations that will implicitly do so.
We need to make sure that the collection exists before we attempt to insert or upsert (update and insert) a document.

In the end, using transactions if we need to rollback, we don't need to keep track of the previous account balance values, as MongoDB will discard all of the changes that we made inside the transaction scope.

Continuing with the same example using Ruby, we have the following code for part 3:

```ruby
require 'mongo'

class MongoBank
  def initialize
    @client = Mongo::Client.new([ '127.0.0.1:27017' ], database:
:mongo_bank)
    db = @client.database
    @collection = db[:accounts]

    # drop any existing data
    @collection.drop

    @collection.insert_one('collection': 'accounts', 'account_id': '1',
'account_name': 'Alex', 'account_balance':100)
    @collection.insert_one('collection': 'accounts', 'account_id': '2',
'account_name': 'Mary', 'account_balance':50)

    transfer('1', '2', 30)
    transfer('1', '2', 300)
  end

  def transfer(source_account, target_account, value)
    puts "transferring #{value} Hypnotons from #{source_account} to
#{target_account}"
    session = @client.start_session

    session.start_transaction(read_concern: { level: :snapshot },
write_concern: { w: :majority })
    @collection.update_one({ account_id: source_account }, { '$inc' => {
account_balance: value*(-1)} }, session: session)
    @collection.update_one({ account_id: target_account }, { '$inc' => {
account_balance: value} }, session: session)

    source_account_balance = @collection.find({ account_id: source_account
}, session: session).first['account_balance']
```

```
    if source_account_balance < 0
      session.abort_transaction
    else
      session.commit_transaction
    end
  end

end

# initialize class
MongoBank.new
```

Alongside all of the points raised in the example in Python, we find that we can also customize `read_concern` and `write_concern` per transaction.

The available `read_concern` levels for multi-document ACID transactions are as follows:

- `majority`: A majority of the servers in a replica set have acknowledged the data. For this to work as expected in transactions, they must also use `write_concern` to `majority`.
- `local`: Only the local server has acknowledged the data.
- `snapshot`: The default `read_concern` levels for transactions as of MongoDB 4.0. If the transaction commits with `majority` as `write_concern`, all transaction operations will have read from a snapshot of majority committed data, otherwise no guarantee can be made.

 Read concern for transactions is set in the transaction level or higher (session or, finally, client). Setting read concern in individual operations is not supported and is generally discouraged.

The available `write_concern` levels for multi-document ACID transactions are the same as everywhere else in MongoDB, except for `w:0` (no acknowledgement), which is not supported at all.

E-commerce using MongoDB

For our second example, we are going to use a more complex use case on a transaction with three different collections.

We are going to simulate a shopping cart and payment transaction process for an e-commerce application using MongoDB. Using the sample code that we'll provide at the end of this section, we will initially populate the database with the following data.

Our first collection is the `users` collection with one document per user:

```
> db.users.find()
{ "_id" : ObjectId("5bc22f35f8d89f2b9e01d0fd"), "user_id" : 1, "name" :
"alex" }
{ "_id" : ObjectId("5bc22f35f8d89f2b9e01d0fe"), "user_id" : 2, "name" :
"barbara" }
```

Then we have the `carts` collection with one document per cart, which is linked via the `user_id` to our users:

```
> db.carts.find()
{ "_id" : ObjectId("5bc2f9de8e72b42f77a20ac8"), "cart_id" : 1, "user_id" :
1 }
{ "_id" : ObjectId("5bc2f9de8e72b42f77a20ac9"), "cart_id" : 2, "user_id" :
2 }
```

The `payments` collection holds any completed payment that has gone through, storing the `cart_id` and the `item_id` to link to the cart that it belonged to and the item that has been paid:

```
> db.payments.find()
{ "_id" : ObjectId("5bc2f9de8e72b42f77a20aca"), "cart_id" : 1, "name" :
"alex", "item_id" : 101, "status" : "paid" }
```

Finally, the `inventories` collection holds a count of the number of items (by `item_id`) that we have currently available, along with their price and a short description:

```
> db.inventories.find()
{ "_id" : ObjectId("5bc2f9de8e72b42f77a20acb"), "item_id" : 101,
"description" : "bull bearing", "price" : 100, "quantity" : 5 }
```

In this example, we are going to demonstrate using MongoDB's schema validation functionality. Using JSON schemata, we can define a set of validations that will be checked against the database level every time a document is inserted or updated. This is a fairly new feature as it was introduced in MongoDB 3.6. In our case, we are going to use it to make sure that we always have a positive number of items in our inventory.

The `validator` object in the MongoDB shell format is as follows:

```
validator = { validator:
  { $jsonSchema:
  { bsonType: "object",
```

```
required: ["quantity"],
properties:
{ quantity:
{ bsonType: ["long"],
minimum: 0,
description: "we can't have a negative number of items in our inventory"
}
}
}
}
}
```

JSON schemata can be used to implement many of the validations that we would usually have in our models in Rails or Django. We can define these keywords as in the following table:

Keyword	Validates on type	Description
enum	All	The enum of allowed values in a field.
type	All	The enum of allowed types in a field.
minimum/maximum	Numeric	The minimum and maximum values for a numeric field.
minLength/maxLength	String	The minimum and maximum length allowed for a string field.
pattern	String	The regex pattern that the string field must match.
required	Objects	The document must contain all the strings defined in the required property array.
minItems/maxItems	Arrays	The minimum and maximum length of items in the array.
uniqueItems	Arrays	If set to true, all items in the array must have unique values.
title	N/A	A descriptive title for the developer's use.
description	N/A	A description for the developer's use.

Using JSON schema, we can offload validations from our models to the database layer and/or use MongoDB validations as an additional layer of security on top of web application validations.

To use a JSON schema, we have to specify it at the time that we are creating our collection, as follows:

```
> db.createCollection("inventories", validator)
```

Returning to our example, our code will simulate having an inventory of five bull bearings and placing two orders; one by user Alex for two bull bearings, followed by a second order by user Barbara for another four bull bearings.

As expected, the second order will not go through because we don't have enough ball bearings in our inventory to fulfill it. We will see this in the following code:

```
from pymongo import MongoClient
from pymongo.errors import ConnectionFailure
from pymongo.errors import OperationFailure

class ECommerce:
    def __init__(self):
        self.client = MongoClient('localhost', 27017, w='majority')
        self.db = self.client.mongo_bank
        self.users = self.db['users']
        self.carts = self.db['carts']
        self.payments = self.db['payments']
        self.inventories = self.db['inventories']
        # delete any existing data
        self.db.drop_collection('carts')
        self.db.drop_collection('payments')
        self.db.inventories.remove()
        # insert new data
        self.insert_data()
        alex_order_cart_id = self.add_to_cart(1,101,2)
        barbara_order_cart_id = self.add_to_cart(2,101,4)
        self.place_order(alex_order_cart_id)
        self.place_order(barbara_order_cart_id)
    def insert_data(self):
        self.users.insert_one({'user_id': 1, 'name': 'alex' })
        self.users.insert_one({'user_id': 2, 'name': 'barbara'})
        self.carts.insert_one({'cart_id': 1, 'user_id': 1})
        self.db.carts.insert_one({'cart_id': 2, 'user_id': 2})
        self.db.payments.insert_one({'cart_id': 1, 'name': 'alex',
 'item_id': 101, 'status': 'paid'})
        self.db.inventories.insert_one({'item_id': 101, 'description': 'bull
bearing', 'price': 100, 'quantity': 5.0})

    def add_to_cart(self, user, item, quantity):
        # find cart for user
        cart_id = self.carts.find_one({'user_id':user})['cart_id']
        self.carts.update_one({'cart_id': cart_id}, {'$inc': {'quantity':
```

```
quantity}, '$set': { 'item': item} })
        return cart_id

    def place_order(self, cart_id):
            while True:
                try:
                    with self.client.start_session() as ses:
                        ses.start_transaction()
                        cart = self.carts.find_one({'cart_id': cart_id},
session=ses)
                        item_id = cart['item']
                        quantity = cart['quantity']
                        # update payments
                        self.db.payments.insert_one({'cart_id': cart_id,
'item_id': item_id, 'status': 'paid'}, session=ses)
                        # remove item from cart
                        self.db.carts.update_one({'cart_id': cart_id},
{'$inc': {'quantity': quantity * (-1)}}, session=ses)
                        # update inventories
                        self.db.inventories.update_one({'item_id': item_id},
{'$inc': {'quantity': quantity*(-1)}}, session=ses)
                        ses.commit_transaction()
                        break
                except (ConnectionFailure, OperationFailure) as exc:
                    print("Transaction aborted. Caught exception during
transaction.")
                    # If transient error, retry the whole transaction
                    if exc.has_error_label("TransientTransactionError"):
                        print("TransientTransactionError, retrying
transaction ...")
                        continue
                    elif str(exc) == 'Document failed validation':
                        print("error validating document!")
                        raise
                    else:
                        print("Unknown error during commit ...")
                        raise
def main():
    ECommerce()
if __name__ == '__main__':
    main()
```

We will break down the preceding example into the interesting parts, as follows:

```
    def add_to_cart(self, user, item, quantity):
        # find cart for user
        cart_id = self.carts.find_one({'user_id':user})['cart_id']
        self.carts.update_one({'cart_id': cart_id}, {'$inc': {'quantity':
```

```
quantity}, '$set': { 'item': item} })
        return cart_id
```

The `add_to_cart()` method doesn't use transactions. The reason is that because we are updating one document at a time, these are guaranteed to be atomic operations.

Then, in the `place_order()` method, we start the session, and then subsequently, a transaction within this session. Similar to the previous use case, we need to make sure that we add the `session=ses` parameter at the end of every operation that we want to be executed in the transaction context:

```
    def place_order(self, cart_id):
while True:
try:
with self.client.start_session() as ses:
ses.start_transaction()
...
# update payments
self.db.payments.insert_one({'cart_id': cart_id, 'item_id': item_id,
'status': 'paid'}, session=ses)
# remove item from cart
self.db.carts.update_one({'cart_id': cart_id}, {'$inc': {'quantity':
quantity * (-1)}}, session=ses)
# update inventories
self.db.inventories.update_one({'item_id': item_id}, {'$inc': {'quantity':
quantity*(-1)}}, session=ses)
ses.commit_transaction()
break
except (ConnectionFailure, OperationFailure) as exc:
print("Transaction aborted. Caught exception during transaction.")
# If transient error, retry the whole transaction
if exc.has_error_label("TransientTransactionError"):
print("TransientTransactionError, retrying transaction ...")
continue
elif str(exc) == 'Document failed validation':
print("error validating document!")
raise
else:
print("Unknown error during commit ...")
raise
```

In this method, we are using the retry able transaction pattern. We start by wrapping the transaction context in a `while True` block, essentially making it loop forever. Then we enclose our transaction in a `try` block that will listen for exceptions.

An exception of type `transient transaction`, which has
the `TransientTransactionError` error label, will result in continued execution in the
`while True` block, essentially retrying the transaction from the very beginning. On the
other hand, a failed validation or any other error will reraise the exception after logging it.

> The `session.commitTransaction()` and
> `session.abortTransaction()` operations will be retried once by
> MongoDB, no matter if we retry the transaction or not.
> We don't need to explicitly call `abortTransaction()` in this example, as
> MongoDB will abort it in the face of exceptions.

In the end, our database looks like the following code block:

```
> db.payments.find()
{ "_id" : ObjectId("5bc307178e72b431c0de385f"), "cart_id" : 1, "name" :
"alex", "item_id" : 101, "status" : "paid" }
{ "_id" : ObjectId("5bc307178e72b431c0de3861"), "cart_id" : 1, "item_id" :
101, "status" : "paid" }
```

The payment that we just made does not have the name field, in contrast to the sample
payment that we inserted in our database before rolling our transactions:

```
> db.inventories.find()
{ "_id" : ObjectId("5bc303468e72b43118dda074"), "item_id" : 101,
"description" : "bull bearing", "price" : 100, "quantity" : 3 }
```

Our inventory has the correct number of bull bearings, three (five minus the two that Alex
ordered), as shown in the following code block:

```
> db.carts.find()
{ "_id" : ObjectId("5bc307178e72b431c0de385d"), "cart_id" : 1, "user_id" :
1, "item" : 101, "quantity" : 0 }
{ "_id" : ObjectId("5bc307178e72b431c0de385e"), "cart_id" : 2, "user_id" :
2, "item" : 101, "quantity" : 4 }
```

Our carts have the correct quantities. Alex's cart (`cart_id=1`) has zero items, whereas
Barbara's cart (`cart_id=2`) still has four, since we don't have enough bull bearings to fulfill
her order. Our payments collection does not have an entry for Barbara's order and the
inventory still has three bull bearings in place.

Our database state is consistent and saving lots of time by implementing the abort
transaction and reconciliation data logic in our application level.

Continuing with the same example in Ruby, we have the following code block:

```ruby
require 'mongo'

class ECommerce
 def initialize
   @client = Mongo::Client.new([ '127.0.0.1:27017' ], database:
:mongo_bank)
   db = @client.database
   @users = db[:users]
   @carts = db[:carts]
   @payments = db[:payments]
   @inventories = db[:inventories]

   # drop any existing data
   @users.drop
   @carts.drop
   @payments.drop
   @inventories.delete_many

   # insert data
   @users.insert_one({ "user_id": 1, "name": "alex" })
   @users.insert_one({ "user_id": 2, "name": "barbara" })

   @carts.insert_one({ "cart_id": 1, "user_id": 1 })
   @carts.insert_one({ "cart_id": 2, "user_id": 2 })

   @payments.insert_one({"cart_id": 1, "name": "alex", "item_id": 101,
"status": "paid" })
   @inventories.insert_one({"item_id": 101, "description": "bull bearing",
"price": 100, "quantity": 5 })

   alex_order_cart_id = add_to_cart(1, 101, 2)
   barbara_order_cart_id = add_to_cart(2, 101, 4)

   place_order(alex_order_cart_id)
   place_order(barbara_order_cart_id)
 end

 def add_to_cart(user, item, quantity)
   session = @client.start_session
   session.start_transaction
   cart_id = @users.find({ "user_id": user}).first['user_id']
   @carts.update_one({"cart_id": cart_id}, {'$inc': { 'quantity': quantity
}, '$set': { 'item': item } }, session: session)
   session.commit_transaction
   cart_id
 end
```

```
def place_order(cart_id)
  session = @client.start_session
  session.start_transaction
  cart = @carts.find({'cart_id': cart_id}, session: session).first
  item_id = cart['item']
  quantity = cart['quantity']
  @payments.insert_one({'cart_id': cart_id, 'item_id': item_id, 'status':
'paid'}, session: session)
  @carts.update_one({'cart_id': cart_id}, {'$inc': {'quantity': quantity *
(-1)}}, session: session)
  @inventories.update_one({'item_id': item_id}, {'$inc': {'quantity':
quantity*(-1)}}, session: session)
  quantity = @inventories.find({'item_id': item_id}, session:
session).first['quantity']
  if quantity < 0
    session.abort_transaction
  else
    session.commit_transaction
  end
 end
end
```

```
ECommerce.new
```

Similar to the Python code sample, we are passing the `session: session` parameter along each operation to make sure that we are operating inside the transaction.

Here, we are not using the retry able transaction pattern. Regardless, MongoDB will retry committing or aborting a transaction once before throwing an exception.

The best practices and limitations of multi-document ACID transactions

There are currently some limitations and best practices when developing using MongoDB transactions in version 4.0.3:

- The transaction timeout is set to 60 seconds.
- As a best practice, any transaction should not try to modify more than 1,000 documents. There is no limitation in reading documents during a transaction.

- The oplog will record a single entry for a transaction, meaning that this is subject to the 16 MB document size limit. This is not such a big problem with transactions that update documents, as only the delta will be recorded in the oplog. It can, however, be an issue when transactions insert new documents, in which case the oplog will record the full contents of the new documents.
- We should add application logic to cater for failing transactions. These could include using retryable writes, or executing some business logic-driven action when the error cannot be retried or we have exhausted our retries (usually, this means a custom 500 error).
- DDL operations such as modifying indexes, collections, or databases will get queued up behind active transactions. Transactions trying to access the namespace while a DDL operation is still pending will immediately abort.
- Transactions only work in replica sets. Starting from MongoDB 4.2, transactions will also be available for sharded clusters.
- Use sparingly; maybe the most important point to consider when developing using MongoDB transactions is that they are not meant as a replacement for good schema design. They should only be used when there is no other way to model our data without them.

Summary

In this chapter, we learned about textbook relational database theory on ACID in the context of MongoDB.

Then, we focused on multi-document ACID transactions and applied them in two use cases using Ruby and Python. We learned about when to use MongoDB transactions and when not to use them, how to use them, their best practices, and their limitations.

In the next chapter, we will deal with one of the most commonly-used features of MongoDB – aggregation.

6
Aggregation

In Chapter 5, *Multi-Document ACID Transactions*, we worked through two use cases of the new transactions capability using code for Ruby and Python. In this chapter, we will dive deeper into the aggregation framework, learning how it can be useful. We will also look at the operators that are supported by MongoDB.

To learn this information, we will use aggregations to process transaction data from the Ethereum blockchain. The complete source code is available at https://github.com/ PacktPublishing/Mastering-MongoDB-4.x-Second-Edition.

In this chapter, we will cover the following topics:

- Why aggregation?
- Different aggregation operators
- Limitations

Why aggregation?

The aggregation framework was introduced by MongoDB in version 2.2 (which is version 2.1 in the development branch). It serves as an alternative to both the MapReduce framework and querying the database directly.

Using the aggregation framework, we can perform GROUP BY operations in the server. Thus, we can project only the fields that are needed in the result set. Using the $match and $project operators, we can reduce the amount of data passed through the pipeline, resulting in faster data processing.

Self-joins—that is, joining data within the same collection—can also be performed using the aggregation framework, as we will see in our use case.

When comparing the aggregation framework to simply using the queries available via the shell or various other drivers, it is important to remember that there is a use case for both.

For selection and projection queries, it's almost always better to use simple queries, as the complexity of developing, testing, and deploying an aggregation framework operation cannot easily outweigh the simplicity of using built-in commands. Finding documents with (`db.books.find({price: 50} {price: 1, name: 1})`), or without (`db.books.find({price: 50})`) projecting only some of the fields, is simple and fast enough to not warrant the usage of the aggregation framework.

On the other hand, if we want to perform GROUP BY and self-join operations using MongoDB, there might be a case for using the aggregation framework. The most important limitation of the `group()` command in the MongoDB shell is that the resulting set has to fit in a document, meaning that it can't be more than 16 MB in size. In addition, the result of any `group()` command can't have more than 20,000 results. Finally, `group()` doesn't work with sharded input collections, which means that when our data size grows we have to rewrite our queries anyway.

In comparison to MapReduce, the aggregation framework is more limited in functionality and flexibility. In the aggregation framework, we are limited by the available operators. On the plus side, the API for the aggregation framework is simpler to understand and use than MapReduce. In terms of performance, the aggregation framework was way faster than MapReduce in earlier versions of MongoDB, but seems to be on a par with the most recent versions after the improvement in performance by MapReduce.

Finally, there is always the option of using the database as data storage and performing complex operations using the application. Sometimes this can be quick to develop, but should be avoided as it will most likely incur memory, networking, and ultimately performance costs down the road.

In the next section, we will describe the available operators before using them in a real use case.

Aggregation operators

In this section, we will learn how to use aggregation operators. Aggregation operators are divided into two categories. Within each stage, we use **expression operators** to compare and process values. Between different stages, we use **aggregation stage operators** to define the data that will get passed on from one stage to the next, as it is considered to be in the same format.

Aggregation stage operators

An aggregation pipeline is composed of different stages. These stages are declared in an array and executed sequentially, with the output of every stage being the input of the next one.

The `$out` stage has to be the final stage in an aggregation pipeline, outputting data to an output collection by replacing or adding to the existing documents:

- `$group`: This is most commonly used to group by identifier expression and to apply the accumulator expression. It outputs one document per distinct group.
- `$project`: This is used for document transformation, and outputs one document per input document.
- `$match`: This is used for filtering documents from input based on criteria.
- `$lookup`: This is used for filtering documents from input. Input can be documents from another collection in the same database selected by an outer left join.
- `$out`: This outputs the documents in this pipeline stage to an output collection by replacing or adding to the documents that already exist in the collection.
- `$limit`: This limits the number of documents passed on to the next aggregation phase based on predefined criteria.
- `$count`: This returns a count of the number of documents at this stage of the pipeline.
- `$skip`: This skips a certain number of documents, preventing them from passing on to the next stage of the pipeline.
- `$sort`: This sorts the documents based on criteria.
- `$redact`: As a combination of `$project` and `$match`, this will redact the selected fields from each document and pass them on to the next stage of the pipeline.
- `$unwind`: This transforms an array of *n* elements to *n* documents, mapping each document to one element of the array. The documents are then passed on to the next stage of the pipeline.
- `$collStats`: This returns statistics regarding the view or collection.
- `$indexStats`: This returns statistics regarding the indexes of the collection.
- `$sample`: This randomly selects a specified number of documents from the input.

- $facet: This combines multiple aggregation pipelines within a single stage.
- $bucket: This splits documents into buckets based on predefined selection criteria and bucket boundaries.
- $bucketAuto: This splits documents into buckets based on predefined selection criteria and attempts to evenly distribute documents among the buckets.
- $sortByCount: This groups incoming documents based on the value of an expression and computes the count of documents in each bucket.
- $addFields: This adds new fields to documents and outputs the same number of documents as input with the added fields.
- $replaceRoot: This replaces all existing fields of the input document (including the standard _id field) with the specified fields.
- $geoNear: This returns an ordered list of documents based on the proximity to a specified field. The output documents include a computed distance field.
- $graphLookup: This recursively searches a collection and adds an array field with the results of the search in each output document.

Expression operators

Within every stage, we can define one or more expression operators to apply our intermediate calculations to. This section will focus on these expression operators.

Expression Boolean operators

Boolean operators are used to pass a true or false value to the next stage of our aggregation pipeline.

We can choose to pass the originating integer, string, or any other type value along as well.

We can use the $and, $or, and $not operators in the same way that we would use them in any programming language.

Expression comparison operators

Comparison operators can be used in conjunction with Boolean operators to construct the expressions that we need to evaluate as true/false for the output of our pipeline's stage.

The most commonly used operators are as follows:

- `$eq ( equal )`
- `$ne ( not equal)`
- `$gt (greater than)`
- `$gte (greater than or equal)`
- `$lt`
- `$lte`

All the aforementioned mentioned operators return a Boolean value of `true` or `false`.

The only operator that doesn't return a Boolean value is `$cmp`, which returns `0` if the two arguments are equivalent, `1` if the first value is greater than the second and `-1` if the second value is greater than the first.

Set expression and array operators

As with most programming languages, set operations ignore duplicate entries and the order of elements, treating them as sets. The order of results is unspecified and duplicates will be deduplicated in the result set. Set expressions do not apply recursively to elements of the set, but only to the top level. This means that if a set contains, for example, a nested array, then this array may or may not contain duplicates.

The available set operators are as follows:

- `$setEquals`: This is `true` if the two sets have the same distinct elements
- `$setIntersection`: This returns the intersection of all input sets (that is, the documents that appear in all of the input sets)
- `$setUnion`: This returns the union of all input sets (that is, the documents that appear in at least one of all of the input sets)
- `$setDifference`: This returns the documents that appear in the first input set but not the second
- `$setIsSubset`: This is `true` if all documents in the first set appear in the second one, even if the two sets are identical
- `$anyElementTrue`: This is `true` if any of the elements in the set evaluate to `true`
- `$allElementsTrue`: This is `true` if all of the elements in the set evaluate to `true`

The available array operators are as follows:

- `$arrayElemAt`: This returns the element at the array index position.
- `$concatArrays`: This returns a concatenated array.
- `$filter`: This returns a subset of the array based on specified criteria.
- `$indexOfArray`: This returns the index of the array that fulfills the search criteria. If it does not, then −1.
- `$isArray`: This returns `true` if the input is an array; otherwise, it returns `false`.
- `$range`: This outputs an array containing a sequence of integers according to user-defined inputs.
- `$reverseArray`: This returns an array with the elements in reverse order.
- `$reduce`: This reduces the elements of an array to a single value according to the specified input.
- `$size`: This returns the number of items in the array.
- `$slice`: This returns a subset of the array.
- `$zip`: This returns a merged array.
- `$in`: This returns `true` if the specified value is in the array; otherwise, it returns `false`.

Expression date operators

Date operators are used to extract date information from date fields when we want to calculate statistics based on the day of the week/month/year using the pipeline:

- `$dayOfYear` is used to get the day of the year within a range of 1 to 366 (for a leap year)
- `$dayOfMonth` is used to get the day of the month within a range of 1 to 31
- `$dayOfWeek` is used to get the day of the week within a range of 1 to 7, with 1 being Sunday and 7 being Saturday (using English days of the week)
- `$isoDayOfWeek` returns the weekday number in the ISO 8601 date format within a range of 1 to 7, with 1 being Monday and 7 being Sunday
- `$week` is the week number within a range of 0 to 53, with 0 being the partial week at the beginning of each year to 53 for a year with a leap week

- $isoWeek returns the week number in the ISO 8601 date format within a range of 1 to 53, 1 being the first week of the year that contains a Thursday and 53 being a leap week, if one exists in the year in question
- $year, $month, $hour, $minute, $milliSecond return the relevant portion of the date in zero-based numbering, except for $month, which returns a value ranging from 1 through 12
- $isoWeekYear returns the year in ISO 8601 date format according to the date that the last week in ISO 8601 date format ends (for example, 2016/1/1 will still return 2015)
- $second returns 0 to 60 inclusive for leap seconds
- $dateToString converts a date input to a string

Expression string operators

Like date operators, string operators are used when we want to transform our data from one stage of the pipeline to the next one. Potential use cases include preprocessing text fields to extract relevant information to be used in later stages of a pipeline:

- $concat: This is used to concatenate strings.
- $split: This is used to split strings based on delimiter. If the delimiter is not found, then the original string is returned.
- $strcasecmp: This is used in case-insensitive string comparisons. It will return 0 if the strings are equal and 1 if the first string is great; otherwise, it will return −1.
- $toLower/$toUpper: These are used to convert a string to all lowercase or all uppercase, respectively.
- $indexOfBytes: This is used to return the byte occurrence of the first occurrence of a substring in a string.
- $strLenBytes: This is the number of bytes in the input string.
- $substrBytes: This returns the specified bytes of the substring.

The equivalent methods for code points (a value in Unicode, regardless of the underlying bytes in its representation) are as follows:

- $indexOfCP
- $strLenCP
- $substrCP

Expression arithmetic operators

During each stage of the pipeline, we can apply one or more arithmetic operators to perform intermediate calculations. These operators are shown in the following list:

- `$abs`: This is the absolute value.
- `$add`: This can add numbers or a number to a date to get a new date.
- `$ceil`/`$floor`: These are the ceiling and floor functions, respectively.
- `$divide`: This is used to divide by two inputs.
- `$exp`: This raises the natural number *e* to the specified exponential power.
- `$pow`: This raises a number to the specified exponential power.
- `$ln`/`$log`/`$log10`: These are used to calculate the natural log, the log on a custom base, or a log base ten, respectively.
- `$mod`: This is the modular value.
- `$multiply`: This is used to multiply by inputs.
- `$sqrt`: This is the square root of the input.
- `$subtract`: This is the result of subtracting the second value from the first. If both arguments are dates, it returns the difference between them. If one argument is a date (this argument has to be the first argument) and the other is a number, it returns the resulting date.
- `$trunc`: This is used to truncate the result.

Aggregation accumulators

Accumulators are probably the most widely used operators, as they allow us to sum, average, get standard deviation statistics, and perform other operations in each member of our group. The following is a list of the aggregation accumulators:

- `$sum`: This is the sum of the numerical values. It ignores non-numerical values.
- `$avg`: This is the average of the numerical values. It ignores non-numerical values.
- `$first`/`$last`: This is the first and last value that passes through the pipeline stage. It is available in the group stage only.
- `$max`/`$min`: These get the maximum and minimum value that passes through the pipeline stage, respectively.
- `$push`: This will add a new element at the end of an input array. It is available in the group stage only.

- `$addToSet`: This will add an element (only if it does not exist) to an array, effectively treating it as a set. It is available in the group stage only.
- `$stdDevPop`/`$stdDevSamp`: These are used to get the population/sample standard deviation in the `$project` or `$match` stages.

These accumulators are available in the group or project pipeline phases except where otherwise noted.

Conditional expressions

Expressions can be used to output different data to the next stage in our pipeline based on Boolean truth tests:

$cond

The `$cond` phrase will evaluate an expression of the format if...then...else, and depending on the result of the `if` statement, it will return the value of the `then` statement or `else` branches. The input can be either three named parameters or three expressions in an ordered list:

$ifNull

The `$ifNull` phrase will evaluate an expression and return the first expression if it is not null or the second expression if the first expression is null. Null can be either a missing field or a field with an undefined value:

$switch

Similar to a programming language's `switch` statement, `$switch` will execute a specified expression when it evaluates to `true`, and breaks out of the control flow.

Type conversion operators

Introduced in MongoDB 4.0, type conversion operators allow us to convert a value to a specified type. The generic syntax of the command is as follows:

```
{
    $convert:
        {
            input: <expression>,
            to: <type expression>,
            onError: <expression>,    // Optional.
            onNull: <expression>      // Optional.
```

```
        }
    }
```

In this syntax, `input` and `to` (the only mandatory arguments) can be any valid expression. In its simplest form, we could, for example, have the following:

```
$convert: { input: "true", to: "bool" }
```

This converts a string with the value `true` to the Boolean value `true`.

The `onError` phrase can again be any valid expression, and specifies the value that MongoDB will return if it encounters an error during conversion, including unsupported type conversions. Its default behavior is to throw an error and stop processing.

The `onNull` phrase can also be any valid expression, and specifies the value that MongoDB will return if the input is null or missing. The default behavior is to return null.

MongoDB also provides some helper functions for the most common `$convert` operations. These functions are as follows:

- `$toBool`
- `$toDate`
- `$toDecimal`
- `$toDouble`
- `$toInt`
- `$toLong`
- `$toObjectId`
- `$toString`

These are even simpler to use. We could rewrite the previous example as the following:

```
{ $toBool: "true" }
```

Other operators

There are some operators that are not as commonly used, but which can be useful in use-case-specific cases. The most important of them are listed in the following sections.

Text search

The $meta operator is used to access text search metadata.

Variable

The $map operator applies a sub-expression to each of the elements of an array and returns the array of the resulting values. It accepts named parameters.

The $let operator defines variables for use within the scope of a subexpression and returns the result of the subexpression. It accepts named parameters.

Literal

The $literal operator will return a value without parsing. It is used for values that the aggregation pipeline may interpret as an expression. For example, you can apply a $literal expression to a string that starts with $ to avoid parsing as a field path.

Parsing data type

The $type operator returns the BSON data type of the field.

Limitations

The aggregation pipeline can output results in the following three distinct ways:

- Inline as a document containing the result set
- In a collection
- Returning a cursor to the result set

Inline results are subject to BSON maximum document size of 16 MB, meaning that we should use this only if our final result is of a fixed size. An example of this would be outputting ObjectId of the top five most ordered items from an e-commerce site.

A contrary example to this would be outputting the top 1,000 most ordered items, along with the product information, including the description and other fields of variable size.

Outputting results into a collection is the preferred solution if we want to perform further processing of the data. We can either output into a new collection or replace the contents of an existing collection. The aggregation output results will only be visible once the aggregation command succeeds; otherwise, it will not be visible at all.

 The output collection cannot be a sharded or capped collection (as of v3.4). If the aggregation output violates indexes (including the built-in index on the unique `ObjectId` per document) or document validation rules, the aggregation will fail.

Each pipeline stage can have documents exceeding the 16 MB limit as these are handled by MongoDB internally. Each pipeline stage, however, can only use up to 100 MB of memory. If we expect more data in our stages, we should set `allowDiskUse:` to `true` to allow excess data to overflow to disk at the expense of performance.

The `$graphLookup` operator does not support datasets over 100 MB and will ignore any setting on `allowDiskUse`.

Aggregation use case

In this rather lengthy section, we will use the aggregation framework to process data from the Ethereum blockchain.

Using our Python code, we have extracted data from Ethereum and loaded it into our MongoDB database. The relation of the blockchain to our database is shown in the following diagram:

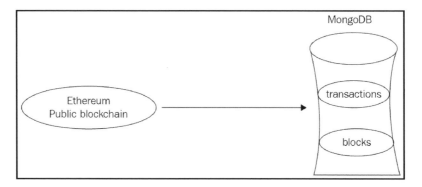

Our data resides in two collections: **blocks** and **transactions**.

A sample block document has the following fields:

- Number of transactions
- Number of contracted internal transactions
- Block hash
- Parent block hash
- Mining difficulty
- Gas used
- Block height

The following code shows the output data from a block:

```
> db.blocks.findOne()
{
"_id" : ObjectId("595368fbcedea89d3f4fb0ca"),
"number_transactions" : 28,
"timestamp" : NumberLong("1498324744877"),
"gas_used" : 4694483,
"number_internal_transactions" : 4,
"block_hash" :
"0x89d235c4e2e4e4978440f3cc1966f1ffb343b9b5cfec9e5cebc331fb810bded3
",
"difficulty" : NumberLong("882071747513072"),
"block_height" : 3923788
}
```

A sample transaction document has the following fields:

- Transaction hash
- The block height it belongs to
- From hash address
- To hash address
- Transaction value
- Transaction fee

The following code shows the output data from a transaction:

```
> db.transactions.findOne()
{
"_id" : ObjectId("59535748cedea89997e8385a"),
"from" : "0x3c540be890df69eca5f0099bbedd5d667bd693f3",
"txfee" : 28594,
"timestamp" : ISODate("2017-06-06T11:23:10Z"),
"value" : 0,
"to" : "0x4b9e0d224dabcc96191cace2d367a8d8b75c9c81",
"txhash" :
"0xf205991d937bcb60955733e760356070319d95131a2d9643e3c48f2dfca39e77
",
"block" : 3923794
}
```

Sample data for our database is available on GitHub at: `https://github.com/
PacktPublishing/Mastering-MongoDB-4.x-Second-Edition`.

As curious developers who are using this novel blockchain technology, we want to analyze Ethereum transactions. We are especially keen to do the following:

- Find the top ten addresses that transactions originate from
- Find the top ten addresses that transactions end in
- Find the average value per transaction, with statistics concerning the deviation
- Find the average fee required per transaction, with statistics concerning the deviation
- Find the time of day that the network is more active according to the number or value of transactions
- Find the day of week that the network is more active according to the number or value of transactions

We find the top ten addresses that transactions originate from. To calculate this metric, we first count the number of occurrences with a 1 count for each one, group them by the value of the `from` field, and output them into a new field called `count`.

After this, we sort by the value of the `count` field in descending (−1) order, and finally, we `limit` the output to the first ten documents that pass through the pipeline. These documents are the top ten addresses that we are looking for.

The following is some sample Python code:

```
def top_ten_addresses_from(self):
    pipeline = [
        {"$group": {"_id": "$from", "count": {"$sum": 1}}},
        {"$sort": SON([("count", -1)])},
        {"$limit": 10},
    ]
    result = self.collection.aggregate(pipeline)
    for res in result:
        print(res)
```

The output of the preceding code is as follows:

```
{u'count': 38, u'_id': u'miningpoolhub_1'}
{u'count': 31, u'_id': u'Ethermine'}
{u'count': 30, u'_id': u'0x3c540be890df69eca5f0099bbedd5d667bd693f3'}
{u'count': 27, u'_id': u'0xb42b20ddbeabdc2a288be7ff847ff94fb48d2579'}
{u'count': 25, u'_id': u'ethfans.org'}
{u'count': 16, u'_id': u'Bittrex'}
{u'count': 8, u'_id': u'0x009735c1f7d06faaf9db5223c795e2d35080e826'}
{u'count': 8, u'_id': u'Oraclize'}
{u'count': 7, u'_id': u'0x1151314c646ce4e0efd76d1af4760ae66a9fe30f'}
{u'count': 7, u'_id': u'0x4d3ef0e8b49999de8fa4d531f07186cc3abe3d6e'}
```

Now we find the top ten addresses that transactions end in. As we did with `from`, the calculation for the `to` addresses is exactly the same, only grouping using the `to` field instead of `from`, as shown in the following code:

```
def top_ten_addresses_to(self):
    pipeline = [
        {"$group": {"_id": "$to", "count": {"$sum": 1}}},
        {"$sort": SON([("count", -1)])},
        {"$limit": 10},
    ]
    result = self.collection.aggregate(pipeline)
    for res in result:
        print(res)
```

The output of the preceding code is as follows:

```
{u'count': 33, u'_id': u'0x6090a6e47849629b7245dfa1ca21d94cd15878ef'}
{u'count': 30, u'_id': u'0x4b9e0d224dabcc96191cace2d367a8d8b75c9c81'}
{u'count': 25, u'_id': u'0x69ea6b31ef305d6b99bb2d4c9d99456fa108b02a'}
{u'count': 23, u'_id': u'0xe94b04a0fed112f3664e45adb2b8915693dd5ff3'}
{u'count': 22, u'_id': u'0x8d12a197cb00d4747a1fe03395095ce2a5cc6819'}
{u'count': 18, u'_id': u'0x91337a300e0361bddb2e377dd4e88ccb7796663d'}
{u'count': 13, u'_id': u'0x1c3f580daeaac2f540c998c8ae3e4b18440f7c45'}
```

```
{u'count': 12, u'_id': u'0xeef274b28bd40b717f5fea9b806d1203daad0807'}
{u'count': 9, u'_id': u'0x96fc4553a00c117c5b0bed950dd625d1c16dc894'}
{u'count': 9, u'_id': u'0xd43d09ec1bc5e57c8f3d0c64020d403b04c7f783'}
```

Let's find the average value per transaction, with statistics concerning the standard deviation. In this example, we are using the `$avg` and `$stdDevPop` operators of the values of the `value` field to calculate the statistics for this field. Using a simple `$group` operation, we output a single document with the ID of our choice (here, `value`) and the `averageValues`, as shown in the following code:

```
def average_value_per_transaction(self):
    pipeline = [
        {"$group": {"_id": "value", "averageValues": {"$avg": "$value"},
"stdDevValues": {"$stdDevPop": "$value"}}},
    ]
    result = self.collection.aggregate(pipeline)
    for res in result:
        print(res)
```

The output of the preceding code is as follows:

```
{u'averageValues': 5.227238976440972, u'_id': u'value', u'stdDevValues':
38.90322689649576}
```

Let's find the average fee required per transaction, returning statistics concerning the deviation. Average fees are similar to average values, replacing `$value` with `$txfee`, as shown in the following code:

```
def average_fee_per_transaction(self):
    pipeline = [
        {"$group": {"_id": "value", "averageFees": {"$avg": "$txfee"},
"stdDevValues": {"$stdDevPop": "$txfee"}}},
    ]
    result = self.collection.aggregate(pipeline)
    for res in result:
        print(res)
```

The output of the preceding code snippet is as follows:

```
{u'_id': u'value', u'averageFees': 320842.0729166667, u'stdDevValues':
1798081.7305142984}
```

We find the time of day that the network is more active according to the number or value of transactions at specific times.

To find out the most active hour for transactions, we use the `$hour` operator to extract the hour field from the `ISODate()` field in which we stored our `datetime` values and called `timestamp`, as shown in the following code:

```
def active_hour_of_day_transactions(self):
    pipeline = [
        {"$group": {"_id": {"$hour": "$timestamp"}, "transactions":
{"$sum": 1}}},
        {"$sort": SON([("transactions", -1)])},
        {"$limit": 1},
    ]
    result = self.collection.aggregate(pipeline)
    for res in result:
        print(res)
```

The output is as follows:

```
{u'_id': 11, u'transactions': 34}
```

The following code will calculate the sum of transaction values for the most active hour of the day:

```
def active_hour_of_day_values(self):
pipeline = [
{"$group": {"_id": {"$hour": "$timestamp"}, "transaction_values": {"$sum":
"$value"}}},
{"$sort": SON([("transactions", -1)])},
{"$limit": 1},
]
result = self.collection.aggregate(pipeline)
for res in result:
print(res)
```

The output of the preceding code is as follows:

```
{u'transaction_values': 33.17773841, u'_id': 20}
```

Let's find the day of the week that the network is more active according to the number of transactions or value of transactions. As we did with the hour of the day, we use the `$dayOfWeek` operator to extract the day of the week from `ISODate()` objects, as shown in the following code. Days are numbered ranging from one for Sunday to seven for Saturday, following the US convention:

```
def active_day_of_week_transactions(self):
    pipeline = [
        {"$group": {"_id": {"$dayOfWeek": "$timestamp"}, "transactions":
```

```
{"$sum": 1}}},
        {"$sort": SON([("transactions", -1)])},
        {"$limit": 1},
    ]
    result = self.collection.aggregate(pipeline)
    for res in result:
        print(res)
```

The output of the preceding code is as follows:

{u'_id': 3, u'transactions': 92}

The following code will calculate the sum of transaction values for the most active day of the week:

```
def active_day_of_week_values(self):
    pipeline = [
        {"$group": {"_id": {"$dayOfWeek": "$timestamp"},
"transaction_values": {"$sum": "$value"}}},
        {"$sort": SON([("transactions", -1)])},
        {"$limit": 1},
    ]

    result = self.collection.aggregate(pipeline)
for res in result:
print(res)
```

The output of the preceding code is as follows:

{u'transaction_values': 547.62439312, u'_id': 2}

The aggregations that we calculated can be described in the following diagram:

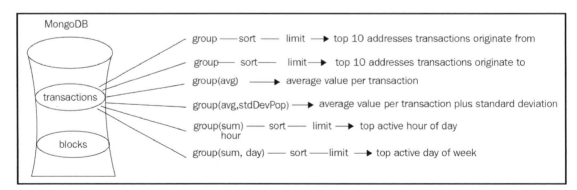

In terms of blocks, we would like to know the following:

- Average number of transactions per block, for both the total overall transactions and the total contracted internal transactions.
- Average gas used per block.
- Average gas used per transaction to a block. Is there a window of opportunity to submit my smart contract in a block?
- Average difficulty per block and how it deviates.
- Average number of transactions per block, both in total and also in contracted internal transactions.

Averaging over the `number_transactions` field, we can get the number of transactions per block, as shown in the following code:

```
def average_number_transactions_total_block(self):
    pipeline = [
        {"$group": {"_id": "average_transactions_per_block", "count":
{"$avg": "$number_transactions"}}},
    ]
    result = self.collection.aggregate(pipeline)
    for res in result:
        print(res)
```

The output of the preceding code is as follows:

```
{u'count': 39.458333333333336, u'_id': u'average_transactions_per_block'}
```

Whereas with the following code, we can get the average number of internal transactions per block:

```
def average_number_transactions_internal_block(self):
    pipeline = [
        {"$group": {"_id": "average_transactions_internal_per_block",
"count": {"$avg": "$number_internal_transactions"}}},
    ]
    result = self.collection.aggregate(pipeline)
    for res in result:
        print(res)
```

The output of the preceding code is as follows:

```
{u'count': 8.0, u'_id': u'average_transactions_internal_per_block'}
```

The average gas used per block can be acquired as follows:

```
def average_gas_block(self):
    pipeline = [
        {"$group": {"_id": "average_gas_used_per_block",
                    "count": {"$avg": "$gas_used"}}},
    ]
    result = self.collection.aggregate(pipeline)
    for res in result:
        print(res)
```

The output is as follows:

```
{u'count': 2563647.9166666665, u'_id': u'average_gas_used_per_block'}
```

The average difficulty per block and how it deviates can be acquired as follows:

```
def average_difficulty_block(self):
    pipeline = [
        {"$group": {"_id": "average_difficulty_per_block",
                    "count": {"$avg": "$difficulty"}, "stddev":
{"$stdDevPop": "$difficulty"}}},
    ]
    result = self.collection.aggregate(pipeline)
    for res in result:
        print(res)
```

The output is as follows:

```
{u'count': 881676386932100.0, u'_id': u'average_difficulty_per_block',
u'stddev': 446694674991.6385}
```

Our aggregations are described in the following schema:

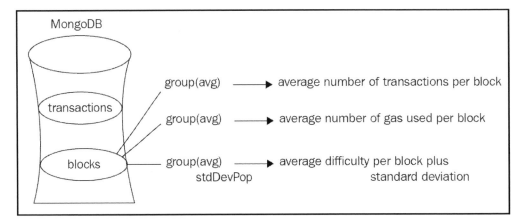

Now that we have the basic statistics calculated, we want to up our game and find out more information about our transactions. Through our sophisticated machine learning algorithms, we have identified some of the transactions as either scams or **initial coin offering (ICO)**, or maybe both.

In these documents, we have marked these attributes in an array called `tags`, as follows:

```
{
  "_id" : ObjectId("59554977cedea8f696a416dd"),
  "to" : "0x4b9e0d224dabcc96191cace2d367a8d8b75c9c81",
  "txhash" :
"0xf205991d937bcb60955733e760356070319d95131a2d9643e3c48f2dfca39e77",
  "from" : "0x3c540be890df69eca5f0099bbedd5d667bd693f3",
  "block" : 3923794,
  "txfee" : 28594,
  "timestamp" : ISODate("2017-06-10T09:59:35Z"),
  "tags" : [
  "scam",
  "ico"
  ],
  "value" : 0
  }
```

Now we want to get the transactions from June, 2017, remove the `_id` field, and produce different documents according to the tags that we have identified. So in our example, we would output two documents in our new collection, `scam_ico_documents`, for separate processing.

The way to do this via the aggregation framework is shown in the following code:

```
def scam_or_ico_aggregation(self):
 pipeline = [
 {"$match": {"timestamp": {"$gte": datetime.datetime(2017,6,1), "$lte":
datetime.datetime(2017,7,1)}}},
 {"$project": {
 "to": 1,
 "txhash": 1,
 "from": 1,
 "block": 1,
 "txfee": 1,
 "tags": 1,
 "value": 1,
 "report_period": "June 2017",
 "_id": 0,
 }

 },
```

```
{"$unwind": "$tags"},
{"$out": "scam_ico_documents"}
]
result = self.collection.aggregate(pipeline)
for res in result:
print(res)
```

Here, we have the following four distinct steps in our aggregation framework pipeline:

1. Using $match, we only extract documents that have a timestamp field value of June 01, 2017.

2. Using $project, we add a new report_period field with a value of June 2017 and remove the _id field by setting its value to 0. We keep the rest of the fields intact by using the value 1, as shown in the preceding code.

3. Using $unwind, we output one new document per tag in our $tags array.

4. Finally, using $out, we output all of our documents to a new scam_ico_documents collection.

Since we used the $out operator, we will get no results in the command line. If we comment out {"$out": "scam_ico_documents"}, we get documents that look like the following:

```
{u'from': u'miningpoolhub_1', u'tags': u'scam', u'report_period': u'June
2017', u'value': 0.52415349, u'to':
u'0xdaf112bcbd38d231b1be4ae92a72a41aa2bb231d', u'txhash':
u'0xe11ea11df4190bf06cbdaf19ae88a707766b007b3d9f35270cde37ceccba9a5c',
u'txfee': 21.0, u'block': 3923785}
```

The final result in our database will look like this:

```
{
  "_id" : ObjectId("5955533be9ec57bdb074074e"),
  "to" : "0x4b9e0d224dabcc96191cace2d367a8d8b75c9c81",
  "txhash" :
"0xf205991d937bcb60955733e760356070319d95131a2d9643e3c48f2dfca39e77",
  "from" : "0x3c540be890df69eca5f0099bbedd5d667bd693f3",
  "block" : 3923794,
  "txfee" : 28594,
  "tags" : "scam",
  "value" : 0,
  "report_period" : "June 2017"
  }
```

Now that we have documents that are clearly separated in the `scam_ico_documents` collection, we can perform further analysis pretty easily. An example of this analysis would be to append more information on some of these scammers. Luckily, our data scientists have come up with some additional information that we have extracted into a new collection `scam_details`, which looks like this:

```
{
  "_id" : ObjectId("5955510e14ae9238fe76d7f0"),
  "scam_address" : "0x3c540be890df69eca5f0099bbedd5d667bd693f3",
  Email_address": example@scammer.com"
  }
```

We can now create a new aggregation pipeline job to join our `scam_ico_documents` with the `scam_details` collection and output these extended results in a new collection, called `scam_ico_documents_extended`, like this:

```
def scam_add_information(self):
 client = MongoClient()
 db = client.mongo_book
 scam_collection = db.scam_ico_documents
 pipeline = [
 {"$lookup": {"from": "scam_details", "localField": "from", "foreignField":
"scam_address", "as": "scam_details"}},
 {"$match": {"scam_details": { "$ne": [] }}},
 {"$out": "scam_ico_documents_extended"}
 ]
 result = scam_collection.aggregate(pipeline)
 for res in result:
 print(res)
```

Here, we are using the following three-step aggregation pipeline:

1. Use the `$lookup` command to join data from the `scam_details` collection and the `scam_address` field with data from our local collection (`scam_ico_documents`) based on the value from the local collection attribute `from` being equal to the value in the `scam_details` collection's `scam_address` field. If these are equal, then the pipeline adds a new field to the document called `scam_details`.

2. Next, we only match the documents that have a `scam_details` field—the ones that matched with the lookup aggregation framework step.

3. Finally, we output these documents in a new collection called `scam_ico_documents_extended`.

These documents will now look like this:

```
> db.scam_ico_documents_extended.findOne()
{
"_id" : ObjectId("5955533be9ec57bdb074074e"),
"to" : "0x4b9e0d224dabcc96191cace2d367a8d8b75c9c81",
"txhash" :
"0xf205991d937bcb60955733e760356070319d95131a2d9643e3c48f2dfca39e77",
"from" : "0x3c540be890df69eca5f0099bbedd5d667bd693f3",
"block" : 3923794,
"txfee" : 28594,
"tags" : "scam",
"value" : 0,
"report_period" : "June 2017",
"scam_details_data" : [
{
"_id" : ObjectId("5955510e14ae9238fe76d7f0"),
"scam_address" : "0x3c540be890df69eca5f0099bbedd5d667bd693f3",
email_address": example@scammer.com"
}]}
```

Using the aggregation framework, we have identified our data and can process it rapidly and efficiently.

The previous steps can be summed up in the following diagram:

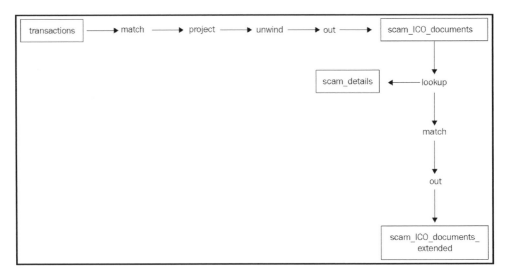

Summary

In this chapter, we dived deep into the aggregation framework. We discussed why and when we should use aggregation as opposed to simply using MapReduce or querying the database. We went through the vast array of options and functionalities for aggregation.

We discussed the aggregation stages and the various operators, such as Boolean operators, comparison operators, set operators, array operators, date operators, string operators, expression arithmetic operators, aggregation accumulators, conditional expressions, and variables, and the literal parsing data type operators.

Using the Ethereum use case, we went through aggregation with working code and learned how to approach an engineering problem to solve it.

Finally, we learned about the limitation that the aggregation framework currently has and when to avoid it.

In the next chapter, we will move on to the topic of indexing and learn how to design and implement performant indexes for our read and write workloads.

7
Indexing

This chapter will explore one of the most important properties of any database: indexing. Similar to book indexes, database indexes allow for quicker data retrieval. In the RDBMS world, indexes are widely used (and sometimes abused) to speed up data access. In MongoDB, indexes play an integral part in schema and query design. MongoDB supports a wide array of indexes that you will learn about in this chapter, including single field, compound, multi-key, geospatial, hashed, partial, and many more. In addition to reviewing the different types of indexes, we will show you how to build and manage indexes for single-server deployments, as well as complex sharded environments.

In this chapter, we will cover the following topics:

- Index internals
- Types of indexes
- Building and managing indexes
- Efficient usage of indexes

Index internals

In most cases, indexes are variations of the B-tree data structure. Invented by Rudolf Bayer and Ed McCreight in 1971, while they were working at Boeing research labs, the **B-tree** data structure allows for searches, sequential access, inserts, and deletes to be performed in logarithmic time. The **logarithmic time** property stands for both the average case performance and the worst possible performance, and it is a great property when applications cannot tolerate unexpected variations in performance behavior.

To further illustrate how important the logarithmic time part is, we will show you the Big-O complexity chart, which is from `http://bigocheatsheet.com/`:

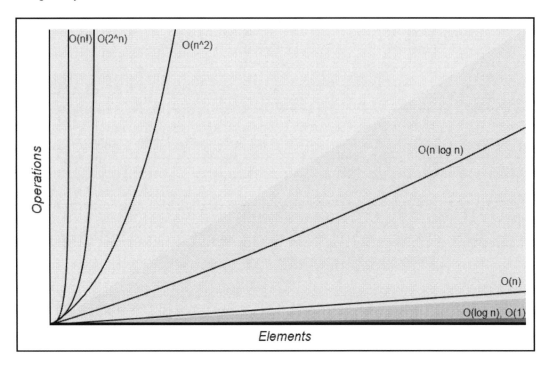

In this diagram, you can see logarithmic time performance as a flat line, parallel to the *x* axis of the diagram. As the number of elements increases, constant time (**O(n)**) algorithms perform worse, whereas quadratic time algorithms (**O(n^2)**) go off the chart. For an algorithm that we rely on to get our data back to us as quickly as possible, time performance is of the utmost importance.

Another interesting property of a B-tree is that it is self-balancing, meaning that it will self-adjust to always maintain these properties. Its precursor and closest relative is the binary search tree, a data structure that only allows two children for each parent node.

Schematically, a B-tree looks like the following diagram, which can also be seen at `https://commons.wikimedia.org/w/index.php?curid=11701365`:

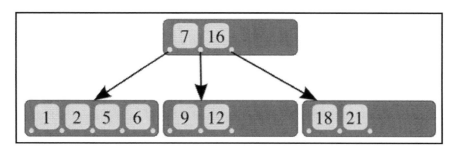

In the preceding diagram, we have a parent node with the values **7** and **16**, pointing to three child nodes.

If we search for the value **9**, knowing that it's greater than **7** and smaller than **16**, we'll be directed to the middle child node that contains the value straight away.

Thanks to this structure, we are approximately halving our search space with every step, ending in a *log n* time complexity. Compared to sequentially scanning through every element, halving the number of elements with each and every step increases our gains exponentially as the number of elements we have to search through increases.

Index types

MongoDB offers a vast array of index types for different needs. In the following sections, we will identify the different types, and the needs that each one of them fulfills.

Single field indexes

The most common and simple type of index is the single field index. An example of a single field and key index is the index on `ObjectId` (`_id`), which is generated by default in every MongoDB collection. The `ObjectId` index is also unique, preventing a second document from having the same `ObjectId` in a collection.

An index on a single field, based on the `mongo_book` database that we used throughout the previous chapters, is defined like this:

```
> db.books.createIndex( { price: 1 } )
```

Here, we create an index on the field name in ascending order of index creation. For a descending order, the same index would be created like this:

```
> db.books.createIndex( { price: -1 } )
```

The ordering for index creation is important if we expect our queries to favor values on the first documents stored in our index. However, due to the extremely efficient time complexity that indexes have, this will not be a consideration for the most common use cases.

An index can be used for exact match queries or range queries on a field value. In the former case, the search can stop as soon as our pointer reaches the value after $O(log\ n)$ time.

In range queries, due to the fact that we are storing values in order in our B-tree index, once we find the border value of our range query in a node of our B-tree, we will know that all of the values in its children will be part of our result set, allowing us to conclude our search.

An example of this is shown as follows:

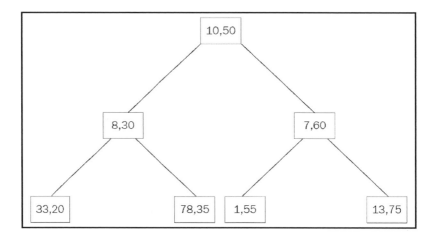

Dropping indexes

Dropping an index is as simple as creating it. We can reference the index by its name or by the fields it is composed from:

```
> db.books.dropIndex( { price: -1 } )

> db.books.dropIndex( "price_index" )
```

Indexing embedded fields

As a document database, MongoDB supports embedding fields and whole documents in nested complex hierarchies inside of the same document. Naturally, it also allows us to index these fields.

In our books collection example, we can have documents like the following:

```
{
"_id" : ObjectId("5969ccb614ae9238fe76d7f1"),
"name" : "MongoDB Indexing Cookbook",
"isbn" : "1001",
"available" : 999,
"meta_data" : {
"page_count" : 256,
"average_customer_review" : 4.8
}
}
```

Here, the meta_data field is a document itself,
with page_count and average_customer_review fields. Again, we can create an index on page_count, as follows:

```
db.books.createIndex( { "meta_data.page_count": 1 } )
```

This can answer queries on equality and range comparisons around the meta_data.page_count field, as follows:

```
> db.books.find({"meta_data.page_count": { $gte: 200 } })
> db.books.find({"meta_data.page_count": 256 })
```

To access embedded fields, we use dot notation, and we need to include quotes ("") around the field's name.

Indexing embedded documents

We can also index the embedded document as a whole, similar to indexing embedded fields:

```
> db.books.createIndex( { "meta_data": 1 } )
```

Here, we are indexing the whole document, expecting queries against its entirety, like the following:

```
> db.books.find({"meta_data": {"page_count":256,
"average_customer_review":4.8}})
```

The key difference is that when we index embedded fields, we can perform range queries on them using the index, whereas when we index embedded documents, we can only perform comparison queries using the index.

The db.books.find({"meta_data.average_customer_review": { $gte: 4.8}, "meta_data.page_count": { $gte: 200 } }) command will not use our meta_data index, whereas db.books.find({"meta_data": {"page_count":256, "average_customer_review":4.8}}) will use it.

Background indexes

Indexes can be created in the foreground, blocking all of the operations in the collection until they are built, or they can be created in the background, allowing for concurrent operations. Building an index in the background is done by passing in the background: true parameter:

```
> db.books.createIndex( { price: 1 }, { background: true } )
```

Background indexes have some limitations that we will revisit in the last section of this chapter, *Building and managing indexes*.

Compound indexes

Compound indexes are a generalization of single-key indexes, allowing for multiple fields to be included in the same index. They are useful when we expect our queries to span multiple fields in our documents, and also for consolidating our indexes when we start to have too many of them in our collection.

Compound indexes can have as many as 31 fields. They cannot have a hashed index type.

A compound index is declared similarly to single indexes, by defining the fields that we want to index and the order of indexing:

```
> db.books.createIndex({"name": 1, "isbn": 1})
```

Sorting with compound indexes

The order of indexing is useful for sorting results. In single field indexes, MongoDB can traverse the index both ways, so it doesn't matter which order we define.

In multi-field indexes, however, ordering can determine whether we can use this index to sort. In the preceding example, a query matching the sort direction of our index creation will use our index as follows:

```
> db.books.find().sort( { "name": 1, "isbn": 1 })
```

It will also use a `sort` query with all of the `sort` fields reversed:

```
> db.books.find().sort( { "name": -1, "isbn": -1 })
```

In this query, since we negated both of the fields, MongoDB can use the same index, traversing it from the end to the start.

The other two sorting orders are as follows:

```
> db.books.find().sort( { "name": -1, "isbn": 1 })
> db.books.find().sort( { "name": 1, "isbn": -1 })
```

They cannot be traversed using the index, as the `sort` order that we want is not present in our index's B-tree data structure.

Reusing compound indexes

An important attribute of compound indexes is that they can be used for multiple queries on prefixes of the fields indexed. This is useful when we want to consolidate indexes that pile up in our collections over time.

Consider the compound (multi-field) index that we created previously:

```
> db.books.createIndex({"name": 1, "isbn": 1})
```

This can be used for queries on name or {name, isbn}:

```
> db.books.find({"name":"MongoDB Indexing"})
> db.books.find({"isbn": "1001", "name":"MongoDB Indexing"})
```

The order of the fields in our query doesn't matter; MongoDB will rearrange the fields to match our query.

However, the order of the fields in our index does matter. A query just for the isbn field cannot use our index:

```
> db.books.find({"isbn": "1001"})
```

The underlying reason is that our fields' values are stored in the index as secondary, tertiary, and so on; each one is embedded inside of the previous ones, just like a **matryoshka**, the Russian nesting doll. This means that when we query on the first field of our multi-field index, we can use the outermost doll to find our pattern, whereas when we are searching for the first two fields, we can match the pattern on the outermost doll, and then dive into the inner one.

This concept is called **prefix indexing**, and along with index intersection, it is the most powerful tool for index consolidation, as you will see later in this chapter.

Multikey indexes

Indexing scalar (single) values was explained in the preceding sections. However, one of the advantages that we get from using MongoDB is the ability to easily store vector values in the form of arrays.

In the relational world, storing arrays is generally frowned upon, as it violates the normal forms. In a document-oriented database such as MongoDB, it is frequently a part of our design, as we can store and query easily on complex structures of data.

Indexing arrays of documents is achieved by using the multikey index. A multikey index can store both arrays of scalar values and arrays of nested documents.

Creating a multikey index is the same as creating a regular index:

```
> db.books.createIndex({"tags":1})
```

Assume that we have created a document in our books collection, using the following command:

```
> db.books.insert({"name": "MongoDB Multikeys Cheatsheet", "isbn": "1002",
"available": 1, "meta_data": {"page_count":128,
"average_customer_review":3.9}, "tags": ["mongodb",
"index","cheatsheet","new"] })
```

Our new index will be a multikey index, allowing us to find documents with any of the tags stored in our array:

```
> db.books.find({tags:"new"})
{
"_id" : ObjectId("5969f4bc14ae9238fe76d7f2"),
"name" : "MongoDB Multikeys Cheatsheet",
"isbn" : "1002",
"available" : 1,
"meta_data" : {
"page_count" : 128,
"average_customer_review" : 3.9
},
"tags" : [
"mongodb",
"index",
"cheatsheet",
"new"
]
}
>
```

We can also create compound indexes with a multikey index, but we can have, at the most, one array in each and every index document. Given that in MongoDB we don't specify the type of each field, this means that creating an index with two or more fields with an array value will fail at creation time, and trying to insert a document with two or more fields as arrays will fail at insertion time.

For example, a compound index on tags, analytics_data will fail to be created if we have the following document in our database:

```
{
"_id" : ObjectId("5969f71314ae9238fe76d7f3"),
"name": "Mastering parallel arrays indexing",
"tags" : [
"A",
"B"
],
"analytics_data" : [
```

```
   "1001",
   "1002"
   ]
   }

> db.books.createIndex({tags:1, analytics_data:1})
{
"ok" : 0,
"errmsg" : "cannot index parallel arrays [analytics_data] [tags]",
"code" : 171,
"codeName" : "CannotIndexParallelArrays"
}
```

Consequently, if we first create the index on an empty collection and try to insert this document, the insert will fail, with the following error:

```
>
db.books.find({isbn:"1001"}).hint("international_standard_book_number_index
").explain()
{
        "queryPlanner" : {
                "plannerVersion" : 1,
                "namespace" : "mongo_book.books",
                "indexFilterSet" : false,
                "parsedQuery" : {
                        "isbn" : {
                                "$eq" : "1001"
                        }
                },
                "winningPlan" : {
                        "stage" : "FETCH",
                        "inputStage" : {
                                "stage" : "IXSCAN",
                                "keyPattern" : {
                                        "isbn" : 1
                                },
                                "indexName" :
"international_standard_book_numbe
r_index",
                                "isMultiKey" : false,
                                "multiKeyPaths" : {
                                        "isbn" : [ ]
                                },
                                "isUnique" : false,
                                "isSparse" : false,
                                "isPartial" : false,
                                "indexVersion" : 2,
                                "direction" : "forward",
```

```
                         "indexBounds" : {
                                  "isbn" : [
                                          "[\"1001\", \"1001\"]"
                                  ]
                          }
                  }
          },
          "rejectedPlans" : [ ]
    },
    "serverInfo" : {
          "host" : "PPMUMCPU0142",
          "port" : 27017,
          "version" : "3.4.7",
          "gitVersion" : "cf38c1b8a0a8dca4a11737581beafef4fe120bcd"
    },
    "ok" : 1
```

Hashed indexes cannot be multikey indexes.

Another limitation that we will likely run into when trying to fine-tune our database is that multikey indexes cannot entirely cover a query. Covering a query with the index means that we can get our result data entirely from the index, without accessing the data in our database at all. This can result in dramatically increased performance, as indexes are most likely to be stored in RAM.

Querying for multiple values in multikey indexes will result in a two-step process, from the index's perspective.

In the first step, index will be used to retrieve the first value of the array, and then a sequential scan will run through the rest of the elements in the array; an example is as follows:

```
> db.books.find({tags: [ "mongodb", "index", "cheatsheet", "new" ] })
```

This will first search for all entries in multikey `index` tags that have a `mongodb` value, and will then sequentially scan through them to find the ones that also have the `index`, `cheatsheet`, and `new` tags.

A multikey index cannot be used as a shard key. However, if the shard key is a prefix index of a multikey index, it can be used. We will cover more on this in `Chapter 13`, *Sharding*.

Special types of indexes

Apart from the generic indexes, MongoDB supports indexes for special use cases. In this section, we will identify and explore how to use them.

Text indexes

Text indexes are special indexes on string value fields, used to support text searches. This book is based on version 3 of the text index functionality, available since version 3.2.

A text index can be specified similarly to a regular index, by replacing the index sort order (-1, 1) with the word `text`, as follows:

```
> db.books.createIndex({"name": "text"})
```

 A collection can have one text index, at the most. This text index can support multiple fields, text or not. It cannot support other special types, such as multikey or geospatial. Text indexes cannot be used for sorting results, even if they are only a part of a compound index.

Since we only have one text index per collection, we need to choose the fields wisely. Reconstructing this text index can take quite some time, and having only one of them per collection makes maintenance quite tricky, as you will see toward the end of this chapter.

Luckily, this index can also be a compound index:

```
> db.books.createIndex( { "available": 1, "meta_data.page_count": 1,
"$**": "text" } )
```

A compound index with `text` fields follows the same rules of sorting and prefix indexing that we explained earlier in this chapter. We can use this index to query on `available`, or the combination of `available` and `meta_data.page_count`, or sort them if the sort order allows for traversing our index in any direction.

We can also blindly index each and every field in a document that contains strings as `text`:

```
> db.books.createIndex( { "$**": "text" } )
```

This can result in unbounded index sizes, and should be avoided; however, it can be useful if we have unstructured data (for example, coming straight from application logs wherein we don't know which fields may be useful, and we want to be able to query as many of them as possible).

Text indexes will apply stemming (removing common suffixes, such as plural s/es for English language words) and remove stop words (a, an, `the`, and so on) from the index.

Text indexing supports more than 20 languages, including Spanish, Chinese, Urdu, Persian, and Arabic. Text indexes require special configurations to correctly index in languages other than English.

Some interesting properties of text indexes are explained as follows:

- **Case-insensitivity and diacritic insensitivity**: A text index is case- and diacritic-insensitive. Version 3 of the text index (the one that comes with version 3.4) supports common *C*, simple *S*, and the special *T* case folding, as described in **Unicode Character Database** (**UCD**) 8.0 case folding. In addition to case-insensitivity, version 3 of the text index supports diacritic insensitivity. This expands insensitivity to characters with accents in both small and capital-letter form. For example, *e, è, é, ê, ë*, and their capital letter counterparts, can all result into being equal when comparing using a text index. In the previous versions of the text index, these were treated as different strings.

- **Tokenization delimiters:** Version 3 of the text index supports the tokenization delimiters, defined as `Dash`, `Hyphen`, `Pattern_Syntax`, `Quotation_Mark`, `Terminal_Punctuation`, and `White_Space`, as described in UCD 8.0 case folding.

Hashed indexes

A hashed index contains `hashed` values of the indexed field:

```
> db.books.createIndex( { name: "hashed" } )
```

This will create a hashed index on the name of each book of our `books` collection. A hashed index is ideal for equality matches, but it cannot work with range queries. If we want to perform a range of queries on fields, we can create a regular index (or a compound index containing the field), and also a hashed index for equality matches. Hashed indexes are used internally by MongoDB for hash-based sharding, as we will discuss in `Chapter 13`, *Sharding*. Hashed indexes truncate floating point fields to integers. Floating points should be avoided for hashed fields wherever possible.

Time to live indexes

Time to live (**TTL**) indexes are used to automatically delete documents after an expiration time. Their syntax is as follows:

```
> db.books.createIndex( { "created_at_date": 1 }, { expireAfterSeconds:
86400 } )
```

The `created_at_date` field values have to be either a date or an array of dates (the earliest one will be used). In this example, the documents will get deleted one day (`86400` seconds) after `created_at_date`.

If the field does not exist or the value is not a date, the document will not expire. In other words, a TTL index silently fails, not returning any errors when it does.

Data gets removed by a background job that runs every 60 seconds. As a result, there is no explicit accuracy guarantee as to how much longer documents will persist past their expiration dates.

 A TTL index is a regular single field index. It can be used for queries like a regular index. A TTL index cannot be a compound index, operate on a capped collection, or use the `_id` field. The `_id` field implicitly contains a timestamp of the created time for the document, but is not a `Date` field. If we want each document to expire at a different, custom date point, we have to set `{expireAfterSeconds: 0}`, and set the TTL index `Date` field manually to the date on which we want the document to expire.

Partial indexes

A partial index on a collection is an index that only applies to the documents that satisfy the `partialFilterExpression` query.

We'll use our familiar `books` collection, as follows:

```
> db.books.createIndex(
  { price: 1, name: 1 },
  { partialFilterExpression: { price: { $gt: 30 } } }
)
```

Using this, we can have an index for just the books that have a price greater than 30. The advantage of partial indexes is that they are more lightweight in creation and maintenance, and use less storage.

The `partialFilterExpression` filter supports the following operators:

- Equality expressions (that is, `field: value`, or using the `$eq` operator)
- The `$exists: true` expression
- The `$gt`, `$gte`, `$lt`, and `$lte` expressions
- `$type` expressions
- The `$and` operator, at the top level only

Partial indexes will only be used if the query can be satisfied as a whole by the partial index.

If our query matches or is more restrictive than the `partialFilterExpression` filter, then the partial index will be used. If the results may not be contained in the partial index, then the index will be totally ignored.

`partialFilterExpression` does not need to be a part of the sparse index fields. The following index is a valid sparse index:

```
> db.books.createIndex({ name: 1 },{ partialFilterExpression: { price: {
$gt: 30 } } })
```

To use this partial index, however, we need to query for both `name` and `price` equal to or greater than `30`.

 Prefer partial indexes to sparse indexes. Sparse indexes offer a subset of the functionality offered by partial indexes. Partial indexes were introduced in MongoDB 3.2, so if you have sparse indexes from earlier versions, it may be a good idea to upgrade them. The `_id` field cannot be a part of a partial index. A shard key index cannot be a partial index. `partialFilterExpression` cannot be combined with the `sparse` option.

Sparse indexes

A sparse index is similar to a partial index, preceding it by several years (it has been available since version 1.8).

A `sparse` index only indexes values that contain the following field:

```
> db.books.createIndex( { "price": 1 }, { sparse: true } )
```

It will only create an index with the documents that contain a `price` field.

Some indexes are always sparse, due to their nature:

- 2d, 2dsphere (version 2)
- geoHaystack
- text

A sparse and unique index will allow for multiple documents missing the index key. It will not allow for documents with the same index field values. A sparse and compound index with geospatial indexes (2d, 2dsphere, and geoHaystack) will index the document as long as it has the geospatial field.

A sparse and compound index with the text field will index the document as long as it has the text field. A sparse and compound index without any of the two preceding cases will index the document as long as it has at least one of the fields.

Avoid creating new sparse indexes in the latest versions of MongoDB; use partial indexes instead.

Unique indexes

A unique index is similar to an RDBMS unique index, forbidding duplicate values for the indexed field. MongoDB creates a unique index by default on the _id field for every inserted document:

```
> db.books.createIndex( { "name": 1 }, { unique: true } )
```

This will create a unique index on a book's name. A unique index can also be a compound embedded field or an embedded document index.

In a compound index, the uniqueness is enforced across the combination of values in all of the fields of the index; for example, the following will not violate the unique index:

```
> db.books.createIndex( { "name": 1, "isbn": 1 }, { unique: true } )
> db.books.insert({"name": "Mastering MongoDB", "isbn": "101"})
> db.books.insert({"name": "Mastering MongoDB", "isbn": "102"})
```

This is because even though the name is the same, our index is looking for the unique combination of name and isbn, and the two entries differ in isbn.

Unique indexes do not work with hashed indexes. Unique indexes cannot be created if the collection already contains duplicate values of the indexed field. A unique index will not prevent the same document from having multiple values.

If a document is missing the indexed field, it will be inserted. If a second document is missing the indexed field, it will not be inserted. This is because MongoDB will store the missing field value as null, only allowing one document to be missing in the field.

Indexes that are a combination of unique and partial will only apply unique indexes after a partial index has been applied. This means that there may be several documents with duplicate values, if they are not a part of partial filtering.

Case-insensitive

Case-sensitivity is a common problem with indexing. We may store our data in mixed caps and need our index to ignore case when looking for our stored data. Until version 3.4, this was dealt with at the application level by creating duplicate fields with all lowercase characters and indexing all lowercase field to simulate a case-insensitive index.

Using the `collation` parameter, we can create case-insensitive indexes, and even collections that behave as case-insensitive.

In general, `collation` allows users to specify language-specific rules for string comparisons. A possible (but not the only) usage is for case-insensitive indexes and queries.

Using our familiar `books` collection, we can create a case-insensitive index on a name, as follows:

```
> db.books.createIndex( { "name" : 1 },
                         { collation: {
                             locale : 'en',
                             strength : 1
                           }
                         } )
```

The `strength` parameter is one of the collation parameters: the defining parameter for case-sensitivity comparisons. Strength levels follow the **International Components for Unicode (ICU)** comparison levels. The values that it accepts are as follows:

Strength Value	Description
1a	Primary level of comparison. Comparison based on string values, ignoring any other differences, such as case and diacritics.
2	Secondary level of comparison, which is the comparison based on the primary level and if this is equal then compare diacritics (that is, accents).
3 (default)	Tertiary level of comparison. Same as level 2, adding case and variants.
4	Quaternary level. Limited for specific use cases to consider the punctuation when levels 1-3 ignore punctuation, or for processing Japanese text.
5	Identical level. Limited for specific use cases: a tie breaker.

Creating the index with `collation` is not enough to get back case-insensitive results. We need to specify `collation` in our query, as well:

```
> db.books.find( { name: "Mastering MongoDB" } ).collation( { locale: 'en',
  strength: 1 } )
```

If we specify the same level of `collation` in our query as our index, then the index will be used. We could specify a different level of `collation`, as follows:

```
> db.books.find( { name: "Mastering MongoDB" } ).collation( { locale: 'en', strength: 2 } )
```

Here, we cannot use the index, as our index has `collation` level 1, and our query looks for `collation` level 2.

If we don't use any `collation` in our queries, we will get results defaulting to level 3, that is, case-sensitive.

Indexes in collections that were created using a different `collation` from the default will automatically inherit this `collation` level.

Suppose that we create a collection with `collation` level 1, as follows:

```
> db.createCollection("case_sensitive_books", { collation: { locale: 'en_US', strength: 1 } } )
```

The following index will also have collation `name: 1`:

```
> db.case_sensitive_books.createIndex( { name: 1 } )
```

Default queries to this collection will be collation `strength: 1`, case-sensitive. If we want to override this in our queries, we need to specify a different level of `collation` in our queries, or ignore the `strength` part altogether. The following two queries will return case-insensitive, default `collation` level results in our `case_sensitive_books` collection:

```
> db.case_sensitive_books.find( { name: "Mastering MongoDB" } ).collation( { locale: 'en', strength: 3 } ) // default collation strength value
> db.case_sensitive_books.find( { name: "Mastering MongoDB" } ).collation( { locale: 'en'  } ) // no value for collation, will reset to global default (3) instead of default for case_sensitive_books collection (1)
```

Collation is a pretty strong and relatively new concept in MongoDB, so we will keep exploring it throughout the different chapters.

Geospatial indexes

Geospatial indexes were introduced early on in MongoDB, and the fact that Foursquare was one of the earliest customers and success stories for MongoDB (then 10gen Inc.) is probably no coincidence. There are three distinct types of geospatial indexes that we will explore in this chapter, and they will be covered in the following sections.

2d geospatial indexes

A `2d` geospatial index stores geospatial data as points on a two-dimensional plane. It is mostly kept for legacy reasons, for coordinate pairs created before MongoDB 2.2, and in most cases, it should not be used with the latest versions.

2dsphere geospatial indexes

A `2dsphere` geospatial index supports queries calculating geometries in an earth-like plane. It is more accurate than the simplistic `2d` index, and can support both GeoJSON objects and coordinate pairs as input.

Its current version, since MongoDB 3.2, is version 3. It is a sparse index by default, only indexing documents that have a `2dsphere` field value. Assuming that we have a location field in our `books` collection, tracking the home address of the main author of each book, we could create an index on this field as follows:

```
> db.books.createIndex( { "location" : "2dsphere" } )
```

The `location` field needs to be a GeoJSON object, like this one:

```
location : { type: "Point", coordinates: [ 51.5876, 0.1643 ] }
```

A `2dsphere` index can also be a part of a compound index, as the first field or otherwise:

```
> db.books.createIndex( { name: 1, location : "2dsphere" } )
```

geoHaystack indexes

`geoHaystack` indexes are useful when we need to search for geographical-based results in a small area. Like searching for a needle in a haystack, with a `geoHaystack` index, we can define buckets of geolocation points and get back all of the results that belong in this area.

We will create a `geoHaystack` index, as follows:

```
> db.books.createIndex( { "location" : "geoHaystack" ,
                          "name": 1 } ,
                        { bucketSize: 2 } )
```

This will create buckets of documents within 2 units of latitude or longitude from each document.

Here, with the preceding example `location`:

```
location : { type: "Point", coordinates: [ 51.5876, 0.1643 ] }
```

Based on the `bucketSize: 2`, every document with the `location [49.5876..53.5876, -2.1643..2.1643]` will belong in the same bucket as our location.

A document can appear in multiple buckets. If we want to use spherical geometry, `2dsphere` is a better solution. `geoHaystack` indexes are sparse, by default.

If we need to calculate the nearest document to our location and it is outside of our `bucketSize` (that is, greater than 2 units of latitude/longitude, in our example), queries will be inefficient, and possibly inaccurate. Use a `2dsphere` index for such queries.

Building and managing indexes

Indexes can be built using the MongoDB shell or any of the available drivers. By default, indexes are built in the foreground, blocking all other operations in the database. This is faster, but is often undesirable, especially in production instances.

We can also build indexes in the background by adding the `{background: true}` parameter in our index commands in the shell. Background indexes will only block the current connection/thread. We can open a new connection (that is, using `mongo` in the command line) to connect to the same database:

```
> db.books.createIndex( { name: 1 }, { background: true } )
```

Background index building can take significantly more time than foreground index building, especially if the indexes can't fit into the available RAM.

Index early and revisit indexes regularly for consolidation. Queries won't see partial index results. Queries will start getting results from an index only after it is completely created.

Do not use the main application code to create indexes, as it can impose unpredictable delays. Instead, get a list of indexes from the application, and mark these for creation during maintenance windows.

Forcing index usage

We can force MongoDB to use an index by applying the `hint()` parameter:

```
> db.books.createIndex( { isbn: 1 }, { background: true } )
{
"createdCollectionAutomatically" : false,
"numIndexesBefore" : 8,
"numIndexesAfter" : 9,
```

```
"ok" : 1
}
```

The output from `createIndex` notifies us that the index was created (`"ok" : 1`), no
collection was automatically created as a part of index creation
(`"createdCollectionAutomatically" : false`), the number of indexes before this
index creation was 8, and now there are nine indexes for this collection, in total.

Now, if we try to search for a book by `isbn`, we can use the `explain()` command to see
the `winningPlan` sub-document, where we can find which query plan was used:

```
> db.books.find({isbn: "1001"}).explain()
...
"winningPlan" : {
"stage" : "FETCH",
"inputStage" : {
"stage" : "IXSCAN",
"keyPattern" : {
"isbn" : 1,
"name" : 1
},
"indexName" : "isbn_1_name_1",
...
```

This means that an index with `isbn` is 1 and `name` is 1 was used instead of our newly
created index. We can also view our index in the `rejectedPlans` sub-document of the
output, as follows:

```
...
"rejectedPlans" : [
{
"stage" : "FETCH",
"inputStage" : {
"stage" : "IXSCAN",
"keyPattern" : {
"isbn" : 1
},
"indexName" : "isbn_1",
...
```

This is, in fact, correct, as MongoDB is trying to reuse an index that is more specific than a
generic one.

We may not be sure though in cases where our `isbn_1` index is performing better than the
`isbn_1_name_1` one.

We can force MongoDB to use our newly created index, as follows:

```
> db.books.find({isbn:
"1001"}).hint("international_standard_book_number_index")
.explain()
{
...
                "winningPlan" : {
                        "stage" : "FETCH",
                        "inputStage" : {
                                "stage" : "IXSCAN",
                                "keyPattern" : {
                                        "isbn" : 1
                        },
...
```

Now, the `winningPlan` sub-document contains our index, `isbn_1`, and there are no `rejectedPlans` elements. It's an empty array in the result set.

We cannot use `hint()` with the special type of text indexes.

Hint and sparse indexes

By design, sparse indexes do not include some documents in the index, based on the presence/absence of a field. Queries that may include documents that are not present in the index will not use a sparse index.

Using `hint()` with a sparse index may result in incorrect counts, since it is forcing MongoDB to use an index that may not include all of the results that we want.

Older versions of `2dsphere`, `2d`, `geoHaystack`, and text indexes are sparse, by default. `hint()` should be used with caution, and after careful consideration of its implications.

Building indexes on replica sets

In replica sets, if we issue a `createIndex()` command, secondaries will begin to create the index after the primary server has finished creating it. Similarly, in sharded environments, primaries will start to build indexes, and secondaries will start after the primary for each shard that is finished.

Recommended approaches to building indexes in replica sets are as follows:

- Stop one secondary from the replica set
- Restart it as a standalone server in a different port
- Build the index from the shell as a standalone index
- Restart the secondary in the replica set
- Allow for the secondary to catch up with the primary

We need to have a large enough oplog size in the primary to make sure that the secondary will be able to catch up once it's reconnected. The oplog size is defined in MB in the configuration, and it defines how many operations will be kept in the log in the primary server. If the oplog size can only hold up to the last 100 operations happening in the primary, and 101 or more operations happen, this means that the secondary will not be able to sync with the primary. This is a consequence of the primary not having enough memory to keep track of its operations and inform the secondary of them. Building indexes in replica sets is a manual process, involving several steps for each primary and secondary server.

This approach can be repeated for each secondary server in the replica set. Then, for the primary server, we can do either of these things:

- Build the index in the background
- Step down the primary by using `rs.stepDown()`, and repeat the preceding process with the server as a secondary

Using approach number two, when the primary steps down, there will be a brief period when our cluster won't be taking any writes. Our application shouldn't timeout during this (usually less than) 30-60 second period.

Building an index in the background in the primary will build it in the background for the secondaries too. This may impact writes in our servers during index creation, but on the plus side, it has no manual steps. It is always a good idea to have a staging environment that mirrors production, and dry run operations that affect the live cluster in staging, in order to avoid surprises.

Managing indexes

In this section, you will learn how to give human-friendly names to your indexes, as well as some special considerations and limitations that we have to keep in mind for indexing.

Naming indexes

By default, index names are assigned by MongoDB automatically, based on the fields indexed and the direction of the index (1, -1). If we want to assign our own `name`, we can do so at creation time:

```
> db.books.createIndex( { isbn: 1 }, { name:
"international_standard_book_number_index" } )
```

Now, we have a new index called `international_standard_book_number_index`, instead of what MongoDB would have named it (`"isbn_1"`).

We can view all of the indexes in our `books` collection by using `db.books.getIndexes()`. A fully qualified index name has to be less than or equal to 128 characters. That also includes `database_name`, `collection_name`, and the dots separating them.

Special considerations

The following are a few limitations to keep in mind concerning indexing:

- Index entries have to be less than 1,024 bytes. This is mostly an internal consideration, but we can keep it in mind if we run into issues with indexing.
- A collection can have up to 64 indexes.
- A compound index can have up to 31 fields.
- Special indexes cannot be combined in queries. This includes special query operators that have to use special indexes, such as `$text` for text indexes and `$near` for geospatial indexes. This is because MongoDB can use multiple indexes to fulfill a query, but not in all cases. There will be more about this issue in the *Index intersection* section.
- Multikey and geospatial indexes cannot cover a query. This means that index data alone will not be enough to fulfill the query, and the underlying documents will need to be processed by MongoDB to get back the complete set of results.
- Indexes have a unique constraint on fields. We cannot create multiple indexes on the same fields, differing only in options. This is a limitation for sparse and partial indexes, as we cannot create multiple variations of these indexes that differ only in the filtering query.

Using indexes efficiently

Creating indexes is a decision that should not be taken lightly. As easy as it is to create indexes via the shell, it can create problems down the line if we end up with too many, or inadequately efficient, indexes. In this section, you will learn how to measure the performance of existing indexes, some tips for improving performance, and how we can consolidate the number of indexes so that we have better-performing indexes.

Measuring performance

Learning how to use the explain() command will help you in both optimizing and understanding the performance of an index. The explain() command, when used in conjunction with a query, will return the query plan that MongoDB would use for this query, instead of the actual results.

It is invoked by chaining it at the end of our query, as follows:

```
> db.books.find().explain()
```

It can take three options: queryPlanner (the default), executionStats, and allPlansExecution.

Let's use the most verbose output, allPlansExecution:

```
> db.books.find().explain("allPlansExecution")
```

Here, we can get information for both the winning query plan and some partial information about query plans that were considered during the planning phase, but were rejected because the query planner considered them slower. The explain() command returns a rather verbose output anyway, allowing for deep insights into how the query plan works to return our results.

At first glance, we need to focus on whether the indexes that should be used are being used, and if the number of scanned documents matches the number of returned documents as much as possible.

For the first one, we can inspect the stage field and look for IXSCAN, which means that an index was used. Then, in the sibling indexName field, we should see the name of our expected index.

For the second one, we need to compare `keysExamined` with the `nReturned` fields. We ideally want our indexes to be as selective as possible with regard to our queries, meaning that to return 100 documents, these would be the 100 documents that our index examines.

Of course, this is a trade-off as indexes increase in number and size in our collection. We can have a limited number of indexes per collection, and we definitely have a limited amount of RAM to fit these indexes, so we must balance the trade-off between having the best available indexes, and these indexes not fitting into our memory and getting slowed down.

Improving performance

Once we get comfortable with measuring the performance of the most common and important queries for our users, we can start to try to improve them.

The general idea is that we need indexes when we expect (or already have) repeatable queries that are starting to run slowly. Indexes do not come for free, as they impose a performance penalty in creation and maintenance, but they are more than worth it for frequent queries, and can reduce the lock percentage in our database, if designed correctly.

Recapping on our suggestions from the previous section, we want our indexes to do the following:

- Fit in the RAM
- Ensure selectivity
- Be used to sort our query results
- Be used in our most common and important queries

Fitting in the RAM can be ensured by using `getIndexes()` in our collections and making sure that we are not creating large indexes by inspecting the system level available RAM and if swap is being used.

Selectivity, as mentioned previously, is ensured by comparing `nReturned` with `keysExamined` in each `IXSCAN` phase of our queries. We want these two numbers to be as close as possible.

Ensuring that our indexes are used to sort our query results is a combination of using compound indexes (which will be used as a whole, and also for any prefix-based query) and declaring the direction of our indexes to be in accordance with our most common queries.

Finally, aligning indexes with our query is a matter of application usage patterns, which can uncover that queries are used most of the time, and then by using `explain()` on these queries to identify the query plan that is being used each time.

Index intersection

Index intersection refers to the concept of using more than one index to fulfill a query. This was added fairly recently, and is not perfect yet; however we can exploit it to consolidate our indexes.

> We can verify whether an index intersection happened in a query by using `explain()` on the query and witnessing an AND_SORTED or AND_HASH stage in the executed query plan.

Index intersection can happen when we use OR (`$or`) queries, by using a different index for each OR clause. Index intersection can happen when we use AND queries, and we have either complete indexes for each AND clause or index prefixes for some (or all) of the clauses.

For example, consider a query on our `books` collection, as follows:

```
> db.books.find({ "isbn":"101", "price": { $gt: 20 }})
```

Here, with two indexes (one on `isbn` and the other on `price`), MongoDB can use each index to get the related results, and then intersect on the index results to get the result set.

With compound indexes, as you learned previously in this chapter, we can use index prefixing to support queries that contain the first *1...n-1* fields of an *n* field compound index.

What we cannot support with compound indexes are queries that are looking for fields in the compound index, missing one or more of the previously defined fields.

> The order matters in compound indexes.

To satisfy these queries, we can create indexes on the individual fields, which will then use index intersection and fulfill our needs. The down side to this approach is that as the number of fields (*n*) increases, the number of indexes that we have to create grows exponentially, thus increasing our need for storage and memory.

Index intersection will not work with `sort()`. We can't use one index for querying and a different index for applying `sort()` to our results.

However, if we have an index that can fulfill a part for the whole of our query and the `sort()` field, then this index will be used.

Further reading

You can refer to the following links for further references:

- `http://bigocheatsheet.com/`
- `https://commons.wikimedia.org/`
- `https://docs.mongodb.com/manual/core/index-intersection/`

Summary

In this chapter, you learned about the foundations of indexing and index internals. We then explored how to use the different index types available in MongoDB, such as single field, compound, and multikey, as well as some special types, such as text, hashed, TTL, partial, parse, unique, case-insensitive, and geospatial.

In the next part of the chapter, you learned how to build and manage indexes using the shell, which is a basic part of administration and database management, even for NoSQL databases. Finally, we discussed how to improve our indexes, at a high level, and also how we can use index intersection in practice, in order to consolidate the number of indexes.

In the next chapter, we will discuss how we can monitor our MongoDB cluster and keep consistent backups. You will also learn how to handle security in MongoDB.

Section 3: Administration and Data Management

3

In this section, we will cover operational concepts and how MongoDB interacts with the data processing ecosystem. We will start by learning how MongoDB deals with monitoring, backup, and security, followed by an overview of the different storage engines that are available in MongoDB. In the MongoDB tooling chapter, we will learn about all the tools, including Stitch and Atlas, that we can use to interact with MongoDB, followed by a chapter that covers a use case about how we can process big data using MongoDB.

This section consists of the following chapters:

- Chapter 8, *Monitoring, Backup, and Security*
- Chapter 9, *Storage Engines*
- Chapter 10, *MongoDB Tooling*
- Chapter 11, *Harnessing Big Data with MongoDB*

8
Monitoring, Backup, and Security

Monitoring, backup, and security should not be an afterthought, but a necessary process before deploying MongoDB in a production environment. In addition, monitoring can (and should) be used to troubleshoot and improve performance at the development stage.

In this chapter, we will discuss the operational aspects of MongoDB. Having a backup strategy that produces correct and consistent backups, as well as making sure that our backup strategy will work in the unfortunate case that a backup is needed, will be covered in this chapter. Finally, we will discuss security for MongoDB for many different aspects, such as authentication, authorization, network-level security, and how to audit our security design.

This chapter will focus on the following three areas:

- Monitoring
- Backup
- Security

Monitoring

When we are designing a software system, we undertake many explicit and implicit assumptions. We always try to make the best decisions based on our knowledge, but there may be some parameters that we have underestimated or didn't take into account.

Using monitoring, we can validate our assumptions and verify that our application performs as intended and scales as expected. Good monitoring systems are also vital for detecting software bugs and to help us detect early potential security incidents.

What should we monitor?

By far, the most important metric to monitor in MongoDB is memory usage. MongoDB (and every database system, for what it's worth) uses system memory extensively to increase performance. No matter whether we use MMAPv1 or WiredTiger storage engines, the memory that's used is the first thing that we should keep our eyes on.

Understanding how computer memory works can help us to evaluate metrics from our monitoring system. These are the most important concepts related to computer memory.

Page faults

RAM is fast, yet expensive. Hard disk drives, or solid state drives, are relatively cheaper and slower, and also provide durability for our data in the case of system and power failures. All of our data is stored on the disk, and when we perform a query, MongoDB will try to fetch data from memory. If the data is not in the memory, then it will fetch the data from the disk and copy it to the memory. This is a **page fault event**, because the data in the memory is organized in pages.

As page faults happen, the memory gets filled up, and eventually, some pages need to be cleared for more recent data to come into the memory. This is called a **page eviction event**. We cannot completely avoid page faults unless we have a really static dataset, but we do want to try to minimize page faults. This can be achieved by holding our working set in memory.

Resident memory

The **resident memory** size is the total amount of memory that MongoDB owns in the RAM. This is the base metric to monitor, and it should be less than 80% of the available memory.

Virtual and mapped memory

When MongoDB asks for a memory address, the operating system will return a virtual address. This may or may not be an actual address in the RAM, depending on where the data resides. MongoDB will use this virtual address to request the underlying data. When we have journaling enabled (which should be almost always), MongoDB will keep another address on record for the journaled data. The virtual memory refers to the size of all of the data requested by MongoDB, including the journaling.

The mapped memory excludes journaling references.

What all of this means is that over time, our mapped memory will be roughly equal to our working set, and the virtual memory will be around twice the amount of our mapped memory.

Working sets

The working set is the data size that MongoDB uses. In the case of a transactional database, this will end up being the data size that MongoDB holds, but there may be cases where we have collections that are not used at all and will not contribute to our working set.

Monitoring memory usage in WiredTiger

Understanding the memory usage in MMAPv1 is relatively straightforward. MMAPv1 uses the `mmap()` system call under the hood to pass on the responsibility of the memory page to the underlying operating system. That is why when we use MMAPv1, the memory usage will grow unbounded, as the operating system is trying to fit as much of our dataset into the memory as possible.

With WiredTiger, on the other hand, we define the internal cache memory usage on startup. By default, the internal cache will be, at a maximum, between half of our RAM, which is in-between 1 GB or 256 MB.

On top of the internal cache, there is also memory that MongoDB can allocate for other operations, like maintaining connections and data processing (in-memory sort, MapReduce, aggregation, and more).

MongoDB processes will also use the underlying operating system's filesystem cache, just like in MMAPv1. The data in the filesystem cache is compressed.

We can view the settings for the WiredTiger cache via the mongo shell, as follows:

```
> db.serverStatus().wiredTiger.cache
```

We can adjust its size by using the `storage.wiredTiger.engineConfig.cacheSizeGB` parameter.

The generic recommendation is to leave the WiredTiger internal cache size at its default. If our data has a high compression ratio, it may be worth reducing the internal cache size by 10% to 20% to free up more memory for the filesystem cache.

Tracking page faults

The number of page faults can remain fairly stable and not affect performance significantly. However, once the number of page faults reaches a certain threshold, our system will be quickly and severely degraded. This is even more evident for HDDs, but it affects **solid-state drives (SSDs)** as well.

The way to ensure that we don't run into problems regarding page faults is to always have a staging environment that is identical to our production in setup. This environment can be used to stress test how many page faults our system can handle, without deteriorating performance. Comparing the actual number of page faults in our production system with the maximum number of page faults that we calculated from our staging system, we can find out how much leeway we have left.

Another way to view page faults is via the shell, looking at the `extra_info` field of the `serverStatus` output:

```
> db.adminCommand({"serverStatus" : 1})['extra_info']
{ "note" : "fields vary by platform", "page_faults" : 3465 }
```

As the `note` states, these fields may not be present in every platform.

Tracking B-tree misses

As you saw in the previous chapter, proper indexing is the best way to keep MongoDB responsive and performant. B-tree misses refer to page faults that happen when we try to access a B-tree index. Indexes are usually used frequently, and are relatively small compared to our working set and the memory available, so they should be in the memory at all times.

If we have an increasing number of B-tree misses or ratio of B-tree hits, or if there is a decrease in the number of B-tree misses, it's a sign that our indexes have grown in size and/or are not optimally designed. B-tree misses can also be monitored via MongoDB Cloud Manager, or in the shell.

In the shell, we can use collection stats to locate it.

I/O wait

I/O wait refers to the time that the operating system waits for an I/O operation to complete. It has a strongly positive correlation with page faults. If we see an I/O wait increasing over time, it's a strong indication that page faults will follow, as well. We should aim to keep the I/O wait at less than 60% to 70% for a healthy operational cluster. Aiming for a threshold like this will buy us some time to upgrade in the case of a suddenly increased load.

Read and write queues

Another way to look at I/O wait and page faults is via read and write queues. When we have page faults and I/O wait, requests will inevitably start to queue for either reads or writes. Queues are the effect, rather than the root cause, so by the time the queues start building up, we know we have a problem to solve.

Lock percentage

This is more of an issue with earlier versions of MongoDB, and less of an issue when using the WiredTiger storage engine. The **lock percentage** shows the percentage of time that the database is locked up, waiting for an operation that uses an exclusive lock to release it. It should generally be low: 10% to 20%, at the most. Over 50% means it's a cause for concern.

Background flushes

MongoDB will flush data to the disk every minute, by default. The **background flush** refers to the time it takes for the data to persist to the disk. It should not be more than 1 second for every 1 minute period.

Modifying the flush interval may help with the background flush time; by writing to the disk more frequently, there will be less data to write. This could, in some cases, make writes faster.

The fact that the background flush time gets affected by the write load means that if our background flush time starts to get too high, we should consider sharding our database to increase the write capacity.

Tracking free space

A common issue when using MMAPv1 (less frequent with WiredTiger) is free disk space. Like the memory, we need to track the disk space usage and be proactive, rather than reactive, with it. Keep monitoring the disk space usage, with proper alerts when it reaches 40%, 60%, or 80% of the disk space, especially for datasets that grow quickly.

Disk space issues are often the ones that cause the most headaches for administrators, DevOps, and developers, because of the time it takes to move data around.

> The `directoryperdb` option can help with data sizing, as we can split our storage into different physically mounted disks.

Monitoring replication

Replica sets use the **operations log (oplog)** to keep the synced state. Every operation gets applied on the primary server, and then gets written in the primary server's oplog, which is a capped collection. Secondaries read this oplog asynchronously and apply the operations one by one.

If the primary server gets overloaded, then the secondaries won't be able to read and apply the operations fast enough, generating replication lag. **Replication lag** is counted as the time difference between the last operation applied on the primary and the last operation applied on the secondary, as stored in the oplog capped collection.

For example, if the time is 4:30:00 PM and the secondary just applied an operation that was applied on our primary server at 4:25:00 PM, this means that the secondary is lagging five minutes behind our primary server.

In our production cluster, the replication lag should be close to (or equal to) zero.

Oplog size

Every member in a replica size will have a copy of the oplog in `db.oplog.rs()`. The reason for this is that if the primary steps down, one of the secondaries will get elected, and it needs to have an up-to-date version of the oplog for the new secondaries to track.

The oplog size is configurable, and we should set it to be as large as possible. The oplog size doesn't affect the memory usage, and can make or break the database in cases of operational issues.

The reason for this is that if the replication lag increases over time, we will eventually get to the point where the secondaries will fall so behind that the primary server won't be able to read from the primary's oplog, as the oldest entry in the primary's oplog will be later than the latest entry that was applied in our secondary server.

In general, the oplog should be at least one to two days' worth of operations. The oplog should be longer than the time it takes for the initial sync, for the same reason that was detailed previously.

Working set calculations

The working set is the strongest indicator of our memory requirements. Ideally, we would like to have our entire dataset in the memory, but most of the time, this is not feasible. The next best thing is to have our working set in memory. The working set can be calculated directly or indirectly.

Directly, we had the `workingSet` flag in `serverStatus`, which we can invoke from the shell, as follows:

```
> db.adminCommand({"serverStatus" : 1, "workingSet" : 1})
```

Unfortunately, this was removed in version 3.0, so we will focus on the indirect method of calculating a working set.

Indirectly, our working set is the size of data that we need to satisfy 95% or more of our user's requests. To calculate this, we need to identify the queries that the users make and which datasets they use from the logs. Adding 30% to 50% to it for index memory requirements, we can arrive at the working set calculation.

Another indirect way of estimating the working size is through the number of page faults. If we don't have page faults, then our working set fits in the memory. Through trial and error, we can estimate the point at which the page faults start to happen and understand how much more of a load our system can handle.

If we can't have the working set in memory, then we should have at least enough memory so that the indexes can fit in memory. In the previous chapter, we described how we can calculate index memory requirements, and how we can use this calculation to size our RAM accordingly.

Monitoring tools

There are several options for monitoring. In this section, we will discuss how we can monitor by using MongoDB's own tools or third-party tools.

Hosted tools

MongoDB, Inc.'s own tool, MongoDB Cloud Manager (formerly MongoDB Monitoring Service), is a robust tool for monitoring all of the metrics that were described previously. MongoDB Cloud Manager has a limited free tier and a 30 day trial period.

Another option for using MongoDB Cloud Manager is via MongoDB Atlas, MongoDB, Inc.'s DBaaS offering. This also has a limited free tier, and is available in all three major cloud providers (Amazon, Google, and Microsoft).

Open source tools

All major open source tools, like **Nagios**, **Munin**, **Cacti**, and others, provide plugin support for MongoDB. Although it is beyond the scope of this book, operations and DevOps should be familiar with both setting up and understanding the metrics that were described previously in order to effectively troubleshoot MongoDB and preemptively resolve issues before they grow out of proportion.

The `mongotop` and `mongostat` commands and scripts in the mongo shell can also be used for ad hoc monitoring. One of the risks with such manual processes, however, is that any failure of the scripts may jeopardize our database. If there are well-known and tested tools for your monitoring needs, please avoid writing your own.

Backups

A quote from a well-known maxim is as follows:

> *"Hope for the best, plan for the worst."*

> *– John Jay (1813)*

This should be our approach when designing our backup strategy for MongoDB. There are several distinct failure events that can happen.

Backups should be the cornerstone of our disaster recovery strategy, in case something happens. Some developers may rely on replication for disaster recovery, as it seems that having three copies of our data is more than enough. We can always rebuild the cluster from the other two copies, in case one of the copies is lost.

This is the case in the event of disks failing. Disk failure is one of the most common failures in a production cluster, and will statistically happen once the disks start reaching their **mean time between failures** (**MTBF**) time.

However, it is not the only failure event that can happen. Security incidents, or purely human errors, are just as likely to happen, and should be a part of our plan, as well. Catastrophic failures by means of losing all replica set members at once, from a fire, a flood, an earthquake, or a disgruntled employee, are events that should not lead to production data loss.

A useful interim option, in the middle ground between replication and implementing proper backups, could be setting up a delayed replica set member. This member can lag several hours or days behind the primary server so that it will not be affected by malicious changes in the primary. The important detail to take into account is that the oplog needs to be configured so that it can hold several hours of delay. Also, this solution is only an interim, as it doesn't take into account the full range of reasons why we need disaster recovery, but can definitely help with a subset of them.

This is called **disaster recovery**. Disaster recovery is a class of failures that require backups to be taken not only regularly, but also by using a process that isolates them (both geographically and in terms of access rules) from our production data.

Backup options

Depending on our deployment strategy, we can choose different options for backups.

Cloud-based solutions

The most straightforward solution arises if we are using a cloud DBaaS solution. In the example of MongoDB, Inc.'s own MongoDB Atlas, we can manage backups from the GUI.

If we host MongoDB in our own servers, we can then use MongoDB, Inc.'s MongoDB Cloud Manager. Cloud Manager is a SaaS that we can point to our own servers to monitor and back up our data. It uses the same oplog that replication uses, and can back up both replica sets and sharded clusters.

If we don't want to (or can't, for security reasons) point our servers to an external SaaS service, we can use MongoDB Cloud Manager's functionality on-premises, using MongoDB Ops Manager. To get MongoDB Ops Manager, we need to get a subscription to the Enterprise Advanced edition of MongoDB for our cluster.

Backups with filesystem snapshots

The most common backup method in the past, and one that is still widely used, relies on the underlying filesystem point-in-time snapshots functionality to back up our data.

EBS on EC2, and **Logical Volume Manager (LVM)** on Linux, support point-in-time snapshots.

 If we use WiredTiger with the latest version of MongoDB, we can have volume-level backups, even if our data and journal files reside in different volumes.

We can make a backup of a replica set as follows:

- To make a backup of a replica set, we need to have a consistent state for our database. This implies that we have all of our writes either committed to the disk or in our journal files.
- If we use WiredTiger storage, our snapshot will be consistent as of the latest checkpoint, which is either 2 GB of data or the last minute backup.

 Ensure that you store the snapshot in an offsite volume for disaster recovery purposes. You need to have enabled journaling to use point-in-time snapshots. It's a good practice to enable journaling regardless.

Making a backup of a sharded cluster

If we want to make a backup of an entire sharded cluster, we need to stop the balancer before starting. The reason is that if there are chunks migrating between different shards at the time that we take our snapshot, our database will be in an inconsistent state, having either incomplete or duplicate data chunks that were in flight at the time we took our snapshot.

Backups from an entire sharded cluster will be approximate-in-time. If we need point-in-time precision, we need to stop all of the writes in our database, something that is generally not possible for production systems.

First, we need to disable the balancer by connecting to our mongos through the mongo shell:

```
> use config
> sh.stopBalancer()
```

Then, if we don't have journaling enabled in our secondaries, or if we have journal and data files in different volumes, we need to lock our secondary mongo instances for all shards and the config server replica set.

> We also need to have a sufficient oplog size in these servers so that they can catch up to the primaries once we unlock them; otherwise, we will need to resync them from scratch.

Given that we don't need to lock our secondaries, the next step is to back up the config server. In Linux (and using LVM), this would be similar to doing the following:

```
$ lvcreate --size 100M --snapshot --name snap-14082017 /dev/vg0/mongodb
```

Then, we need to repeat the same process for a single member from each replica set in each shard.

Finally, we need to restart the balancer using the same mongo shell that we used to stop it:

```
> sh.setBalancerState(true)
```

Without going into too much detail here, it's evident that making a backup of a sharded cluster is a complicated and time-consuming procedure. It needs prior planning and extensive testing to make sure that it not only works with minimal disruption, but also that our backups are usable and can be restored back to our cluster.

Making backups using mongodump

The `mongodump` tool is a command-line tool that can make a backup of the data in our MongoDB cluster. As such, the downside is that all of the indexes need to be recreated on restore, which may be a time-consuming operation.

The major downside that the `mongodump` tool has is that in order to write data to the disk, it needs to bring data from the internal MongoDB storage to the memory first. This means that in the case of production clusters running under strain, `mongodump` will invalidate the data residing in the memory from the working set with the data that would not be residing in the memory under regular operations. This degrades the performance of our cluster.

On the plus side, when we use `mongodump`, we can continue taking writes in our cluster, and if we have a replica set, we can use the `--oplog` option to include the entries that occur during the `mongodump` operation in its output oplog.

If we go with that option, we need to use `--oplogReplay` when we use the `mongorestore` tool to restore our data back to the MongoDB cluster.

`mongodump` is a great tool for single-server deployments, but once we get to larger deployments, we should consider using different (and better planned) approaches to back up our data.

Backing up by copying raw files

If we don't want to use any of the preceding options that were outlined, our last resort is to copy the raw files using `cp/rsync`, or something equivalent. This is generally not recommended, for the following reasons:

- We need to stop all of the writes before copying files
- The backup size will be larger, since we need to copy indexes and any underlying padding and fragmentation storage overhead
- We cannot get point-in-time recovery by using this method for replica sets, and copying data from sharded clusters in a consistent and predictable manner is extremely difficult

> Making a backup by copying raw files should be avoided, unless no other option really exists.

Making backups using queuing

Another strategy that's used in practice is utilizing a queuing system, intercepting our database and the frontend software system. Having something like an ActiveMQ queue before the inserts/updates/deletes in our database means that we can safely send out data to different sinks, which are MongoDB servers or log files in a separate repository. Like the delayed replica set method, this method can be useful for a class of backup problems, but can fail for some others.

> This is a useful interim solution, but it should not be used as a permanent one.

EC2 backup and restore

MongoDB Cloud Manager can automate making backups from EC2 volumes; and, since our data is in the cloud, why not use the Cloud Manager anyway?

If we can't use it for some reason, we can write a script to make backup by implementing the following steps:

1. Assuming that we have journaling enabled (and we really should) and we have already mapped `dbpath`, containing data and journal files to a single EBS volume, we first need to find the EBS block instances associated with the running instance by using `ec2-describe-instances`.
2. The next step is to find the logical volumes that `dbpath` of our MongoDB database is mapped to using `lvdisplay`.
3. Once we have identified the logical devices from the logical volumes, we can use `ec2-create-snapshot` to create new snapshots. We need to include each and every logical device that maps to our `dbpath` directory.

To verify that our backups work, we need to create new volumes based on the snapshots and mount the new volumes there. Finally, the `mongod` process should be able to start mounting the new data, and we should connect by using MongoDB to verify these.

Incremental backups

Making full backups every time may be viable for some deployments, but as the size reaches a certain threshold, full backups take too much time and space.

At this point, we will want to make full backups every once in a while (maybe one per month, for example) and incremental backups in-between (for example, nightly).

Both Ops Manager and Cloud Manager support incremental backups, and if we get to this size, it may be a good idea to use a tool to make our backups instead of rolling out our own.

If we don't want to (or can't) use these tools, we have the option of restoring via the oplog, as follows:

1. Make a full backup with any method that was described previously
2. Lock writes on the secondary server of our replica set
3. Note the latest entry in the oplog
4. Export the entries in the oplog after the latest entry in the oplog:

   ```
   > mongodump --host <secondary> -d local -c oplog.rs -o /mnt/mongo-
   oldway_backup
       --query '{ "ts" : { $gt :  Timestamp(1467999203, 391) } }'
   ```

5. Unlock writes on the secondary server

To restore, we can use the `oplog.rs` file that we just exported, and use `mongorestore` with the option `--oplogReplay`:

```
> mongorestore -h <primary> --port <port> --oplogReplay
<data_file_position>
```

 This method requires locking writes, and may not work in future versions.

An even better solution is to use the **Logical Volume Management (LVM)** filesystem with incremental backups, but this depends on the underlying LVM implementation, which we may or may not be able to tweak.

Security

Security is a multifaceted goal in a MongoDB cluster. For the rest of this chapter, we will examine different attack vectors and how we can protect against them. In addition to these best practices, developers and administrators must always use common sense so that security interferes only as much as is required for operational goals.

Authentication

Authentication refers to verifying the identity of a client. This prevents the impersonation of someone in order to gain access to their data.

The simplest way to authenticate is by using a `username` and `password` pair. This can be done via the shell in two ways, the first of which is as follows:

```
> db.auth( <username>, <password> )
```

Passing in a comma-separated `username` and `password` will assume the default values for the rest of the fields:

```
> db.auth( {
    user: <username>,
    pwd: <password>,
    mechanism: <authentication mechanism>,
    digestPassword: <boolean>
} )
```

If we pass a document object, we can define more parameters than `username/password`.

The (authentication) `mechanism` parameter can take several different values, with the default being `SCRAM-SHA-1`. The parameter value `MONGODB-CR` is used for backwards compatibility with versions earlier than 3.0.

MONGODB-x.509 is used for TLS/SSL authentication. Users and internal replica set servers can be authenticated by using SSL certificates, which are self-generated and signed, or comes from a trusted third-party authority.

To configure x.509 for internal authentication of replica set members, we need to supply one of the following parameters.

The following is for the configuration file:

```
security.clusterAuthMode / net.ssl.clusterFile
```

The following is used on the command line:

```
--clusterAuthMode and --sslClusterFile
> mongod --replSet <name> --sslMode requireSSL --clusterAuthMode x509 --
sslClusterFile <path to membership certificate and key PEM file> --
sslPEMKeyFile <path to SSL certificate and key PEM file> --sslCAFile <path
to root CA PEM file>
```

MongoDB Enterprise Edition, the paid offering from MongoDB, Inc., adds two more options for authentication, as follows:

- The first added option is **Generic Security Service Application Program Interface (GSSAPI)** Kerberos. Kerberos is a mature and robust authentication system that can be used for Windows-based Active Directory deployments, among others.
- The second added option is PLAIN (LDAP SASL). LDAP is just like Kerberos: a mature and robust authentication mechanism. The main consideration when using the PLAIN authentication mechanism is that the credentials are transmitted in plain text over the wire. This means that we should secure the path between the client and server via VPN or a TSL/SSL connection to avoid a man in the middle stealing our credentials.

Authorization

After we have configured the authentication to verify that the users are who they claim they are when connecting to our MongoDB server, we need to configure the rights that each one of them will have in our database.

This is the **authorization** aspect of permissions. MongoDB uses role-based access control to control permissions for different user classes.

Every role has permissions to perform some actions on a resource.

A resource can be a collection/collections or a database/databases.

The command's format is as follows:

```
{ db: <database>, collection: <collection> }
```

If we specify `""` (an empty string) for either `db` or `collection`, it means any `db` or `collection`. An example of this is as follows:

```
{ db: "mongo_books", collection: "" }
```

This would apply our action in every `collection` in the `mongo_books` database.

If the database is not the `admin` database, this will not include the system collections. System collections, such as `<db>.system.profile`, `<db>.system.js`, `admin.system.users`, and `admin.system.roles`, need to be defined explicitly.

Similar to the preceding option, we can define the following:

```
{ db: "", collection: "" }
```

We define this to apply our rule to all of the collections across all of the databases, except for system collections, of course.

We can also apply rules across an entire cluster, as follows:

```
{ resource: { cluster : true }, actions: [ "addShard" ] }
```

The preceding example grants privileges for the addShard action (adding a new shard to our system) across the entire cluster. The cluster resource can only be used for actions that affect the entire cluster, rather than a collection or database (for example, shutdown, replSetReconfig, appendOplogNote, resync, closeAllDatabases, and addShard).

What follows is an extensive list of cluster-specific actions, and some of the most widely used actions.

The list of the most widely used actions is as follows:

- find
- insert
- remove
- update
- bypassDocumentValidation
- viewRole/viewUser
- createRole/dropRole
- createUser/dropUser
- inprog
- killop
- replSetGetConfig/replSetConfigure/replSetStateChange/resync
- getShardMap/getShardVersion/listShards/moveChunk/removeShard/addShard
- dropDatabase/dropIndex/fsync/repairDatabase/shutDown
- serverStatus/top/validate

Cluster-specific actions are as follows:

- unlock
- authSchemaUpgrade
- cleanupOrphaned
- cpuProfiler
- inprog
- invalidateUserCache
- killop
- appendOplogNote
- replSetConfigure
- replSetGetConfig
- replSetGetStatus
- replSetHeartbeat
- replSetStateChange
- resync
- addShard
- flushRouterConfig
- getShardMap
- listShards
- removeShard
- shardingState
- applicationMessage
- closeAllDatabases
- connPoolSync
- fsync
- getParameter
- hostInfo
- logRotate
- setParameter
- shutdown
- touch
- connPoolStats
- cursorInfo

- `diagLogging`
- `getCmdLineOpts`
- `getLog`
- `listDatabases`
- `netstat`
- `serverStatus`
- `top`

If this sounds too complicated, that's because it is! The flexibility that MongoDB allows for configuring different actions on resources means that we need to study and understand the extensive lists, as described previously.

Thankfully, some of the most common actions and resources are bundled in built-in roles.

We can use these built-in roles to establish the baseline of permissions that we will give to our users, and then fine-grain these based on the extensive list.

User roles

There are two different generic user roles that we can specify, as follows:

- `read`: A read-only role across non-system collections and the following system collections: `system.indexes`, `system.js`, and `system.namespaces` collections
- `readWrite`: A read and modify role across non-system collections and the `system.js` collection

Database administration roles

There are three database-specific administration roles, as follows:

- `dbAdmin`: The basic admin user role that can perform schema-related tasks, indexing, and gathering statistics. A `dbAdmin` cannot perform user and role management.
- `userAdmin`: Create and modify roles and users. This is complementary to the `dbAdmin` role.

A `userAdmin` can modify itself to become a superuser in the database, or, if scoped to the `admin` database, the MongoDB cluster.

- `dbOwner`: Combining `readWrite`, `dbAdmin`, and `userAdmin` roles, this is the most powerful admin user role.

Cluster administration roles

The following are the cluster-wide administration roles that are available:

- `hostManager`: Monitor and manage servers in a cluster.
- `clusterManager`: Provides management and monitoring actions on the cluster. A user with this role can access the config and local databases, which are used in sharding and replication, respectively.
- `clusterMonitor`: Read-only access for monitoring tools provided by MongoDB, such as MongoDB Cloud Manager and the Ops Manager agent.
- `clusterAdmin`: Provides the greatest cluster management access. This role combines the privileges that are granted by the `clusterManager`, `clusterMonitor`, and `hostManager` roles. Additionally, the role provides the `dropDatabase` action.

Backup and restore roles

Role-based authorization roles can be defined in the backup and restore granularity level, as well:

- `backup`: Provides privileges that are needed to back up the data. This role provides sufficient privileges to use the MongoDB Cloud Manager backup agent, the Ops Manager backup agent, or `mongodump`.
- `restore`: Provides the privileges that are needed to restore data with `mongorestore`, without the `--oplogReplay` option or `system.profile` collection data.

Roles across all databases

Similarly, the following is the set of available roles across all databases:

- readAnyDatabase: Provides the same read-only permissions as read, except it applies to all but the local and config databases in the cluster. The role also provides the listDatabases action on the cluster as a whole.
- readWriteAnyDatabase: Provides the same read and write permissions as readWrite, except it applies to all but the local and config databases in the cluster. The role also provides the listDatabases action on the cluster as a whole.
- userAdminAnyDatabase: Provides the same access to user administration operations as userAdmin, except it applies to all but the local and config databases in the cluster. Since the userAdminAnyDatabase role allows users to grant any privilege to any user, including themselves, the role also indirectly provides superuser access.
- dbAdminAnyDatabase: Provides the same access to database administration operations as dbAdmin, except it applies to all but the local and config databases in the cluster. The role also provides the listDatabases action on the cluster as a whole.

Superuser

Finally, the following are the superuser roles that are available:

- root: Provides access to the operations and all of the resources of the readWriteAnyDatabase, dbAdminAnyDatabase, userAdminAnyDatabase, clusterAdmin, restore, and backup combined
- __internal: Similar to the root user, any __internal user can perform any action against any object across the server

Superuser roles should be avoided, as they can have potentially destructive permissions across all of the databases on our server.

Network-level security

Apart from MongoDB-specific security measures, there are best practices that have been established for network-level security:

- Only allow communication between servers, and only open the ports that are used for communicating between them.
- Always use TLS/SSL for communication between servers. This prevents man-in-the-middle attacks from impersonating a client.
- Always use different sets of development, staging, and production environments and security credentials. Ideally, create different accounts for each environment, and enable two-factor authentication in both staging and production environments.

Auditing security

No matter how much we plan our security measures, a second or third pair of eyes from someone outside of our organization can give a different view of our security measures and uncover problems that we may have underestimated or overlooked. Don't hesitate to involve security experts and white hat hackers to do penetration testing in your servers.

Special cases

Medical or financial applications require added levels of security for data privacy reasons.

If we are building an application in the healthcare space, accessing users' personally identifiable information, we may need to get HIPAA certified.

If we are building an application that interacts with payments and manages cardholder information, we may need to become PCI/DSS compliant.

The specifics of each certification are outside the scope of this book, but it is important to know that MongoDB has use cases in these fields that fulfill the requirements, and, as such, it can be the right tool with proper design beforehand.

Overview

Summing up the best practice recommendations involving security, we have the following:

- **Enforce authentication**: Always enable authentication in production environments.
- **Enable access control**: First, create a system administrator, and then use that administrator to create more limited users. Give as few permissions as are needed for each user role.
- **Define fine-grained roles in access control**: Do not give more permissions than are needed for each user.
- **Encrypt communication between clients and servers**: Always use TLS/SSL for communication between clients and servers in production environments. Always use TLS/SSL for communication between `mongod` and `mongos` or config servers, as well.
- **Encrypt data at rest**: MongoDB Enterprise Edition offers the functionality to encrypt data when stored, using WiredTiger encryption at rest.

 Alternatively, we can encrypt data using filesystem, device, or physical encryption. In the cloud, we often get the option for encryption, as well (for example, with EBS on Amazon EC2).

- **Limit network exposure**: MongoDB servers should only be connected to the application servers and any other servers that are needed for operations. Ports other than the ones that we set up for MongoDB communications should not be open to the outside world. If we want to debug MongoDB usage, it's important to have a proxy server with controlled access set up to communicate with our database.
- **Audit servers for unusual activity**: MongoDB Enterprise Edition offers a utility for auditing. By using it, we can output events to the console, a JSON file, a BSON file, or the syslog. In any case, it's important to make sure that audit events are stored in a partition that is not available to the system's users.
- Use a dedicated operating system user to run MongoDB. Make sure that the dedicated operating system user can access MongoDB, but doesn't have unnecessary permissions.
- Disable JavaScript server-side scripts if they are not needed.

MongoDB can use JavaScript for server-side scripts with the following commands: `mapReduce()`, `group()`, and `$where`. If we don't need these commands, we should disable server-side scripting by using the `--noscripting` option on the command line.

Summary

In this chapter, you learned about three operational aspects of MongoDB: monitoring, backup, and security.

We discussed the metrics that we should monitor in MongoDB, and how to monitor them. Following that, we discussed how to make backups and ensure that we can use them to restore our data. Finally, you learned about security with the authentication and authorization concepts, as well as network-level security and how to audit it.

As important as it is to design, build, and extend our application as needed, it is equally important to make sure that we have peace of mind during operations and are safeguarded from unexpected events, such as human error and internal or external malicious users.

In the next chapter, you will learn about pluggable storage engines, a new concept that was introduced in version 3.0 of MongoDB. Pluggable storage engines allow different use cases to be served, especially in application domains that have specific and stringent requirements concerning data handling and privacy.

Storage Engines

9

MongoDB introduced the concept of pluggable storage engines in version 3.0. After the acquisition of WiredTiger, it introduced its storage engine as optional at first, and then as the default storage engine for the current version of MongoDB. In this chapter, we will dive deeply into the concept of storage engines, why they matter, and how we can choose the best one according to our workload.

We will cover the following topics:

- Pluggable storage engines
- WiredTiger
- Encrypted
- In-memory
- MMAPv1
- Locking in MongoDB

Pluggable storage engines

With MongoDB breaking out from the web application paradigm into domains with different requirements, storage has become an increasingly important consideration.

Using multiple storage engines can be seen as an alternative way to using different storage solutions and databases in our infrastructure stack. This way, we can reduce operational complexity and development time to market with the application layer being agnostic of the underlying storage layer.

MongoDB currently offers four different storage engines that we will examine in further detail in the following sections.

WiredTiger

As of version 3.2, WiredTiger is the default storage engine, and also the best choice for most workloads. By providing document-level locking, it overcomes one of the most significant drawbacks earlier versions of MongoDB had—lock contention under high load.

We will explore some of WiredTiger's benefits in the following sections.

Document-level locking

Locking is so important that we will explain the performance implications that fine-grained locking has in further detail at the end of this section. Having document-level locking as opposed to MMAPv1 collection-level locking can make a huge difference in many real-world use cases, and is one of the main reasons to choose WiredTiger over MMAPv1.

Snapshots and checkpoints

WiredTiger uses **Multi-Version Concurrency Control** (**MVCC**). MVCC is based upon the concept that the database keeps multiple versions of an object so that readers will be able to view consistent data that doesn't change during a read.

In a database, if we have multiple readers accessing data at the same time that writers are modifying the data, we can end up with a case where readers view an inconsistent view of this data. The simplest and easiest way to solve this problem is to block all readers until the writers are done modifying data.

This will, of course, cause severe performance degradation. MVCC solves this problem by providing a snapshot of the database for each reader. When the read starts, each reader is guaranteed to view data as exactly it was at the point in time that the read started. Any changes made by writers will only be seen by readers after the write has been completed, or, in database terms, after the transaction is committed.

To achieve this goal, when a write is coming in, updated data will be kept in a separate location on disk and MongoDB will mark the affected document as obsolete. MVCC is said to provide point-in-time consistent views. This is equivalent to a read committed isolation level in traditional RDBMS systems.

For every operation, WiredTiger will snapshot our data at the exact moment that it happens and provide a consistent view of application data to the application. When we write data, WiredTiger will create a snapshot every 2 GB of journal data or 60 seconds, whichever comes first. WiredTiger relies on its built-in journal to recover any data after the latest checkpoint in case of failure.

> We can disable journaling using WiredTiger, but if the server crashes, we will lose any data after the last checkpoint is written.

Journaling

As explained in the *Snapshots and checkpoints* section, journaling is the cornerstone of WiredTiger crash recovery protection.

WiredTiger compresses the journal using the snappy compression algorithm. We can use the following setting to set a different compression algorithm:

```
storage.wiredTiger.engineConfig.journalCompressor
```

We can also disable journaling for WiredTiger by setting the following to `false`:

```
storage.journal.enabled
```

> If we use a replica set, we may be able to recover our data from a secondary that will get elected as a primary and start taking writes in the event that our primary fails. It is recommended to always use journaling, unless we understand and can take the risk of suffering through the consequences of not using it.

Data compression

MongoDB uses the snappy compression algorithm by default to compress data and prefixes for indexes. Index-prefixed compression means that identical index key prefixes are stored only once per page of memory. Compression not only reduces our storage footprint, but will increase I/O operations per second, as less data needs to be stored and moved to and from disk. Using more aggressive compression can lead to performance gains if our workload is I/O bound and not CPU bound.

We can define `.zlib` compression instead of snappy or no compression by setting the following parameter to `false`:

```
storage.wiredTiger.collectionConfig.blockCompressor
```

> Data compression uses less storage at the expense of CPU. `.zlib` compression achieves better compression at the expense of higher CPU usage, as opposed to the default snappy compression algorithm.

We can disable index prefixes compression by setting the following parameter to `false`:

```
storage.wiredTiger.indexConfig.prefixCompression
```

We can also configure storage per-index during creation using the following parameter:

```
{ <storage-engine-name>: <options> }
```

Memory usage

WiredTiger is significantly different to MMAPv1 in how it uses RAM. MMAPv1 is essentially using the underlying operating system's filesystem cache to page data from disk to memory and vice versa.

WiredTiger, on the contrary, introduces the new concept of the WiredTiger internal cache.

The WiredTiger internal cache is, by default, the larger of the following:

- 50% of RAM minus 1 GB
- 256 MB

This means if our server has 8 GB RAM we will get the following:

$$max(3\ GB\ ,\ 256\ MB) = WiredTiger\ will\ use\ 3\ GB\ of\ RAM$$

And if our server has 2,512 MB RAM we will get the following:

$$max(256\ MB,\ 256\ MB) = WiredTiger\ will\ use\ 256\ MB\ of\ RAM$$

Essentially, for any server that has less than 2,512 MB RAM, WiredTiger will use 256 MB for its internal cache.

We can change the size of the WiredTiger internal cache by setting the following:

```
storage.wiredTiger.engineConfig.cacheSizeGB
```

We can also do this from the command line using the following:

```
--wiredTigerCacheSizeGB
```

Apart from the WiredTiger internal cache that is uncompressed for higher performance, MongoDB also uses the filesystem cache that is compressed, just like MMAPv1, and will end up using all available memory in most cases.

The WiredTiger internal cache can provide similar performance to in-memory storage. As such, it is important to grow it as much as possible.

We can achieve better performance when using WiredTiger with multi-core processors. This is also a big win compared to MMAPv1, which does not scale as well.

We can, and should, use Docker or other containerization technologies to isolate the mongod processes from each other and make sure that we know how much memory each process can, and should, use in a production environment. It is not recommended to increase the WiredTiger internal cache above its default value. The filesystem cache should not be less than 20% of the total RAM.

readConcern

WiredTiger supports multiple readConcern levels. Just like writeConcern, which is supported by every storage engine in MongoDB, with readConcern, we can customize how many servers in a replica set must acknowledge the query results for the document to be returned in the result set.

Available options for read concern are as follows:

- local: Default option. Will return most recent data from the server. Data may, or may not, have propagated to the other servers in a replica set, and we run the risk of a rollback.
- linearizable:
  - Only applicable for reads from the primary
  - Only applicable in queries that return a single result
  - Data returns satisfy two conditions:
    - majority, writeConcern

- Data was acknowledged before the start of the read operation

In addition, if we have set `writeConcernMajorityJournalDefault` to `true`, we are guaranteed that the data won't get rolled back.

If we have set `writeConcernMajorityJournalDefault` to `false`, MongoDB will not wait for `majority` writes to be durable before acknowledging the write. In this case our data may be rolled back in the event of a loss of a member from the replica set. Data returned has already been propagated and acknowledged from `majority` of the servers before read has started.

We need to use `maxTimeMS` when using `linearizable` and `majority` read concern levels in case we can't establish `majority writeConcern` to avoid blocking, forever waiting for the response. In this case, the operation will return a timeout error.

MMAPv1 is the older storage engine and is considered, in many aspects, as being deprecated, but many deployments are still using it.

`local` and `linearizable` read concerns are available for MMAPv1 as well.

WiredTiger collection-level options

When we create a new collection, we can pass in options to WiredTiger like this:

```
> db.createCollection(
  "mongo_books",
  { storageEngine: { wiredTiger: { configString: "<key>=<value>" } } }
)
```

This helps to create our `mongo_books` collection with a key-value pair from the available ones that WiredTiger exposes through its API. Some of the most widely used key-value pairs are the following:

Key	Value
block_allocation	Best or first
allocation_size	512 bytes through to 4 KB; default 4 KB

`block_compressor`	None, `.lz4`, `.snappy`, `.zlib`, `.zstd`, or custom compressor identifier string depending on configuration
`memory_page_max`	512 bytes through to 10 TB; default 5 MB
`os_cache_max`	Integer greater than zero; default zero

This is taken directly from the definition in the WiredTiger documents located at `http://source.wiredtiger.com/mongodb-3.4/struct_w_t___s_e_s_s_i_o_n.html`:

```
int WT_SESSION::create()
```

Collection-level options allow for flexibility in configuring storage but should be used with extreme care and after careful testing in development/staging environments.

 Collection-level options will get propagated to secondaries if applied to a primary in a replica set. `block_compressor` can also be configured from the command line globally for the database using the `--wiredTigerCollectionBlockCompressor` option.

WiredTiger performance strategies

As discussed earlier in this chapter, WiredTiger uses an internal cache to optimize performance. On top of it, there is always the filesystem cache that the operating system (and MMAPv1) uses to fetch data from disk.

By default, we have 50% of RAM dedicated to the filesystem cache and 50% to the WiredTiger internal cache.

The filesystem cache will keep data compressed as it is stored on disk. The internal cache will decompress it as follows:

- **Strategy 1**: Allocate 80% or more to the internal cache. This has the goal of fitting our working set in WiredTiger's internal cache.
- **Strategy 2**: Allocate 80% or more to the filesystem cache. Our goal here is to avoid using the internal cache as much as possible, and rely on the filesystem cache for our needs.
- **Strategy 3**: Use an SSD as the underlying storage for fast seek time and keep defaults at 50-50% allocation.
- **Strategy 4**: Enable compression in our storage layer through MongoDB's configuration to save on storage, and potentially improve our performance by having a smaller working set size.

Our workload will dictate whether we need to deviate from the default Strategy 1 to any of the rest. In general, we should use SSDs wherever possible, and with MongoDB's configurable storage, we can even use SSDs for some of the nodes where we need the best performance and keep HDDs for analytics workloads.

WiredTiger B-tree versus LSM indexes

B-tree is the most common data structure for indexes across different database systems. WiredTiger offers the option to use a **Log Structured Merge (LSM)** tree instead of a B-tree for indexing.

An LSM tree can provide better performance when we have a workload of random inserts that would otherwise overflow our page cache and start paging in data from disk to keep our index up to date.

LSM indexes can be selected from the command line like this:

```
> mongod --wiredTigerIndexConfigString "type=lsm,block_compressor=zlib"
```

The preceding command chooses `lsm` as `type`, and `block_compressor` is `zlib` for indexes in this `mongod` instance.

Encrypted

The encrypted storage engine was added to support a series of special use cases, mostly revolving around finance, retail, healthcare, education, and government.

We need to have encryption for the rest of our data if we have to comply to a set of regulations, including the following:

- PCI DSS for handling credit card information
- HIPAA for healthcare applications
- NIST for government
- FISMA for government
- STIG for government

This can be done in several ways, and cloud service providers, such as EC2, provide EBS storage volumes with built-in encryption. Encrypted storage supports Intel's AES-NI equipped CPUs for acceleration of the encryption/decryption process.

The encryption algorithms supported are the following:

- AES-256, CBC (default)
- AES-256, GCM
- FIPS, FIPS-140-2

Encryption is supported at page level for better performance. When a change is made in a document, instead of re-encrypting/decrypting the entire underlying file, only the page that is affected gets modified.

Encryption key management is a huge aspect of encrypted storage security. Most specifications previously mentioned require key rotation at least once per year.

MongoDB's encrypted storage uses an internal database key per node. This key is wrapped by an external (master) key that must be used to start the node's `mongod` process. By using the underlying operating system's protection mechanisms such as `mlock` or `VirtualLock`, MongoDB can guarantee that the external key will never be leaked from memory to disk by page faults.

The external (master) key can be managed either by using the **Key Management Interoperability Protocol** (**KMIP**) or by using local key management via a keyfile.

MongoDB can achieve key rotation by performing rolling restarts of the replica set members. Using KMIP, MongoDB can rotate only the external key and not the underlying database files. This delivers significant performance benefits.

Using KMIP is the recommended approach for encrypted data storage. Encrypted storage is based on WiredTiger, so all its advantages can be enjoyed using encryption as well. Encrypted storage is a part of MongoDB Enterprise Edition, the paid offering by MongoDB.

Using MongoDB's encrypted storage gives the advantage of increased performance versus encrypted storage volumes. MongoDB's encrypted storage has an overhead of around 15% as compared to 25% or more for third-party encrypted storage solutions.

In most cases, if we need to use encrypted storage, we will know it well in advance from the application design phase, and we can perform benchmarks against different solutions to choose the one that best fits our use case.

In-memory

MongoDB storage in-memory is a risky task with high rewards. Keeping data in-memory can be up to 100,000 times faster than durable storage on disk.

Another advantage of using in-memory storage is that we can achieve predictable latency when we write or read data. Some use cases dictate for latency that does not deviate from normal, no matter what the operation is.

On the other hand, by keeping data in-memory we are open to power loss and application failure where we can lose all of our data. Using a replica set can safeguard against some classes of errors, but we will always be more exposed to data loss if we store in data as opposed to storing on disk.

However, there are some use cases in which we may not care that much about losing older data. For example, in the financial world we may have the following:

- High-frequency trading/algorithmic trading, where higher latency in the case of high traffic can lead to transactions not being fulfilled
- In fraud detection systems, we are concerned about real-time detection being as fast as possible and we can safely store only the cases that require further investigation, or the definitely positive ones, to durable storage
- Credit card authorizations, trade ordering reconciliation, and other high-traffic systems that demand a real-time answer

In the web applications ecosystem we have the following:

- In intrusion detection systems, such as fraud detection, we are concerned with detecting intrusion as fast as possible without so much concern for false positive cases.
- In the case of the product search cache, losing data is not mission-critical, but rather a small inconvenience from the customer's perspective.
- For real-time personalized product recommendations, there is a low-risk operation in terms of data loss. We can always rebuild the index even if we suffer data loss.

A major disadvantage of an in-memory storage engine is that our dataset has to fit in-memory. This means we must know and keep track of our data usage so we don't exceed the memory of our server.

Overall, using the MongoDB in-memory storage engine may be useful in some edge use cases, but lacking durability in a database system can be a blocking factor in its adoption.

In-memory storage is part of MongoDB Enterprise Edition, the paid offering by MongoDB.

MMAPv1

With the introduction of WiredTiger and its many benefits, such as document-level locking, many MongoDB users are questioning whether it's worth discussing MMAPv1 anymore.

In reality, the only cases where we should consider using MMAPv1 instead of WiredTiger would be the following:

- **Legacy systems**: If we have a system that fits our needs, we may upgrade to MongoDB 3.0+ and not transition to WiredTiger.
- **Version downgrade**: Once we upgrade to MongoDB 3.0+ and convert our storage to WiredTiger, we cannot downgrade to a version lower than 2.6.8. This should be kept in mind if we want the flexibility to downgrade at a later time.

As shown previously, WiredTiger is a better choice than MMAPv1, and we should use it whenever we get the chance. This book is oriented around WiredTiger, and assumes we will be able to use the latest stable version of MongoDB (3.4 at the time of writing).

 MMAPv1, as of version 3.4, only supports collection-level locking, as opposed to the document-level locking supported by WiredTiger. This can lead to a performance penalty in high contention database loads and is one of the main reasons why we should use WiredTiger whenever possible.

MMAPv1 storage optimization

MongoDB, by default, uses the power-of-two allocation strategy. When a document is created it will get allocated a power of size two. That is, `ceiling(document_size)`.

For example, if we create a document of 127 bytes, MongoDB will allocate 128 bytes (2^7), while if we create a document of 129 bytes, MongoDB will allocate 256 bytes (2^8). This is helpful when updating documents, as we can update them and not move the underlying document on disk until it exceeds the space allocated.

If a document is moved on disk (that is, adding a new subdocument or an element in an array of the document that forces the size to exceed the allocated storage), a new power-of-two allocation size will be used.

If the operation doesn't affect its size (that is, changing an integer value from one to two), the document will remain stored in the same physical location on disk. This concept is called **padding**. We can configure padding using the compact administration command as well.

When we move documents on disk, we have non-contiguous blocks of data stored, essentially holes in storage. We can prevent this from happening by setting paddingFactor at collection level.

paddingFactor has a default value of 1.0 (no padding) and a maximum of 4.0 (expanding size by three times as much as the original document size). For example, paddingFactor of 1.4 will allow the document to expand by 40% before getting moved on to a new location on disk.

For example, with our favorite books collection, to get 40% more space, we would do the following:

```
> db.runCommand ( { compact: 'books', paddingFactor: 1.4 } )
```

We can also set padding in terms of bytes per document. This way we get *x* bytes padding from the initial creation of each document in our collection:

```
> db.runCommand ( { compact: 'books', paddingBytes: 300 } )
```

This will allow a document created at 200 bytes to grow to 500 bytes, while a document created at 4,000 bytes will be allowed to grow to 4,300 bytes.

We can eliminate holes altogether by running a compact command with no parameters, but this means that every update that increases document size will have to move documents, essentially creating new holes in storage.

Mixed usage

When we have an application with MongoDB as the underlying database, we can set it up to use different replica sets for different operations at application level, matching their requirements.

For example, in our financial application, we can use one connection pool for the fraud detection module utilizing in-memory nodes, and a different one for the rest of our system, shown as follows:

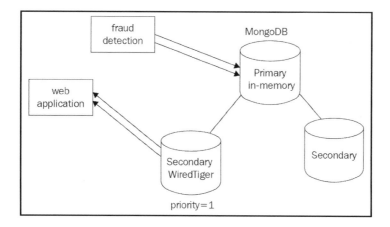

In addition, storage engine configuration in MongoDB is applied per node, which allows for some interesting setups.

As shown in the preceding architectural diagram, we can use a mix of different storage engines in different members of a replica set. In this case, we are using the in-memory engine for optimal performance in the primary node, while one of the secondaries uses WiredTiger to ensure data durability. We can use `priority=1` in the in-memory secondary node to make sure that, if the primary fails, the secondary will get elected right away. If we don't do it, we risk having a failing primary server exactly when we have high load in the system, and the secondary has not kept up with the primary's writes in-memory.

The mixed storage approach is widely used in the microservice architecture. By decoupling service and database and using the appropriate database for each use case, we can easily horizontally scale our infrastructure.

All storage engines support a common baseline functionality, such as the following:

- Querying
- Indexing
- Replication
- Sharding
- Ops and Cloud Manager support
- Authentication and authorization semantics

Other storage engines

Modular MongoDB architecture allows for third parties to develop their own storage engines.

RocksDB

RocksDB is an embedded database for key-value data. It's a fork of `LevelDB` storing key-value pairs in arbitrary byte arrays. It was started at Facebook in 2012, and now serves as the backend for the interestingly named **CockroachDB**, the open source DB inspired by Google Spanner.

MongoRocks is a project backed by Percona and Facebook aiming to bring RocksDB backend to MongoDB. RocksDB can achieve higher performance than WiredTiger for some workloads, and is worth investigating.

TokuMX

Another widely used storage engine is TokuMX by Percona. TokuMX was designed with both MySQL and MongoDB in mind, but since 2016, Percona has focused its efforts on the MySQL version, instead switching over to **RocksDB** for MongoDB storage support.

Locking in MongoDB

Document-level and collection-level locking is mentioned throughout this chapter and also in several other chapters in this book. It is important to understand how locking works and why it is important.

Database systems use the concept of locks to achieve ACID properties. When there are multiple read or write requests coming in parallel, we need to lock our data so that all readers and writers have consistent and predictable results.

MongoDB uses multi-granularity locking. The available granularity levels in descending order are as follows:

- Global
- Database
- Collection
- Document

The locks that MongoDB and other databases use are the following, in order of granularity:

- *IS*: Intent shared
- *IX*: Intent exclusive
- *S*: Shared
- *X*: Exclusive

If we use locking at a granularity level with *S* or *X* locks, then all higher levels need to be locked with an intent lock of the same type.

Other rules for locks are as follows:

- A single database can simultaneously be locked in *IS* and *IX* mode
- An exclusive (*X*) lock cannot coexist with any other lock
- A shared (*S*) lock can only coexist with *IS* locks

Reads and writes requesting locks are generally queued in **first-in, first-out (FIFO)** order. The only optimization that MongoDB will actually do is reordering requests according to the next request in queue to be serviced.

What this means is that if we have an *IS(1)* request coming up next and our current queue has the following *IS(1)->IS(2)->X(3)->S(4)->IS(5)* as shown in the following screenshot:

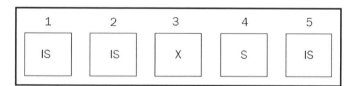

Then MongoDB will reorder requests like this, *IS(1)->IS(2)->S(4)->IS(5)->X(3)* as shown in the following screenshot:

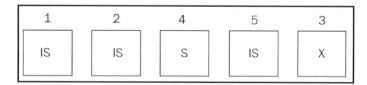

If, during servicing, the *IS(1)* request, new *IS*, or *S* requests come in, let's say *IS(6)* and *S(7)*, in that order, they will still be added at the end of the queue and won't be considered until the *X(3)* request is done with.

Our new queue will now look like *IS(2)->S(4)->IS(5)->X(3)->IS(6)->S(7)*:

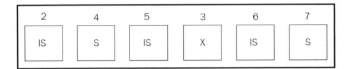

This is done to prevent the starvation of the *X(3)* request that would end up getting pushed back in the queue all the time because new *IS* and *S* requests come in. It is important to understand the difference between intent locks and locks themselves. WiredTiger storage engine will only use intent locks for global, database, and collection levels.

It uses intent locks at higher levels (that is, collection, database, global), when a new request comes in and according to the compatibility matrix as follows:

Mode	NL	IS	IX	S	SIX	X
NL	Yes	Yes	Yes	Yes	Yes	Yes
IS	Yes	Yes	Yes	Yes	Yes	No
IX	Yes	Yes	Yes	No	No	No
S	Yes	Yes	No	Yes	No	No
SIX	Yes	Yes	No	No	No	No
X	Yes	No	No	No	No	No

MongoDB will first acquire intention locks in all ancestors before acquiring the lock on the document itself. This way, when a new request comes in, it can quickly identify if it cannot be serviced based on less granular locks.

WiredTiger will use *S* and *X* locks at the document level. The only exception to that is for typically infrequent and/or short-lived operations involving multiple databases. These will still require a global lock, similar to the behavior MongoDB had in pre 2.x versions.

 Administrative operations, such as dropping a collection, still require an exclusive database lock.

MMAPv1, as explained previously, uses collection-level locks. Operations that span a single collection, but may or may not be spanning a single document, will still lock up the entire collection. This is the main reason why WiredTiger is the preferred storage solution for all new deployments.

Lock reporting

We can inspect lock status using any of the following tools and commands:

- `db.serverStatus()` through the `locks` document

- `db.currentOp()` through the `locks` field

- `mongotop`

- `mongostat`

- MongoDB Cloud Manager

- MongoDB Ops Manager

Lock contention is a really important metric to keep track of, as it can bring our database to its knees if it grows out of control.

 If we want to terminate an operation, we have to use the `db.killOp()` shell command.

Lock yield

A database with a database-level lock will not be really useful under stress, and will end being locked up most of the time. A smart solution to that in the early versions of MongoDB was getting operations to yield their locks on the basis of some heuristics.

`update()` commands affecting multiple documents would yield their X lock to improve concurrency.

MMAPv1's predecessor in earlier versions of MongoDB would use these heuristics to predict whether data was already in-memory before performing the requested operation. If it wasn't, it would yield the lock until the underlying operating system pages data in-memory, and then re-acquire the lock to continue with servicing the request.

The most notable exceptions to these are index scans, where the operation will not yield its lock and will just block on waiting for the data to get loaded from disk.

Since WiredTiger is only using intent locks at collection level and above, it doesn't really need these heuristics, as intent locks don't block other readers and writers.

Commonly used commands and locks

The commonly used commands and locks are as follows:

Command	Lock
find()	S
it() (query cursor)	S
insert()	X
remove()	X
update()	X
mapreduce()	Both S and X, depending on the case. Some MapReduce chunks can run in parallel.
index()	• **Foreground indexing**: Database lock. • **Background indexing**: No lock, except for administrative commands that will return an error. Also, background indexing will take considerably more time.
aggregate()	S

Commands requiring a database lock

The following commands require a database lock. We should plan in advance before issuing them in a production environment:

- db.collection.createIndex() in the (default) foreground mode
- reIndex
- compact
- db.repairDatabase()
- db.createCollection() if creating a multiple GB capped collection
- db.collection.validate()
- db.copyDatabase(), which may lock more than one database

We also have some commands that lock the entire database for a really short period of time:

- db.collection.dropIndex()
- db.getLastError()
- db.isMaster()
- Any rs.status() command
- db.serverStatus()

- `db.auth()`
- `db.addUser()`

These commands shouldn't take more than a few milliseconds to operate and so we shouldn't worry about it, unless we have automated scripts with these commands in place, in which case we must take note to throttle how often they would occur.

 In a sharded environment, each `mongod` applies its own locks, thus greatly improving concurrency.

In replica sets, our primary server must take all write operations. For these to be replicated correctly to the secondaries we must lock the local database that holds the oplog of operations at the same time that we lock our primary document/collection/database. This is usually a short-lived lock that, again, we shouldn't worry about.

Secondaries in replica sets will fetch write operations from the primary local database's oplog, apply the appropriate *X* lock, and apply service reads once the *X* locks are done with.

From the long preceding explanation, it's evident that locking should be avoided at all costs in MongoDB. We should design our database so that we avoid as many *X* locks as possible, and when we need to take *X* locks over one or multiple databases, do so in a maintenance window with a backup plan in case operations take longer than expected.

Further reading

You can refer to the following links for further reference:

- `https://docs.mongodb.com/manual/faq/concurrency/`
- `https://docs.mongodb.com/manual/core/storage-engines/`
- `https://www.mongodb.com/blog/post/building-applications-with-mongodbs-pluggable-storage-engines-part-1`
- `https://www.mongodb.com/blog/post/building-applications-with-mongodbs-pluggable-storage-engines-part-2`
- `https://docs.mongodb.com/manual/core/wiredtiger/`
- `https://docs.mongodb.com/manual/reference/method/db.collection.createIndex/#createindex-options`
- `https://docs.mongodb.com/manual/core/mmapv1/`

- `https://docs.mongodb.com/manual/reference/method/db.createCollection/#create-collection-storage-engine-options`
- `http://source.wiredtiger.com/mongodb-3.4/struct_w_t___s_e_s_s_i_o_n.html`
- `https://webassets.mongodb.com/microservices_white_paper.pdf?_ga=2.158920114.90404900.1503061618-355279797.1491859629`
- `https://webassets.mongodb.com/storage_engines_adress_wide_range_of_use_cases.pdf?_ga=2.125749506.90404900.1503061618-355279797.1491859629`
- `https://docs.mongodb.com/manual/reference/method/db.createCollection/#create-collection-storage-engine-options`
- `http://source.wiredtiger.com/mongodb-3.4/struct_w_t___s_e_s_s_i_o_n.html`
- `https://docs.mongodb.com/manual/reference/read-concern/`
- `https://www.percona.com/live/17/sessions/comparing-mongorocks-wiredtiger-and-mmapv1-performance-and-efficiency`
- `https://www.percona.com/blog/2016/06/01/embracing-mongorocks/`
- `https://www.percona.com/software/mongo-database/percona-tokumx`
- `https://www.slideshare.net/profyclub_ru/4-understanding-and-tuning-wired-tiger-the-new-high-performance-database-engine-in-mongodb-henrik-ingo-mongodb`

Summary

In this chapter, we learned about different storage engines in MongoDB. We identified the pros and cons of each one and the use cases for choosing each storage engine.

We learned about using multiple storage engines, how we can use them, and the benefits. A big part of this chapter was also dedicated to database locking, how it can happen, why it is bad, and how we can avoid it.

We split our operations by the lock they need. This way, when we design and implement our application, we can make sure that we have a design that locks our database as little as possible.

In the next chapter, we will learn about MongoDB and how we can use it to ingest and process big data.

10
MongoDB Tooling

Features, stability, and great driver support are all important; however, there is another area that is key to a software product succeeding, and that is the ecosystem built around it. MongoDB (originally under the name 10gen Inc.) introduced the MMS more than 8 years ago, in 2011, and it was seen as an innovation at the time. In this chapter, we will go through the following suite of different tools that are available for MongoDB and explore how they can improve productivity:

- MongoDB Enterprise Kubernetes Operator
- MongoDB Mobile
- MongoDB Stitch
- MongoDB Sync

Introduction

MongoDB Monitoring Service (MMS) is a mostly free **Software as a Service (SaaS)** solution that can monitor and access the diagnostics of any database that is signed up to it. When it was introduced, it greatly helped 10gen's engineers to troubleshoot any problems that the customers had. Since then, tooling has been a centerpiece of MongoDB's evolution.

MongoDB Atlas

MongoDB Atlas is MongoDB's **Database as a Service (DBaaS)** offering. It is available as a multi-cloud offering, supporting **Amazon Web Service (AWS)**, Microsoft Azure, and Google Cloud Platform.

Using DBaaS, patches and minor version upgrades are applied automatically, without any downtime. Using the **graphical user interface (GUI)**, a developer can deploy geographically distributed database instances to avoid having any single point of failure. For websites with significant traffic, this can also help by placing database servers closer to the users who are accessing their data. This is a key part of MongoDB's strategy and offering as they embrace having data close to the user.

Similar to most DBaaS offerings, Atlas allows users to scale a deployment using a GUI. Every deployment lives on its own **Virtual Private Cloud (VPC)** and can leverage MongoDB Enterprise Server features such as encryption key management, **Lightweight Directory Access Protocol (LDAP)**, and auditing features.

The live migration service can be used to migrate datasets from existing deployments on-premises, in any of the three supported cloud providers or other DBaaS services, such as **mLab**, **Compose**, and **ObjectRocket**, using the same GUI.

Creating a new cluster

Creating a new cluster using MongoDB Atlas is as simple as clicking and selecting through configuration options. In the following screenshot, we can see all the options that are available when creating a new cluster:

The following screenshot shows **Zone configuration summary**:

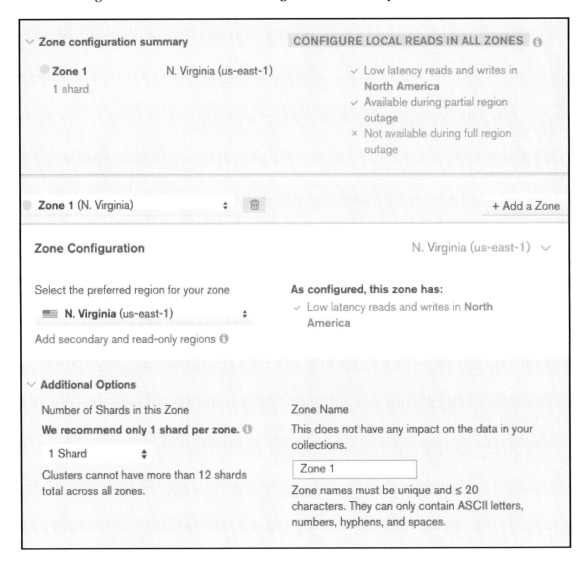

One of the game-changing settings in MongoDB Atlas is the ability to instantly provision geographically distributed servers across different zones and date centers (for all three major cloud providers) with the goal of having our data closest to our users. This can be useful for performance and regulatory reasons (such as **General Data Protection Regulation (GDPR)**, for the European Union).

By enabling global writes, we can start configuring this setting. Using any of the two templates—global performance or excellent global performance—an admin can create server configurations that will be less than 120 or less than 80 milliseconds from any user around the world. An administrator can also define their own custom assignments from regions to data centers.

In **Zone configuration summary**, we can see an overview of how our settings will affect performance. **M30** is the shard-enabled MongoDB Atlas plan and this configuration is creating (under the hood) a shard per zone. We can create more shards per zone but this is not recommended at this time.

Enabling configure local reads in all zones will create local read-only replica set nodes in every region other than the zone that is used to write data to. So, if we have three zones (*A*, *B*, and *C*), we end up with writes for *A* going to *A*, but reads from *A* happening either from a server in zone *A*, or *B* or *C*, depending on which server is geographically closer to the user. The same goes for zones *B* and *C*.

This section is probably the most important for complex, multi-region deployments and should be treated with extreme care.

The next section is configuring the servers that we want to use for our clusters:

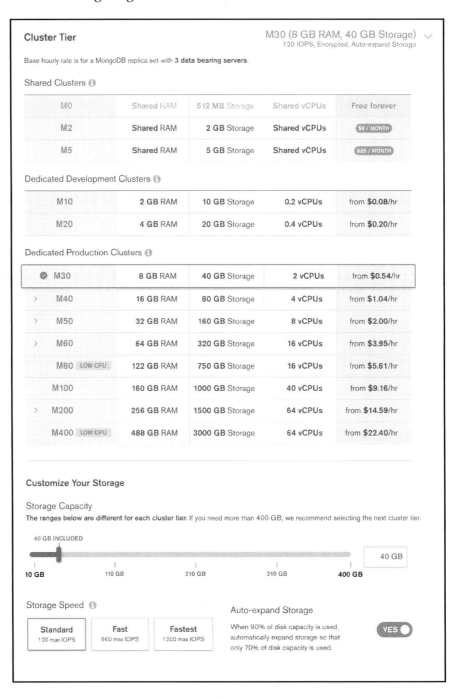

This is similar to how we will select servers in EC2 or Microsoft Azure. The main point to note is that we can select custom IOPS (the number of I/O operations per second) performance, and that we should select the **Auto-expand Storage** option to avoid running out of disk capacity. Together with this option, it's always useful to keep an eye on storage allocation to avoid excessive charges at the end of a billing cycle.

In the next panel, we can configure backup and advanced options for our cluster. The following screenshot shows **Additional Settings** for continuous backup:

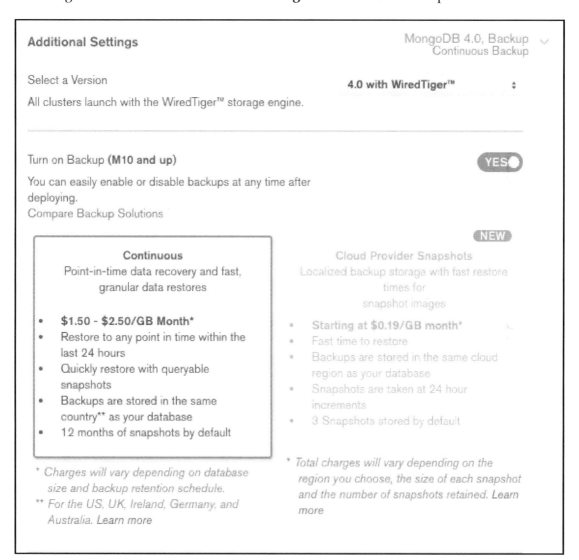

The following screenshot shows the **Advanced Settings** option for enabling **BI Connector**:

Advanced Settings

Enable Business Intelligence Connector **(M10 and up)**   NO

The BI Connector allows you to visualize your data on
relational business intelligence tools (e.g. Tableau,
MicroStrategy, Qlik).

| **BI Connector** | $27.18/day for sustained monthly usage |
| **pricing for M30** | or $77.02/day, up to $826.93/month maximum |

Encryption at Rest using your Key Management **(M10 and up)**   NO

Encrypt with your configured AWS KMS or Azure Key
Vault to ensure that database files written to the filesystem
and any backup snapshots are encrypted by the
WiredTiger™ Encrypted Storage Engine using keys that
you control.

The following screenshot shows **More Configuration Options** that are available:

⌄ More Configuration Options

Set Oplog Size

Set the maximum size of this cluster's oplog. *View documentation*

2048 **MB** 30,720 MB available

Set Minimum TLS Protocol Version

Configure this cluster to only accept connections using selected protocols below. *View documentation*

TLS 1.1 and ab ⇕

Enforce Index Key Limit

Documents can only be updated or inserted if, for all indexed fields, the corresponding index entries do not exceed 1024 bytes.

If disabled (`failIndexKeyTooLong=false`), documents with indexed fields exceeding the index limit will be inserted or modified successfully, but not indexed. *View documentation*

Require Indexes for All Queries

Do not run queries that require a collection scan; return an error instead. *View documentation*

Allow Server-Side JavaScript

Operations that perform server-side execution of JavaScript are allowed (e.g. `$where` query operator, **mapReduce**, etc.). *View documentation*

Important notes

MongoDB has provided some useful tips for in MongoDB Atlas, including the following:

- Use the latest version of MongoDB whenever possible.
- Use the latest **Transport Layer Security** (**TLS**) version available, which is 1.3 at the time of writing.
- Encryption at rest cannot be used together with continuous backups. We need to select cloud provider snapshots to be able to use this feature.
- It's probably a good idea to disable server-side JavaScript, unless we know why we need it, for example, when we have legacy MapReduce jobs in place.
- Requiring indexes for all queries can be useful if we have a well-defined business case and requirements for how we will use the database, and/or we expect our dataset to be so large that querying without indexes is practically impossible.
- Finally, we get to select the name of our cluster. This cannot be changed after creation so it's important to agree with fellow team members before we click on the **Create Cluster** button.

After a bit of waiting, our cluster will be operational, and we will be able to connect to it via a plain old MongoDB URI.

MongoDB Cloud Manager

Formerly known as **MongoDB Management Service** (**MMS**) and before that as **MongoDB Monitoring Service** (**MMS**), Cloud Manager is a managed SaaS for on-premises MongoDB deployments.

Atlas as a DBaaS solution can provide an end-to-end solution for database management. For many use cases this may not be feasible. In this case, it may make sense to use some of the features in a pay-as-you-go fashion.

Cloud Manager has a limited free tier and several paid ones.

Here are some of the key features of Cloud Manager:

- Automated backups
- More than 100 database metrics and **Key Performance Indicators** (**KPIs**) that can be used to track MongoDB's performance
- Customized alerts that integrate with third-party systems such as PagerDuty, email, and SMS
- A unified operations view, either via directly querying its JSON API, or by integrating it with popular performance tracking solutions such as New Relic (`https://www.newrelic.com`)

Premium plans also offer advice around performance and indexing. Cloud Manager's only requirement is to install the required agents in our application.

MongoDB Ops Manager

Ops Manager is, in many ways, different to Cloud Manager. In contrast to Cloud Manager, it is a downloadable executable for Windows Server, **Red Hat Enterprise Linux** (**RHEL**), or Ubuntu.

Following on this, users need to install and manage the service within their own infrastructure.

Aside from this difference, Ops Manager can also help achieve similar goals to Cloud Manager:

- Monitoring on more than 100 performance metrics
- Automation on installing and upgrading clusters; plus index maintenance can be achieved with zero downtime
- For continuous, incremental backups with point-in-time recovery
- Query optimization
- Index suggestions

A sample Ops Manager topology is as follows:

Aside from the Ops Manager and the MongoDB nodes, we also need snapshot storage if we have enabled backups.

Ops Manager can be a better alternative to Cloud Manager if we want an on-premises solution for security, or for other reasons. This is included as part of the MongoDB Enterprise Server paid solution.

MongoDB Charts

MongoDB Charts is a tool to generate visualizations from MongoDB data. It enables non-technical people to query a MongoDB database using a GUI and share the results with colleagues.

MongoDB Charts can create a series of charts, including the following:

- A column and bar chart reference
- A line and area chart reference
- Grid charts:
    - A heatmap reference
    - A scatter chart reference
- A donut chart reference
- Text charts: Number chart reference

Like Ops Manager, it's a standalone executable utilizing Docker that needs to be installed and managed on-premises.

> Use replica set secondaries for charts queries. Ideally, use a secondary, hidden, non-electable node as an analytics node in replica sets.

MongoDB Compass

MongoDB Compass is similar to MongoDB Charts, with less functionality around charting, but more heavily oriented towards running ad hoc queries and connecting to our database without the need for a command-line interface.

Compass provides the ability to query MongoDB through a GUI and visually construct queries. It can provide rich visualizations on result datasets, and help with constructing aggregation queries through a point and click interface.

Compass also provides visualizations for most administrative queries around query and index performance, so that it can be used to monitor and troubleshoot clusters from a database administrator perspective. It exposes an API that can be used to import or develop plugins.

A useful feature for non-technical users is the ability to download a read-only edition so that we can limit access to non-destructive operations. There is also an isolated edition of this tool that can be used to restrict connections to a single chosen server. These requests will also be TLS-encrypted.

Compass is available for Windows, OSX, Red Hat, and Ubuntu as an executable download. MongoDB Compass has a limited free edition, and the full feature set is available via a MongoDB subscription package.

MongoDB Connector for Business Intelligence (BI)

MongoDB Connector for BI is one of the most useful tools for non-developers. It is a part of the MongoDB Enterprise Advanced subscription and enables integration with BI tools using standard SQL queries.

It enables MongoDB integrations with enterprise tools such as Tableau, Qlik, Spotfire, Cognos, MicroStrategy, and SAP BusinessObjects.

It is available as an executable download for Amazon Linux, Debian, OSX, Red Hat, SUSE, Ubuntu, and Windows platforms, and can work with both on-premises databases and MongoDB Atlas. Once installed and configured correctly, it can provide an **Open Database Connectivity (ODBC) Data Source Name (DSN)** that most BI tools can use to connect to.

An introduction to Kubernetes

Kubernetes (`https://kubernetes.io`) is an open source container-orchestration system for automating deployment, scaling, and the management of containerized applications. In layman's terms, we can use Kubernetes (often referred to as k8s) to manage applications deployed via containers. Kubernetes was initially developed at Google and is now maintained by the **Cloud Native Computing Foundation (CNCF)**.

The most widely-used container technology is probably Docker. We can download and install Docker on any PC and, through a few commands, install a Docker image that will be isolated from our host system and contain our application code. Docker performs operating system level virtualization, where all containers are run by the host's operating system kernel. This results in containers being more lightweight than a full virtual machine (VM).

Multiple Docker containers can be orchestrated using **Docker Swarm**. This is similar to Kubernetes and sometimes the two systems are directly compared with each other.

MongoDB provides tools that can help administrators deploy and manage MongoDB clusters using Kubernetes.

Enterprise Kubernetes Operator

Starting from MongoDB 4.0, the MongoDB Enterprise Operator for Kubernetes enables a user to deploy and manage MongoDB clusters directly from the Kubernetes API. This circumvents the need to directly connect to Cloud Manager or Ops Manager, and simplifies the deployment and management of Kubernetes clusters.

 Cloud Manager is, in most aspects, the SaaS equivalent of Ops Manager.

Enterprise Kubernetes Operator can be installed using Helm, the package manager for Kubernetes. First, we have to clone the GitHub repository from MongoDB: `https://github.com/mongodb/mongodb-enterprise-kubernetes.git`.

After we change the directory to our local copy, we can issue the following command:

```
helm install helm_chart/ --name mongodb-enterprise
```

We will then have the local copy installed; the next step is to configure it.

By configuring our local installation, we need to apply a Kubernetes `ConfigMap` file. The configuration settings that we need to copy from Ops Manager or Cloud Manager are as follows:

- **Base URL**: The URL of your Ops Manager or Cloud Manager. For Cloud Manager, this will be `http://cloud.mongodb.com`; for Ops Manager, this should be similar to `http://<MY_SERVER_NAME>:8080/`.
- **Project ID**: The ID of an Ops Manager project that the Enterprise Kubernetes Operator will deploy into. This should be created within the Ops Manager or Cloud Manager, and is a unique ID to organize a MongoDB cluster and provide a security boundary for the project. It should be a 24-digit hexadecimal string.
- **User**: An existing Ops Manager username. This is the email of a user in Ops Manager that we want the Enterprise Kubernetes Operator to use when connecting to Ops Manager.
- **Public API key**: This is used by the Enterprise Kubernetes Operator to connect to the Ops Manager REST API endpoint.

This is created by clicking on the username on the **Ops Manager** console and selecting **Account**. On the next screen, we can click on **Public API Access**, and then click on the **Generate** key button and provide a description. The next screen will display the public API key that we need.

This is the only chance that we will ever have to view this API key, so we need to write it down, otherwise, we will need to regenerate a new key.

Once we have these values, we can create the Kubernetes `ConfigMap` file with any name we want, as long as it's a `.yaml` file. In our case, we will name it `mongodb-project.yaml`.

Its structure will be as follows:

```
apiVersion: v1
kind: ConfigMap
metadata:
 name:<<any sample name we choose(1)>>
 namespace: mongodb
data:
 projectId:<<Project ID from above>>
 baseUrl: <<BaseURI from above>>
```

Then we can apply this file to Kubernetes using the following command:

```
kubectl apply -f mongodb-project.yaml
```

The last step we need to take is to create the Kubernetes secret. This can be done using the following command:

```
kubectl -n mongodb create secret generic <<any sample name for credentials
we choos>> --from-literal="user=<<User as above>>" --from-
literal="publicApiKey=<<our public api key as above>>"
```

We need to note down the credentials name as we will need it in the subsequent steps.

Now we are ready to deploy our replica set using Kubernetes! We can create a `replica-set.yaml` file with the following structure:

```
apiVersion: mongodb.com/v1
kind: MongoDbReplicaSet
metadata:
 name: <<any replica set name we choose>>
 namespace: mongodb
spec:
 members: 3
 version: 3.6.5
persistent: false
```

```
project: <<the name value (1) that we chose in metadata.name of ConfigMap
file above>>
credentials: <<the name of credentials secret that we chose above>>
```

We apply the new configuration using `kubectl apply`:

kubectl apply -f replica-set.yaml

We will be able to see our new replica set in Ops Manager.

 To troubleshoot and identify issues in MongoDB using Kubernetes we can use `kubectl logs` to inspect logs, and `kubectl exec` to shell into one of the containers that is running MongoDB.

MongoDB Mobile

MongoDB Mobile is the mobile version of the MongoDB database. It's aimed at smartphones and IoT sensors via Embedded MongoDB. MongoDB Mobile has two core parts:

- A MongoDB database server that runs locally on the device, enabling offline access to data. This database is a stripped-down version of the MongoDB Server Community Edition, without any of the features that are not needed for Mobile (for example, replication).
- Native Java and Android SDKs to provide low-level access to the database and interact with the local Mobile database and any MongoDB Stitch backend.

Mobile SDK has two modes of operation. In local mode, the SDK only allows access to the local Mobile database, and cannot sync with any external source in Atlas. In remote mode, the SDK can access both MongoDB Atlas and MongoDB Mobile databases and Sync between them.

Here are some limitations of MongoDB Mobile over the server version:

- No support for replication
- No support for sharding
- No database authentication; however, the MongoDB Mobile database only accepts connections originating from the application
- No SSL

- No encryption at rest
- No change streams support
- No server-side JavaScript evaluation (this is for performance reasons)
- No multi-document ACID transactions

To set up MongoDB Mobile, we need to download and install the MongoDB Stitch SDK first. Then, creating and querying a local MongoDB database is as easy as a few lines of code (this example is in Android):

```
Import packages:
// Base Stitch Packages
import com.mongodb.stitch.android.core.Stitch;
import com.mongodb.stitch.android.core.StitchAppClient;
// Packages needed to interact with MongoDB and Stitch
import com.mongodb.client.MongoClient;
import com.mongodb.client.MongoCollection;
// Necessary component for working with MongoDB Mobile
import
com.mongodb.stitch.android.services.mongodb.local.LocalMongoDbService;
```

Initialize the database as follows:

```
// Create the default Stitch Client
final StitchAppClient client =
  Stitch.initializeDefaultAppClient("<APP ID>");
// Create a Client for MongoDB Mobile (initializing MongoDB Mobile)
final MongoClient mobileClient =
  client.getServiceClient(LocalMongoDbService.clientFactory);
```

Next, get a reference to the database:

```
MongoCollection<Document> localCollection =
  mobileClient.getDatabase("my_db").getCollection("my_collection");
```

Insert document as follows:

```
localCollection.insertOne(document);
```

Then, find the first document by using `first()`:

```
Document doc = localCollection.find().first();
```

MongoDB Mobile is most powerful when used in conjunction with MongoDB Stitch, which we will explore in the next section.

MongoDB Stitch

MongoDB Stitch is MongoDB's serverless platform offering. It is based on four distinct areas of functionality:

- The first area is QueryAnywhere. QueryAnywhere allows client-side applications to access MongoDB using its query language. We can define data access rules on the Stitch server on a per collection basis to allow us to filter results based on user data (userId).
- The second area is Stitch functions. These are simple JavaScript functions that can execute without a server inside the Stitch platform. By using Stitch functions, we can implement application logic, expose APIs, and build integrations with third-party services. This service is mostly similar to Amazon's AWS Lambda.
- The third area is Stitch triggers. Similar to MongoDB server's change streams and triggers as they are used in relational databases, Stitch triggers execute user-defined functions in real time by responding to changes in database state.
- Finally, there is Stitch Mobile Sync, which bridges the Stitch serverless offering with Mobile MongoDB. By using it, we can develop a Mobile service with a local MongoDB database residing in the smartphone, which is perfectly synced with our MongoDB Atlas-powered database in the cloud.

This way, we can query data locally in the app with no lag, or even while being offline, and rely on Stitch Mobile Sync to keep our data store up to date.

 Stitch can be used on the web (JavaScript), Android, and macOS (Swift).

QueryAnywhere

QueryAnywhere allows querying MongoDB server data directly from a client application. A key differentiation and functionality that allows us to do this securely is the ability to define data access rules to filter results based on the content of a document or the logged-in user.

Rules

MongoDB rules are a combination of a role, and the permissions assigned to that role. Roles define a set of users that will have the same read/write access to a document. Roles in Stitch can be defined with an **apply-when** rule.

This can be defined using the %% variable notation:

```
{
   "createdBy": "%%user.id"
}
```

Each role can have one or more permissions that define which fields they can read and/or write in a document.

MongoDB Stitch also offers four templates that have predefined roles and permissions around the most common use cases:

- Users can only read and write their own data.
- Users can read all data, but only write their own data.
- Users can only read all data.
- Users can read and write their own data. Users that belong to a sharing list can read that data.

 Authorization is applied before the rules. If a user is not authorized to access a collection, their rules will not be evaluated at all.

Functions

Stitch functions can be used to execute server-side application logic. They are written in JavaScript ES6+ and don't require server.

Here are some key limitations of functions:

- They stop execution once they return
- They can run for up to 60 seconds, using up to 256 MB of memory
- They cannot import modules or use some of the core JavaScript functionality, such as global object types, mathematical, number, string, array, and object APIs

Stitch functions can be imported via the CLI or from Stitch UI. For a simple function that we have named multiply, we could add this code in the UI:

```
exports = function(a, b) {
  return a * b;
};
```

And then we could call it from another function, webhook, or trigger within Stitch:

```
context.functions.execute("multiply", a, b);
```

We can also trigger its execution within a Stitch JSON expression using `%function`:

```
{
  "%%true": {
    "%function": {
      "name": "multiply",
      "arguments": [3,4]
    }
  }
}
```

We can even call this function from our client application using Stitch SDK (JavaScript, Android, or macOS):

```
const client = Stitch.defaultAppClient;
client.callFunction("multiply", [3, 4]).then(result => {
console.log(result) // Output: 12
});
```

Triggers

Triggers are building upon Stitch functions to execute when a database collection changes for database triggers, or execute authentication logic when a user is modified using authentication triggers.

Database triggers can execute on one or more of the INSERT, UPDATE, REPLACE, and DELETE database operations.

 These values all need to be case sensitive.

We need to define the **linked function**, which is the function that will execute once the trigger fires. An interesting option for the UPDATE operation is `fullDocument`. When set to `true`, this will include the full result of the operation. This is, as always, subject to the 16 MB document size limit, so updates to documents really close to the 16 MB limit may fail as the result will exceed the limit.

Authentication triggers, on the other hand, allow us to execute custom code on authentication events. These can be triggered on CREATE, LOGIN, and DELETE operation types from the following providers:

- oauth2-google
- oauth2-facebook
- custom-token
- local-userpass
- api-key
- anon-user

 Authentication operation types are case sensitive and need to be all uppercase. Up to 50 triggers per second can be concurrently executed. If we try to invoke more, they will get into a queue to be processed in a **first-in first-out (FIFO)** fashion.

Triggers are quite similar to RDBMS trigger functionality, with the added bonus that they are easy and flexible to manage via the Stitch trigger's GUI console.

Mobile Sync

One of the newest additions in MongoDB Stitch Mobile Sync can be used to sync data seamlessly between MongoDB Mobile and the server's backend (at the moment of writing this, it has to be hosted on MongoDB Atlas). Mobile Sync is also based on change streams to listen to data changing between local and remote databases. As data changes in the local Mobile database, we may run into conflicts between the local and remote state. This is why we need to define some handlers to specify what should happen in that case. There are three interfaces that we need to implement for our models:

- ConflictHandler
- ErrorListener
- ChangeEventListener

ConflictHandler has a method that arguments documentId of the document that conflicts the local and remote events, returns a resolution to the conflict as shown:

```
DocumentT resolveConflict(BsonValue documentId,
                          ChangeEvent<DocumentT> localEvent,
                          ChangeEvent<DocumentT> remoteEvent)
```

`ErrorListener` does not return anything and is called when an error happens for
`documentId` and non-network related exception:

```
void onError(BsonValue documentId,Exception error)
```

Finally, `ChangeEventListener` also does not return any values and is called when any
change `event` happens for the given `documentId`:

```
void onEvent(BsonValue documentId, ChangeEvent<DocumentT> event)
```

Summary

In this chapter, we went through different MongoDB tools and learned how to use them to
increase productivity. Starting from MongoDB Atlas, the hosted DBaaS solution, we
followed on with Cloud Manager and Ops Manager, and explored how they differ from
each other.

Then, we dived into MongoDB Charts and MongoDB Compass—the GUI-driven MongoDB
administration tools. We learned about MongoDB Connector for BI and how can it prove to
be useful for our purposes. Then we discussed Kubernetes, how it compares to Docker and
Docker Swarm, and how we can use Kubernetes with MongoDB Enterprise Operator. The
next section was dedicated to MongoDB Mobile and Stitch—two major enhancements in
MongoDB 4.0. We introduced practical examples of using Stitch's functionality, especially
around QueryAnywhere, triggers, and functions. Finally, we briefly introduced Mobile
Sync, one of the latest additions to MongoDB's arsenal, and looked at how it can be used to
sync our Mobile applications with a cloud-based database.

In the next chapter, we are going to switch gears and deal with how we can use big data
with MongoDB to ingest and process large streaming and batch datasets.

11
Harnessing Big Data with MongoDB

MongoDB is often used in conjunction with big data pipelines because of its performance, flexibility, and lack of rigorous data schemas. This chapter will explore the big data landscape, and how MongoDB fits alongside message queuing, data warehousing, and extract, transform, load pipelines.

The topics that we will discuss in this chapter are as follows:

- What is big data?
- Message queuing systems
- Data warehousing
- A big data use case using Kafka, Spark on top of HDFS, and MongoDB

What is big data?

In the last five years, the number of people accessing and using the internet has almost doubled from a little under 2 billion to around 3.7 billion. Half of the global population are now online.

With the number of internet users increasing, and with networks evolving, more data is being added to existing datasets each year. In 2016, global internet traffic was 1.2 zettabytes (which is 1.2 billion terabytes) and it is expected to grow to 3.3 zettabytes by 2021.

This enormous amount of data that is generated every year means that it is imperative that databases and data stores in general can scale and process our data efficiently.

The term **big data** was first coined in the 1980's by John Mashey (`http://static.usenix.org/event/usenix99/invited_talks/mashey.pdf`), and mostly came into play in the past decade with the explosive growth of the internet. Big data typically refers to datasets that are too large and complex to be processed by traditional data processing systems, and so need some kind of specialized system architecture to be processed.

Big data's defining characteristics are as follows, in general:

- Volume
- Variety
- Velocity
- Veracity
- Variability

Variety and variability refer to the fact that our data comes in different forms and our datasets have internal inconsistencies. These need to be smoothed out by a data cleansing and normalization system before we can actually process our data.

Veracity refers to the uncertainty of the quality of data. Data quality may vary, with perfect data for some dates and missing datasets for others. This affects our data pipeline and how much we can invest in our data platforms, since, even today, one out of three business leaders don't completely trust the information they use to make business decisions.

Finally, velocity is probably the most important defining characteristic of big data (other than the obvious volume attribute) and it refers to the fact that big datasets not only have large volumes of data, but also grow at an accelerated pace. This makes traditional storage using, for example, indexing a difficult task.

The big data landscape

Big data has evolved into a complex ecosystem affecting every sector of the economy. Going from hype to unrealistic expectations and back to reality, we now have big data systems implemented and deployed in most Fortune 1000 companies that deliver real value.

If we segment the companies that participate in the big data landscape by industry, we would probably come up with the following sections:

- Infrastructure
- Analytics
- Applications-enterprise
- Applications-industry
- Cross-infrastructure analytics
- Data sources and APIs
- Data resources
- Open source

From an engineering point of view, we are probably more concerned about the underlying technologies than their applications in different industry sectors.

Depending on our business domain, we may have data coming in from different sources, such as transactional databases, IoT sensors, application server logs, other websites via a web service API, or just plain web page content extraction:

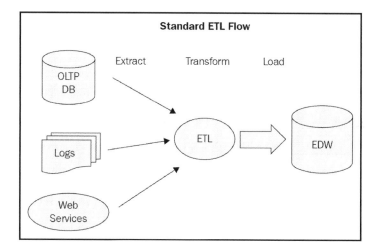

Message queuing systems

In most of the flows previously described, we have data being **extracted, transformed, loaded** (ETL) into an **enterprise data warehouse** (EDW). To extract and transform this data, we need a message queuing system to deal with spikes in traffic, endpoints being temporarily unavailable, and other issues that may affect the availability and scalability of this part of the system.

Message queues also provide decoupling between producers and consumers of messages. This allows for better scalability by partitioning our messages into different topics/queues.

Finally, using message queues, we can have location-agnostic services that don't care where the message producers sit, which provide interoperability between different systems.

In the message queuing world, the most popular systems in production at the time of writing this book are RabbitMQ, ActiveMQ, and Kafka. We will provide a small overview of them before we dive into our use case to bring all of them together.

Apache ActiveMQ

Apache ActiveMQ is an open source message broker, written in Java, together with a full **Java Message Service (JMS)** client.

It is the most mature implementation out of the three that we examine here, and has a long history of successful production deployments. Commercial support is offered by many companies, including Red Hat.

It is a fairly simple queuing system to set up and manage. It is based on the JMS client protocol and is the tool of choice for Java EE systems.

RabbitMQ

RabbitMQ, on the other hand, is written in Erlang and is based on the **Advanced Message Queuing Protocol (AMQP)** protocol. AMQP is significantly more powerful and complicated than JMS, as it allows peer-to-peer messaging, request/reply, and publish/subscribe models for one-to-one or one-to-many message consumption.

RabbitMQ has gained popularity in the past 5 years, and is now the most searched-for queuing system.

RabbitMQ's architecture is outlined as follows:

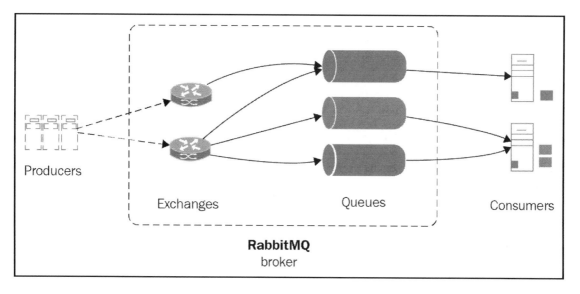

Scaling in RabbitMQ systems is performed by creating a cluster of RabbitMQ servers. Clusters share data and state, which are replicated, but message queues are distinct per node. To achieve high availability we can also replicate queues in different nodes.

Apache Kafka

Kafka, on the other hand, is a queuing system that was first developed by LinkedIn for its own internal purposes. It is written in Scala and is designed from the ground up for horizontal scalability and the best performance possible.

Focusing on performance is a key differentiator for Apache Kafka, but it means that in order to achieve performance, we need to sacrifice something. Messages in Kafka don't hold unique IDs, but are addressed by their offset in the log. Apache Kafka consumers are not tracked by the system; it is the responsibility of the application design to do so. Message ordering is implemented at the partition level and it is the responsibility of the consumer to identify if a message has been delivered already.

Semantics were introduced in version 0.11 and are part of the latest 1.0 release so that messages can now be both strictly ordered within a partition and always arrive exactly once for each consumer:

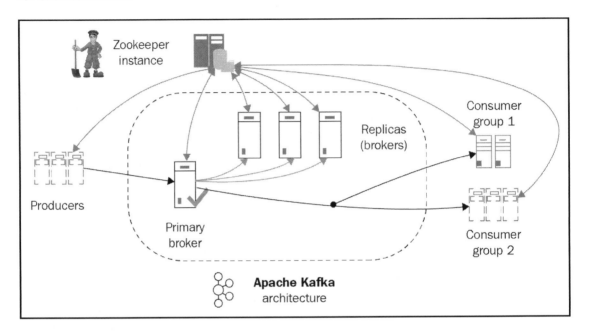

Data warehousing

Using a message queuing system is just the first step in our data pipeline design. At the other end of message queuing, we would typically have a data warehouse to process the vast amount of data that arrives. There are numerous options there, and it is not the main focus of this book to go over these or compare them. However, we will skim through two of the most widely-used options from the Apache Software Foundation: Apache Hadoop and Apache Spark.

Apache Hadoop

The first, and probably still most widely used, framework for big data processing is Apache Hadoop. Its foundation is the **Hadoop Distributed File System (HDFS)**. Developed at Yahoo! in the 2000s, it originally served as an open source alternative to **Google File System (GFS)**, a distributed filesystem that was serving Google's needs for distributed storage of its search index.

Hadoop also implemented a MapReduce alternative to Google's proprietary system, Hadoop MapReduce. Together with HDFS, they constitute a framework for distributed storage and computations. Written in Java, with bindings for most programming languages and many projects that provide abstracted and simple functionality, and sometimes based on SQL querying, it is a system that can reliably be used to store and process terabytes, or even petabytes, of data.

In later versions, Hadoop became more modularized by introducing **Yet Another Resource Negotiator (YARN)**, which provides the abstraction for applications to be developed on top of Hadoop. This has enabled several applications to be deployed on top of Hadoop, such as **Storm**, **Tez**, **OpenMPI**, **Giraph**, and, of course, **Apache Spark**, as we will see in the following sections.

Hadoop MapReduce is a batch-oriented system, meaning that it relies on processing data in batches, and is not designed for real-time use cases.

Apache Spark

Apache Spark is a cluster-computing framework from the University of California, Berkeley's AMPLab. Spark is not a substitute for the complete Hadoop ecosystem, but mostly for the MapReduce aspect of a Hadoop cluster. Whereas Hadoop MapReduce uses on-disk batch operations to process data, Spark uses both in-memory and on-disk operations. As expected, it is faster with datasets that fit in memory. This is why it is more useful for real-time streaming applications, but it can also be used with ease for datasets that don't fit in memory.

Apache Spark can run on top of HDFS using YARN or in standalone mode, as shown in the following diagram:

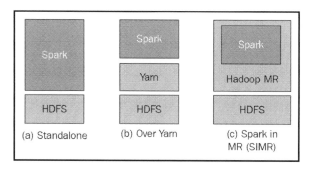

This means that in some cases (such as the one that we will use in our following use case) we can completely ditch Hadoop for Spark if our problem is really well defined and constrained within Spark's capabilities.

Spark can be up to 100 times faster than Hadoop MapReduce for in-memory operations. Spark offers user-friendly APIs for Scala (its native language), Java, Python, and Spark SQL (a variation of the SQL92 specification). Both Spark and MapReduce are resilient to failure. Spark uses RDDs that are distributed across the whole cluster.

As we can see from the overall Spark architecture, as follows, we can have several different modules of Spark working together for different needs, from SQL querying to streaming and machine learning libraries.

Comparing Spark with Hadoop MapReduce

The Hadoop MapReduce framework is more commonly compared to Apache Spark, a newer technology that aims to solve problems in a similar problem space. Some of their most important attributes are summarized in the following table:

	Hadoop MapReduce	Apache Spark
Written in	Java	Scala
Programming model	MapReduce	RDD
Client bindings	Most high-level languages	Java, Scala, Python
Ease of use	Moderate, with high-level abstractions (Pig, Hive, and so on)	Good
Performance	High throughput in batch	High throughput in streaming and batch mode
Uses	Disk (I/O bound)	Memory, degrading performance if disk is needed
Typical node	Medium	Medium-large

As we can see from the preceding comparison, there are pros and cons for both technologies. Spark arguably has better performance, especially in problems that use fewer nodes. On the other hand, Hadoop is a mature framework with excellent tooling on top of it to cover almost every use case.

MongoDB as a data warehouse

Apache Hadoop is often described as the 800 lb gorilla in the room of big data frameworks. Apache Spark, on the other hand, is more like a 200 lb cheetah for its speed, agility, and performance characteristics, which allow it to work well in a subset of the problems that Hadoop aims to solve.

MongoDB, on the other hand, can be described as the MySQL equivalent in the NoSQL world, because of its adoption and ease of use. MongoDB also offers an aggregation framework, MapReduce capabilities, and horizontal scaling using sharding, which is essentially data partitioning at the database level. So naturally, some people wonder why we don't use MongoDB as our data warehouse to simplify our architecture.

This is a pretty compelling argument, and it may or may not be the case that it makes sense to use MongoDB as a data warehouse. The advantages of such a decision are as follows:

- Simpler architecture
- Less need for message queues, reducing latency in our system

The disadvantages are as follows:

- MongoDB's MapReduce framework is not a replacement for Hadoop's MapReduce. Even though they both follow the same philosophy, Hadoop can scale to accommodate larger workloads.
- Scaling MongoDB's document storage using sharding will hit a wall at some point. Whereas Yahoo! has reported using 42,000 servers in its largest Hadoop cluster, the largest MongoDB commercial deployments stand at 5 billion (Craigslist), compared to 600 nodes and petabytes of data for Baidu, the internet giant dominating, among others, the Chinese internet search market.

There is more than an order of magnitude of difference in terms of scaling.

MongoDB is mainly designed around being a real-time querying database based on stored data on disk, whereas MapReduce is designed around using batches, and Spark is designed around using streams of data.

A big data use case

Putting all of this into action, we will develop a fully working system using a data source, a Kafka message broker, an Apache Spark cluster on top of HDFS feeding a Hive table, and a MongoDB database. Our Kafka message broker will ingest data from an API, streaming market data for an XMR/BTC currency pair. This data will be passed on to an Apache Spark algorithm on HDFS to calculate the price for the next ticker timestamp, based on the following:

- The corpus of historical prices already stored on HDFS
- The streaming market data arriving from the API

This predicted price will then be stored in MongoDB using the MongoDB Connector for Hadoop. MongoDB will also receive data straight from the Kafka message broker, storing it in a special collection with the document expiration date set to one minute. This collection will hold the latest orders, with the goal of being used by our system to buy or sell, using the signal coming from the Spark ML system.

So, for example, if the price is currently 10 and we have a bid for 9.5, but we expect the price to go down at the next market tick, then the system would wait. If we expect the price to go up in the next market tick, then the system would increase the bid price to 10.01 to match the price in the next ticker.

Similarly, if the price is 10 and we bid for 10.5, but expect the price to go down, we would adjust our bid to 9.99 to make sure we don't overpay for it. But, if the price is expected to go up, we would immediately buy to make a profit at the next market tick.

Schematically, our architecture looks like this:

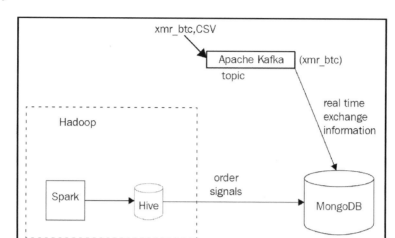

The API is simulated by posting JSON messages to a Kafka topic named xmr_btc. On the other end, we have a Kafka consumer importing real-time data to MongoDB.

We also have another Kafka consumer importing data to Hadoop to be picked up by our algorithms, which send recommendation data (signals) to a Hive table. Finally, we export data from the Hive table into MongoDB.

Setting up Kafka

The first step in setting up the environment for our big data use case is to establish a Kafka node. Kafka is essentially a FIFO queue, so we will use the simplest single node (broker) setup. Kafka organizes data using topics, producers, consumers, and brokers.

The important Kafka terminologies are as follows:

- A **broker** is essentially a node.
- A **producer** is a process that writes data to the message queue.
- A **consumer** is a process that reads data from the message queue.
- A **topic** is the specific queue that we write to and read data from.

A Kafka topic is further subdivided into a number of partitions. We can split data from a particular topic into multiple brokers (nodes), both when we write to the topic and also when we read our data at the other end of the queue.

After installing Kafka on our local machine, or any cloud provider of our choice (there are excellent tutorials for EC2 to be found just a search away), we can create a topic using this single command:

```
$ kafka-topics  --create --zookeeper localhost:2181 --replication-factor 1
--partitions 1 --topic xmr-btc
Created topic "xmr-btc".
```

This will create a new topic called `xmr-btc`.

Deleting the topic is similar to creating one, by using this command:

```
$ kafka-topics --delete --zookeeper localhost:2181 --topic xmr-btc
```

We can then get a list of all topics by issuing the following command:

```
$ kafka-topics --list --zookeeper localhost:2181
xmr-btc
```

We can then create a command-line producer for our topic, just to test that we can send messages to the queue, like this:

```
$ kafka-console-producer --broker-list localhost:9092 --topic xmr-btc
```

Data on every line will be sent as a string encoded message to our topic, and we can end the process by sending a `SIGINT` signal (typically *Ctrl + C*).

Afterwards we can view the messages that are waiting in our queue by spinning up a consumer:

```
$ kafka-console-consumer --zookeeper localhost:2181 --topic xmr-btc --from-
beginning
```

This consumer will read all messages in our xmr-btc topic, starting from the beginning of history. This is useful for our test purposes, but we will change this configuration in real-world applications.

 You will keep seeing zookeeper, in addition to kafka, mentioned in the commands. Apache Zookeeper comes together with Apache Kafka, and is a centralized service that is used internally by Kafka for maintaining configuration information, naming, providing distributed synchronization, and providing group services.

Now we have set up our broker, we can use the code at https://github.com/agiamas/mastering-mongodb/tree/master/chapter_9 to start reading (consuming) and writing (producing) messages to the queue. For our purposes, we are using the ruby-kafka gem, developed by Zendesk.

For simplicity, we are using a single class to read from a file stored on disk and to write to our Kafka queue.

Our produce method will be used to write messages to Kafka as follows:

```
def produce
  options = { converters: :numeric, headers: true }
    CSV.foreach('xmr_btc.csv', options) do |row|
      json_line = JSON.generate(row.to_hash)
      @kafka.deliver_message(json_line, topic: 'xmr-btc')
    end
end
```

Our consume method will read messages from Kafka as follows:

```
def consume
  consumer = @kafka.consumer(group_id: 'xmr-consumers')
  consumer.subscribe('xmr-btc', start_from_beginning: true)
  trap('TERM') { consumer.stop }
  consumer.each_message(automatically_mark_as_processed: false) do
|message|
    puts message.value
    if valid_json?(message.value)
      MongoExchangeClient.new.insert(message.value)
      consumer.mark_message_as_processed(message)
    end
  end
  consumer.stop
end
```

Notice that we are using the consumer group API feature (added in Kafka 0.9) to get multiple consumers to access a single topic by assigning each partition to a single consumer. In the event of a consumer failure, its partitions will be reallocated to the remaining members of the group.

The next step is to write these messages to MongoDB, as follows:

1. First, we create our collection so that our documents expire after one minute. Enter the following in the mongo shell:

```
> use exchange_data
> db.xmr_btc.createIndex( { "createdAt": 1 }, { expireAfterSeconds:
60 })
{
"createdCollectionAutomatically" : true,
"numIndexesBefore" : 1,
"numIndexesAfter" : 2,
"ok" : 1
}
```

This way, we create a new database called exchange_data with a new collection called xmr_btc that has auto-expiration after one minute. For MongoDB to auto-expire documents, we need to provide a field with a datetime value to compare its value against the current server time. In our case, this is the createdAt field.

2. For our use case, we will use the low-level MongoDB Ruby driver. The code for MongoExchangeClient is as follows:

```
class MongoExchangeClient
  def initialize
    @collection = Mongo::Client.new([ '127.0.0.1:27017' ], database:
:exchange_data).database[:xmr_btc]
  end
  def insert(document)
    document = JSON.parse(document)
    document['createdAt'] = Time.now
    @collection.insert_one(document)
  end
end
```

This client connects to our local database, sets the createdAt field for the TTL document expiration, and saves the message to our collection.

With this setup, we can write messages to Kafka, read them at the other end of the queue, and write them into our MongoDB collection.

Setting up Hadoop

We can install Hadoop and use a single node for the use case in this chapter using the instructions from Apache Hadoop's website at `https://hadoop.apache.org/docs/stable/hadoop-project-dist/hadoop-common/SingleCluster.html`.

After following these steps, we can browse the HDFS files in our local machine at `http://localhost:50070/explorer.html#/`. Assuming that our signals data is written in HDFS under the `/user/<username>/signals` directory, we will use the MongoDB Connector for Hadoop to export and import it into MongoDB.

MongoDB Connector for Hadoop is the officially supported library, allowing MongoDB data files or MongoDB backup files in BSON to be used as the source or destination for Hadoop MapReduce tasks.

This means that we can also easily export to, and import data from, MongoDB when we are using higher-level Hadoop ecosystem tools such as Pig (a procedural high-level language), Hive (a SQL-like high-level language), and Spark (a cluster-computing framework).

Steps for Hadoop setup

The different steps to set up Hadoop are as follows:

1. Download the JAR from the Maven repository at `http://repo1.maven.org/maven2/org/mongodb/mongo-hadoop/mongo-hadoop-core/2.0.2/`.

2. Download `mongo-java-driver` from `https://oss.sonatype.org/content/repositories/releases/org/mongodb/mongodb-driver/3.5.0/`.

3. Create a directory (in our case, named `mongo_lib`) and copy these two JARs in there with the following command:

   ```
   export
   HADOOP_CLASSPATH=$HADOOP_CLASSPATH:<path_to_directory>/mongo_lib/
   ```

Alternatively, we can copy these JARs under the `share/hadoop/common/` directory. As these JARs will need to be available in every node, for clustered deployment, it's easier to use Hadoop's `DistributedCache` to distribute the JARs to all nodes.

4. The next step is to install Hive from `https://hive.apache.org/downloads.html`. For this example, we used a MySQL server for Hive's metastore data. This can be a local MySQL server for development, but it is recommended that you use a remote server for production environments.

5. Once we have Hive set up, we just run the following command:

   ```
   > hive
   ```

6. Then, we add the three JARs (`mongo-hadoop-core`, `mongo-hadoop-driver`, and `mongo-hadoop-hive`) that we downloaded earlier:

   ```
   hive> add jar /Users/dituser/code/hadoop-2.8.1/mongo-hadoop-
   core-2.0.2.jar;
   Added [/Users/dituser/code/hadoop-2.8.1/mongo-hadoop-
   core-2.0.2.jar] to class path
   Added resources: [/Users/dituser/code/hadoop-2.8.1/mongo-hadoop-
   core-2.0.2.jar]
   hive> add jar /Users/dituser/code/hadoop-2.8.1/mongodb-
   driver-3.5.0.jar;
   Added [/Users/dituser/code/hadoop-2.8.1/mongodb-driver-3.5.0.jar]
   to class path
   Added resources: [/Users/dituser/code/hadoop-2.8.1/mongodb-
   driver-3.5.0.jar]
   hive> add jar /Users/dituser/code/hadoop-2.8.1/mongo-hadoop-
   hive-2.0.2.jar;
   Added [/Users/dituser/code/hadoop-2.8.1/mongo-hadoop-
   hive-2.0.2.jar] to class path
   Added resources: [/Users/dituser/code/hadoop-2.8.1/mongo-hadoop-
   hive-2.0.2.jar]
   hive>
   ```

And then, assuming our data is in the table exchanges:

customerid	int
pair	String
time	TIMESTAMP
recommendation	int

> We can also use Gradle or Maven to download the JARs in our local project. If we only need MapReduce, then we just download the mongo-hadoop-core JAR. For Pig, Hive, Streaming, and so on, we must download the appropriate JARs from http://repo1.maven.org/maven2/org/mongodb/mongo-hadoop/. Some useful Hive commands include the following: show databases; and
> create table exchanges(customerid int, pair String, time TIMESTAMP, recommendation int);

7. Now that we are all set, we can create a MongoDB collection backed by our local Hive data:

```
hive> create external table exchanges_mongo (objectid STRING,
customerid INT,pair STRING,time STRING, recommendation INT) STORED
BY 'com.mongodb.hadoop.hive.MongoStorageHandler' WITH
SERDEPROPERTIES('mongo.columns.mapping'='{"objectid":"_id",
"customerid":"customerid","pair":"pair","time":"Timestamp",
"recommendation":"recommendation"}')
tblproperties('mongo.uri'='mongodb://localhost:27017/exchange_data.
xmr_btc');
```

8. Finally, we can copy all data from the exchanges Hive table into MongoDB as follows:

```
hive> Insert into table exchanges_mongo select * from exchanges;
```

This way, we have established a pipeline between Hadoop and MongoDB using Hive, without any external server.

Using a Hadoop to MongoDB pipeline

An alternative to using the MongoDB Connector for Hadoop is to use the programming language of our choice to export data from Hadoop, and then write into MongoDB using the low-level driver or an ODM, as described in previous chapters.

For example, in Ruby, there are a few options:

- **WebHDFS** on GitHub, which uses the WebHDFS or the **HttpFS** Hadoop API to fetch data from HDFS
- System calls, using the Hadoop command-line tool and Ruby's `system()` call

Whereas in Python, we can use the following:

- **HdfsCLI**, which uses the WebHDFS or the HttpFS Hadoop API
- **libhdfs**, which uses a JNI-based native C wrapped around the HDFS Java client

All of these options require an intermediate server between our Hadoop infrastructure and our MongoDB server, but, on the other hand, allow for more flexibility in the ETL process of exporting/importing data.

Setting up Spark to MongoDB

MongoDB also offers a tool to directly query Spark clusters and export data to MongoDB. Spark is a cluster computing framework that typically runs as a YARN module in Hadoop, but can also run independently on top of other filesystems.

MongoDB Spark Connector can read and write to MongoDB collections from Spark using Java, Scala, Python, and R. It can also use aggregation and run SQL queries on MongoDB data after creating a temporary view for the dataset backed by Spark.

Using Scala, we can also use Spark Streaming, the Spark framework for data-streaming applications built on top of Apache Spark.

Further reading

You can refer to the following references for further information:

- https://www.cisco.com/c/en/us/solutions/collateral/service-provider/visual-networking-index-vni/vni-hyperconnectivity-wp.html
- http://www.ibmbigdatahub.com/infographic/four-vs-big-data
- https://spreadstreet.io/database/
- http://mattturck.com/wp-content/uploads/2017/05/Matt-Turck-FirstMark-2017-Big-Data-Landscape.png
- http://mattturck.com/bigdata2017/
- https://dzone.com/articles/hadoop-t-etl
- https://www.cloudamqp.com/blog/2014-12-03-what-is-message-queuing.html
- https://www.linkedin.com/pulse/jms-vs-amqp-eran-shaham
- https://www.cloudamqp.com/blog/2017-01-09-apachekafka-vs-rabbitmq.html
- https://trends.google.com/trends/explore?date=allq=ActiveMQ,RabbitMQ,ZeroMQ
- https://thenextweb.com/insider/2017/03/06/the-incredible-growth-of-the-internet-over-the-past-five-years-explained-in-detail/#.tnw_ALaObAUG
- https://static.googleusercontent.com/media/research.google.com/en//archive/mapreduce-osdi04.pdf
- https://en.wikipedia.org/wiki/Apache_Hadoop#Architecture
- https://wiki.apache.org/hadoop/PoweredByYarn
- https://www.slideshare.net/cloudera/introduction-to-yarn-and-mapreduce-2?next_slideshow=1
- https://www.mongodb.com/blog/post/mongodb-live-at-craigslist
- https://www.mongodb.com/blog/post/mongodb-at-baidu-powering-100-apps-across-600-nodes-at-pb-scale
- http://www.datamation.com/data-center/hadoop-vs.-spark-the-new-age-of-big-data.html
- https://www.mongodb.com/mongodb-data-warehouse-time-series-and-device-history-data-medtronic-transcript
- https://www.mongodb.com/blog/post/mongodb-debuts-in-gartner-s-magic-quadrant-for-data-warehouse-and-data-management-solutions-for-analytics
- https://www.infoworld.com/article/3014440/big-data/five-things-you-need-to-know-about-hadoop-v-apache-spark.html
- https://www.quora.com/What-is-the-difference-between-Hadoop-and-Spark

- https://iamsoftwareengineer.wordpress.com/2015/12/15/hadoop-vs-spark/?iframe=truetheme_preview=true
- https://www.infoq.com/articles/apache-kafka
- https://stackoverflow.com/questions/42151544/is-there-any-reason-to-use-rabbitmq-over-kafka
- https://medium.com/@jaykreps/exactly-once-support-in-apache-kafka-55e1fdd0a35f
- https://www.slideshare.net/sbaltagi/apache-kafka-vs-rabbitmq-fit-for-purpose-decision-tree
- https://techbeacon.com/what-apache-kafka-why-it-so-popular-should-you-use-it
- https://github.com/zendesk/ruby-kafka
- http://zhongyaonan.com/hadoop-tutorial/setting-up-hadoop-2-6-on-mac-osx-yosemite.html
- https://github.com/mtth/hdfs
- http://wesmckinney.com/blog/outlook-for-2017/
- http://wesmckinney.com/blog/python-hdfs-interfaces/
- https://acadgild.com/blog/how-to-export-data-from-hive-to-mongodb/
- https://sookocheff.com/post/kafka/kafka-in-a-nutshell/
- https://www.codementor.io/jadianes/spark-mllib-logistic-regression-du107neto
- http://ondra-m.github.io/ruby-spark/
- https://amodernstory.com/2015/03/29/installing-hive-on-mac/
- https://www.infoq.com/articles/apache-spark-introduction
- https://cs.stanford.edu/~matei/papers/2010/hotcloud_spark.pdf

Summary

In this chapter, we learned about the big data landscape and how MongoDB compares with, and fares against, message-queuing systems and data warehousing technologies. Using a big data use case, we learned how to integrate MongoDB with Kafka and Hadoop from a practical perspective.

In the next chapter, we will turn to replication and cluster operations, and discuss replica sets, the internals of elections, and the setup and administration of our MongoDB cluster.

Section 4: Scaling and High Availability

4

In this section, we will start by covering replication and how we can use it to make sure that we won't suffer any data losses. Sharding is the next topic, which helps us to achieve horizontal scaling in MongoDB. Finally, we will learn best practices and tips for high availability and fault tolerance when using MongoDB.

This section consists of the following chapters:

- Chapter 12, *Replication*
- Chapter 13, *Sharding*
- Chapter 14, *Fault Tolerance and High Availability*

12
Replication

Replication has been one of the most useful features of MongoDB since the very early days. In general, replication refers to the process of synchronizing data across different servers. The benefits of replication include protection from data loss and high availability of data. Replication also provides disaster recovery, an avoidance of downtime for maintenance, scaling reads (since we can read from multiple servers), and scaling writes (only if we can write to multiple servers).

In this chapter, we will cover the following topics:

- An architectural overview, elections, and the use cases for replication
- Setting up a replica set
- Connecting to a replica set
- Replica set administration
- The best practices for deploying replica sets using cloud providers
- Replica set limitations

Replication

There are different approaches to replication. The approach that MongoDB takes is logical replication with a master-slave, which we will explain in more detail later in this chapter.

Logical or physical replication

With replication, we synchronize data across multiple servers, providing data availability and redundancy. Even if we lose a server due to a hardware or software failure, by using replication, we will have multiple copies that we can use to restore our data. Another advantage of replication is that we can use one of the servers as a dedicated reporting, or backup, server.

In logical replication, we have our master/primary server performing operations; the slave/secondary server tails a queue of operations from the master and applies the same operations in the same order. Using of MongoDB as an example, the **operations log** (**oplog**) keeps track of operations that have happened on the primary server and applies them in the exact same order on the secondary server.

Logical replication is useful for a wide array of applications, such as information sharing, data analysis, and **Online Analytical Processing** (**OLAP**) reporting.

In physical replication, data gets copied on the physical level, at a lower level than database operations. This means that we are not applying the operations, but copying the bytes that were affected by these operations. It also means that we can gain better efficiency, since we are using low-level structures to transfer data. We can also ensure that the state of the database is exactly the same, since they are identical, byte for byte.

What is typically missing from physical replication is knowledge about the database structure, which means that it is harder (if not impossible) to copy some collections from a database and ignore others.

Physical replication is typically suited for more rare circumstances, like disaster recovery, wherein a full and exact copy of everything (including data, indexes, the internal state of the database in a journal, and redoing/undoing logs) is of crucial importance to bringing the application back to the exact state it was in.

Different high availability types

In high availability, there are several configurations that we can use. Our primary server is called the **hot server**, as it can process each and every request coming in. Our secondary server can be in any of the following states:

- Cold
- Warm
- Hot

A **secondary cold server** is a server that is there just in case the primary server goes offline, without any expectation of it holding the data and state that the primary server had.

A **secondary warm server** receives periodic updates of data from the primary server, but typically, it is not entirely up to date with the primary server. It can be used for some non-real-time analytics reporting to offload the main server, but typically, it will not be able to pick up the transactional load of the primary server if it goes down.

A **secondary hot server** always keeps an up-to-date copy of the data and state from the primary server. It usually waits in a hot standby state, ready to take over when the primary server goes down.

MongoDB has both the hot and warm server types of functionality, as we will explore in the following sections.

Most database systems employ a similar notion of primary/secondary servers, so conceptually, everything from MongoDB gets applied there, too.

An architectural overview

MongoDB's replication is provided in the following diagram:

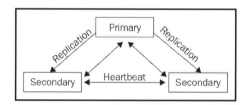

The primary server is the only one that can take writes at any time. The secondary servers are in a hot standby state, ready to take over if the primary server fails. Once the primary server fails, an election takes place regarding which secondary server will become primary.

We can also have **arbiter nodes**. Arbiter nodes do not hold any data, and their sole purpose is to participate in the election process.

We must always have an odd number of nodes (including arbiters). Three, five, and seven are all fine, so that in the event of the primary (or more servers) failing, we have a majority of votes in the election process.

When the other members of a replica set don't hear from the primary for more than 10 seconds (configurable), an eligible secondary will start the election process to vote for a new primary. The first secondary to hold the election and win the majority will become the new primary. All remaining servers will now replicate from the new primary server, keeping their roles as secondaries but syncing up from the new primary.

Starting with MongoDB 3.6, client drivers can retry write operations a **single time** if they detect that the primary is down. A replica set can have up to 50 members, but only up to seven of them can vote in the election process.

The setup for our replica set after the new election will be as follows:

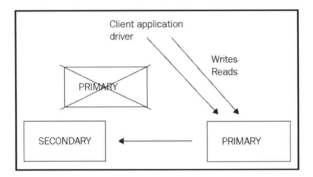

In the next section, we will discuss how elections work.

How do elections work?

All of the servers in a replica set maintain regular communication with every other member via a heartbeat. The heartbeat is a small packet that's regularly sent to verify that all members are operating normally.

Secondary members also communicate with the primary to get the latest updates from the oplog and apply them to their own data.

The information here refers to the latest replication election protocol, version 1, which was introduced in MongoDB v3.2.

Schematically, we can see how this works.

When the primary member goes down, all of the secondaries will miss a heartbeat or more. They will be waiting up until the `settings.electionTimeoutMillis` time passes (the default is 10 seconds), and then the secondaries will start one or more rounds of elections to find the new primary.

For a server to be elected as primary from the secondaries, it must have two properties:

- Belong in a group of voters that have *50% + 1* of the votes
- Be the most up-to-date secondary in this group

In a simple example of three servers with one vote each, once we lose the primary, the other two servers will each have one vote (so, in total, two-thirds), and as such, the one with the most up-to-date oplog will be elected as primary.

Now, consider a more complex setup, as follows:

- Seven servers (one primary, six secondaries)
- One vote each

We lose the primary server, and the six remaining servers have network connectivity issues, resulting in a network partition:

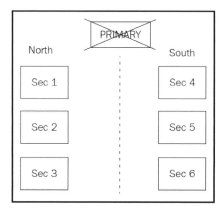

These partitions can be described as follows:

- Partition **North**: Three servers (one vote each)
- Partition **South**: Three servers (one vote each)

Neither partition has any knowledge of what happened to the rest of the servers. Now, when they hold elections, no partition can establish a majority, as they have three out of seven votes. No primary will get elected from either partition. This problem can be overcome by having, for example, one server with three votes.

Now, our overall cluster setup looks as follows:

- **Server #1**: one vote
- **Server #2**: one vote
- **Server #3**: one vote
- **Server #4**: one vote
- **Server #5**: one vote
- **Server #6**: one vote
- **Server #7**: three votes

After losing Server #1, our partitions now look as follows:

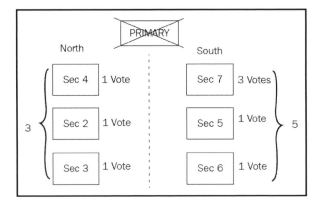

Partition **North** is as follows:

- **Server #2**: One vote
- **Server #3**: One vote
- **Server #4**: One vote

Partition **South** is as follows:

- **Server #5**: One vote
- **Server #6**: One vote
- **Server #7**: Three votes

Partition **South** has three servers, with a total of five out of nine votes. The secondary among servers #5, #6, and #7 that is most up to date (according to its oplog entries) will be elected as the primary.

What is the use case for a replica set?

MongoDB offers most of the advantages of using a replica set, some of which are listed as follows:

- Protection from data loss
- High availability of data
- Disaster recovery
- Avoidance of downtime for maintenance
- Scaling reads, since we can read from multiple servers
- Helping to design for geographically dispersed services
- Data privacy

The most notable item that's missing from the list is scaling writes. This is because, in MongoDB, we can only have one primary, and only this primary can take writes from our application server.

When we want to scale write performance, we typically design and implement sharding, which will be the topic of the next chapter. Two interesting properties of the way that MongoDB replication is implemented are geographically dispersed services and data privacy.

It is not uncommon for our application servers to be located in multiple data centers across the globe. Using replication, we can have a secondary server as close to the application server as possible. What this means is that our reads will be fast, as if they were local, and we will get a latency performance penalty just for our writes. This requires some planning at the application level, of course, so that we can maintain two different pools of connections to our database, which can be easily done by either using the official MongoDB drivers or using higher-level ODMs.

The second interesting property of MongoDB's replication design is implementing data privacy. When we have servers geographically dispersed across different data centers, we can enable replication per database. By keeping a database out of the replication process, we can make sure that our data stays confined in the data center that we need. We can also set up different replication schemas per database in the same MongoDB server so that we have multiple replication strategies according to our data privacy needs, excluding some servers from our replica sets if they are not allowed by our data privacy regulations.

Setting up a replica set

In this section, we will go over the most common deployment procedures to set up a replica set. These involve either converting a standalone server into a replica set or setting up a replica set from scratch.

Converting a standalone server into a replica set

To convert a standalone server into a replica set, we first need to cleanly shut down the mongo server:

```
> use admin
> db.shutdownServer()
```

Then, we start the server with the `--replSet` configuration option via the command line (which we will do here), or by using a configuration file, as we will explain in the next section:

1. First, we connect (via the mongo shell) to the new replica set enabled instance, as follows:

   ```
   > rs.initiate()
   ```

2. Now, we have the first server of our replica set. We can add the other servers (which must have also been started with `--replSet`) by using the mongo shell, as follows:

   ```
   > rs.add("<hostname><:port>")
   ```

Double-check the replica set configuration by using `rs.conf()`. Verify the replica set status by using `rs.status()`.

Creating a replica set

Starting a MongoDB server as a part of a replica set is as easy as setting it in the configuration via the command line:

```
> mongod --replSet "xmr_cluster"
```

This is fine for development purposes. For production environments, it's recommended that we use a configuration file instead:

```
> mongod --config <path-to-config>
```

Here, the `<path-to-config>` can be as follows:

```
/etc/mongod.conf
```

This configuration file has to be in a YAML format.

 YAML does not support tabs. Convert tabs to spaces by using your editor of choice.

A simple configuration file sample is as follows:

```
systemLog:
   destination: file
   path: "/var/log/mongodb/mongod.log"
   logAppend: true
storage:
   journal:
       enabled: true
processManagement:
   fork: true
net:
   bindIp: 127.0.0.1
   port: 27017
replication:
   oplogSizeMB: <int>
   replSetName: <string>
```

Root-level options define the sections that leaf-level options apply to by nesting. Regarding replication, the mandatory options are `oplogSizeMB` (the oplog size for the member, in MB) and `replSetName` (the replica set name, such as `xmr_cluster`).

We can also set the following on the same level as `replSetName`:

```
secondaryIndexPrefetch: <string>
```

This is only available for the MMAPv1 storage engine, and it refers to the indexes on secondaries that will get loaded into memory before applying operations from the oplog.

It defaults to `all`, and the available options are `none` and `_id_only`, in order to load no indexes into memory and only load the default index that was created on `_id` fields:

```
enableMajorityReadConcern: <boolean>
```

This is the configuration setting for enabling the read preference of `majority` for this member.

After we have started all of the replica set processes on different nodes, we log in to one of the nodes using `mongo` from the command line with the appropriate `host:port`. Then, we need to initiate the cluster from one member.

We can use configuration files, as follows:

```
> rs.initiate()
```

Or, we can pass in the configurations as a document parameter, as follows:

```
> rs.initiate( {
  _id : "xmr_cluster",
  members: [ { _id : 0, host : "host:port" } ]
})
```

We can verify that the cluster was initiated by using `rs.conf()` in the shell.

Following that, we add each other member to our replica set by using the `host:port` that we defined in our networking setup:

```
> rs.add("host2:port2")
> rs.add("host3:port3")
```

The minimum number of servers that we must use for an HA replica set is 3. We could replace one of the servers with an arbiter, but this is not recommended. Once we have added all of the servers and have waited a bit, we can check the status of our cluster by using `rs.status()`. By default, the oplog will be 5% of the free disk space. If we want to define it when we create our replica set, we can do so by passing the command-line parameter `--oplogSizeMB` or `replication.oplogSizeMB` in our configuration file. An oplog size cannot be more than 50 GB.

Read preference

By default, all writes and reads go/come from the primary server. Secondary servers replicate data, but are not used for querying.

In some cases, it may be beneficial to change this and start to take reads from secondaries.

The MongoDB official drivers support five levels of read preference:

Read Preference Mode	Description
primary	This is the default mode, where reads come from the primary server of the replica set.
primaryPreferred	With this mode, applications will read from the primary, unless it is unavailable, in which case reads will come from secondary members.
secondary	Reads come exclusively from secondary servers.
secondaryPreferred	With this mode, applications will read from secondary members, unless they are unavailable, in which case reads will come from the primary member.
nearest	Applications will read from the member of the replica set that is nearest in terms of network latency, not taking into account the member's type.

Using any read preference other than primary can be beneficial for asynchronous operations that are not extremely time-sensitive. For example, reporting servers can take reads from secondaries instead of the primary, as we may be fine with a small delay in our aggregation data, with the benefit of incurring more read load on our primary server.

Geographically distributed applications will also benefit from reading from secondaries, as these will have significantly lower latency. Although it's probably counter-intuitive, just changing the read preference from primary to secondary will not significantly increase the total read capacity of our cluster. This is because all of the members of our cluster are taking the same write load from clients' writes, and replication for the primary and secondaries, respectively.

More importantly, however, reading from a secondary may return stale data, which has to be dealt with at the application level. Reading from different secondaries that may have variable replication lag (compared to our primary writes) may result in reading documents out of their insertion order (**non-monotonic reads**).

With all of the preceding caveats, it is still a good idea to test reading from secondaries if our application design supports it. An additional configuration option that can help us to avoid reading stale data is `maxStalenessSeconds`.

Based on a coarse estimation from each secondary as to how far behind the primary it is, we can set this to a value of 90 (seconds) or more to avoid reading stale data. Given that secondaries know how far behind they are from the primary (but don't accurately or aggressively estimate it), this should be treated as an approximation, rather than something we base our design o.

Write concern

By default, the write operations in MongoDB replica sets will be acknowledged once the write has been acknowledged by the primary server. If we want to change this behavior, we can do so in two different ways:

- We can request a different write concern per operation, in cases where we want to make sure that a write has propagated to multiple members of our replica set before marking it as complete, as follows:

```
> db.mongo_books.insert(
  { name: "Mastering MongoDB", isbn: "1001" },
  { writeConcern: { w: 2, wtimeout: 5000 } }
)
```

  In the preceding example, we are waiting for the write to be confirmed by two servers (the primary, plus any one of the secondaries). We are also setting a timeout of `5000` milliseconds to avoid our write from blocking in cases where the network is slow or we just don't have enough servers to acknowledge the request.

- We can also change the default write concern across the entire replica set, as follows:

```
> cfg = rs.conf()
> cfg.settings.getLastErrorDefaults = { w: "majority", wtimeout:
5000 }
> rs.reconfig(cfg)
```

  Here, we set the write concern to `majority` with a timeout of 5 seconds. The write concern `majority` makes sure that our writes will propagate to at least $n/2+1$ servers, where n is the number of our replica set members.

The write concern `majority` is useful if we have a read preference of `majority` as well, as it ensures that every write with `w:` `"majority"` will also be visible with the same read preference. If we set `w>1`, it's useful to also set `wtimeout:` `<milliseconds>` with it. `wtimeout` will return from our write operation once the timeout has been reached, thus not blocking our client for an indefinite period of time. It's recommended to set `j:` `true`, as well. `j:` `true` will wait for our write operation to be written to the journal before acknowledging it. `w>1`, along with `j:` `true`, will wait for the number of servers that we have specified to write to the journal before acknowledgement.

Custom write concerns

We can also identify our replica set members with different tags (that is, `reporting`, East Coast Servers, and HQ servers) and specify a custom write concern per operation, as follows:

1. Use the usual procedure for connecting to the primary via the mongo shell, as follows:

    ```
    > conf = rs.conf()
    > conf.members[0].tags = { "location": "UK", "use": "production",
    "location_uk":"true"   }
    > conf.members[1].tags = { "location": "UK", "use": "reporting",
    "location_uk":"true"   }
    > conf.members[2].tags = { "location": "Ireland", "use":
    "production"   }
    ```

2. We can now set a custom write concern, as follows:

    ```
    > conf.settings = { getLastErrorModes: { UKWrites : {
    "location_uk": 2} } }
    ```

3. After applying this, we use the `reconfig` command:

    ```
    > rs.reconfig(conf)
    ```

4. We can now start by setting `writeConcern` in our writes, as follows:

```
> db.mongo_books.insert({<our insert object>}, { writeConcern: { w:
"UKWrites" } })
```

This means that our write will only be acknowledged if the `UKWrites` write concern is satisfied, which, in turn, will be satisfied by at least two servers, with the tag `location_uk` verifying it. Since we only have two servers located in the UK, we can make sure that with this custom write concern, we have written our data to all of our UK-based servers.

Priority settings for replica set members

MongoDB allows us to set different priority levels for each member. This allows for some interesting applications and topologies to be implemented.

To change the priority after we have set up our cluster, we have to connect to our primary using the mongo shell and get the configuration object (in this case, `cfg`):

```
> cfg = rs.conf()
```

Then, we can change the `members` sub-document `priority` attribute to the value of our choice:

```
> cfg.members[0].priority = 0.778
> cfg.members[1].priority = 999.9999
```

The default `priority` is 1 for every member. The priority can be set from 0 (never become a primary) to 1000, in floating-point precision.

Higher priority members will be the first to call an election when the primary steps down, and are also the most likely to win the election.

Custom priorities should be configured with consideration of the different network partitions. Setting priorities the wrong way may lead to elections not being able to elect a primary, thus stopping all writes to our MongoDB replica set.

If we want to prevent a secondary from becoming a primary, we can set its priority to 0, as we will explain in the following section.

Zero priority replica set members

In some cases (for example, if we have multiple data centers), we will want some of the members to never be able to become a primary server.

In a scenario with multiple data center replications, we may have our primary data center with one primary and one secondary based in the UK, and a secondary server located in Russia. In this case, we don't want our Russia-based server to become primary, as it would incur latency on our application servers based in the UK. In this case, we will set up our Russia-based server with `priority` as 0.

Replica set members with `priority` as 0 also can't trigger elections. In all other aspects, they are identical to every other member in the replica set. To change the `priority` of a replica set member, we must first get the current replica set configuration by connecting (via the mongo shell) to the primary server:

```
> cfg = rs.conf()
```

This will provide the config document that contains the configuration for every member in our replica set. In the `members` sub-document, we can find the `priority` attribute, which we have to set to 0:

```
> cfg.members[2].priority = 0
```

Finally, we need to reconfigure the replica set with the updated configuration:

```
rs.reconfig(cfg)
```

Make sure that you have the same version of MongoDB running in every node, otherwise there may be unexpected behavior. Avoid reconfiguring the replica set cluster during high volume periods. Reconfiguring a replica set may force an election for a new primary, which will close all active connections, and may lead to a downtime of 10-30 seconds. Try to identify the lowest traffic time window to run maintenance operations like reconfiguration, and always have a recovery plan in case something goes wrong.

Hidden replica set members

Hidden replica set members are used for special tasks. They are invisible to clients, will not show up in the `db.isMaster()` mongo shell command and similar administrative commands, and, for all purposes, will not be taken into account by clients (that is, read preference options).

They can vote for elections, but will never become a primary server. A hidden replica set member will only sync up to the primary server, and doesn't take reads from the clients. As such, it has the same write load as the primary server (for replication purposes), but no read load on its own.

Due to the previously mentioned characteristics, reporting is the most common application of a hidden member. We can connect directly to this member and use it as the data source of truth for OLAP.

To set up a hidden replica set member, we follow a similar procedure to `priority` to 0. After we have connected to our primary via the mongo shell, we get the configuration object, identify the member in the members sub-document that corresponds to the member we want to set as `hidden`, and subsequently set its `priority` to 0 and its `hidden` attribute to `true`. Finally, we have to apply the new configuration by calling `rs.reconfig(config_object)` with `config_object` that we used as a parameter:

```
> cfg = rs.conf()
> cfg.members[0].priority = 0
> cfg.members[0].hidden = true
> rs.reconfig(cfg)
```

A `hidden` replica set member can also be used for backup purposes. However, as you will see in the next section, we may want to use other options, either at the physical level or to replicate data at the logical level. In those cases, consider using a delayed replica set instead.

Delayed replica set members

In many cases, we will want to have a node that holds a copy of our data at an earlier point in time. This helps to recover from a big subset of human errors, like accidentally dropping a collection, or an upgrade going horrendously wrong.

A delayed replica set member has to be `priority` = 0 and `hidden` = `true`. A delayed replica set member can vote for elections, but will never be visible to clients (`hidden` = `true`) and will never become a primary (`priority` = 0).

An example is as follows:

```
> cfg = rs.conf()
> cfg.members[0].priority = 0
> cfg.members[0].hidden = true
> cfg.members[0].slaveDelay = 7200
> rs.reconfig(cfg)
```

This will set the `members[0]` to a delay of 2 hours. Two important factors for deciding the delta time period between the primary and delayed secondary server are as follows:

- Enough oplog size in the primary
- Enough time for the maintenance to finish before the delayed member starts picking up data

The following table shows the delay of the replica set in hours:

Maintenance window, in hours	Delay	Oplog size on primary, in hours
0.5	[0.5,5)	5

Production considerations

Deploy each `mongod` instance on a separate physical host. If you are using VMs, make sure that they map to different underlying physical hosts. Use the `bind_ip` option to make sure that your server maps to a specific network interface and port address.

Use firewalls to block access to any other port and/or only allow access between application servers and MongoDB servers. Even better, set up a VPN so that your servers communicate with each other in a secure, encrypted fashion.

Connecting to a replica set

Connecting to a replica set is not fundamentally different from connecting to a single server. In this section, we will show some examples that use the official `mongo-ruby-driver`. We will use the following steps for the replica set, as follows:

1. First, we need to set our `host` and `options` objects:

```
client_host = ['hostname:port']
client_options = {
 database: 'signals',
 replica_set: 'xmr_btc'
}
```

In the preceding example, we are getting ready to connect to `hostname:port`, in the database signals in `replica_set xmr_btc`.

2. Calling the initializer on `Mongo::Client` will now return a `client` object that contains a connection to our replica set and database:

```
client = Mongo::Client.new(client_host, client_options)
```

The `client` object has the same options it has when connecting to a single server.

 MongoDB uses auto-discovery after connecting to our `client_host` to identify the other members of our replica set, regardless of whether they are the primary or secondaries. The `client` object should be used as a singleton, created once and reused across our code base.

3. Having a singleton `client` object is a rule that can be overridden in some cases. We should create different `client` objects if we have different classes of connections to our replica set.

An example would be having a `client` object for most operations, and then another `client` object for operations that are fine with only reading from secondaries:

```
client_reporting = client.with(:read => { :mode => :secondary })
```

4. This Ruby MongoDB `client` command will return a copy of the `MongoDB:Client` object with a read preference secondary that can be used, for example, for reporting purposes.

Some of the most useful options that we can use in our `client_options` initialization object are as follows:

Option	Description	Type	Default
replica_set	As used in our example: the replica set name.	String	None
write	The write concern options as a hash object; the available options are w, wtimeout, j, and fsync. That is, to specify writes to two servers, with journaling, flushing to disk (fsync) true, and a timeout of 1 second: { write: { w: 2, j: true, wtimeout: 1000, fsync: true } }	Hash	{ w: 1 }

read	The read preference mode as a hash. Available options are `mode` and `tag_sets`. That is, to limit reads from secondary servers that have tag `UKWrites`:
	`{ read:`
	`  { mode: :secondary,`
	`    tag_sets: [ "UKWrites" ]`
	`  }`
	`}`
		Hash	`{ mode: primary }`

user	The name of the user to authenticate with.	String	None
password	The password of the user to authenticate with.	String	None
connect	Using `:direct`, we can force treat a replica set member as a standalone server, bypassing auto-discovery. Other options include: `:direct`, `:replica_set`, and `:sharded`.	Symbol	None
heartbeat_frequency	How often replica set members will communicate to check whether they are all alive.	Float	`10`
database	Database connection.	String	`admin`

Similar to connecting to a standalone server, there are also options for SSL and authentication that are used in the same way.

We can also configure the connection pool by setting the following code:

```
min_pool_size(defaults to 1 connection),
max_pool_size(defaults to 5),
wait_queue_timeout(defaults to 1 in seconds).
```

The MongoDB driver will try to reuse existing connections, if available, or it will open a new connection. Once the pool limit has been reached, the driver will block, waiting for a connection to be released to use it.

Replica set administration

The administration of a replica set can be significantly more complex than what is needed for single-server deployments. In this section, instead of trying to exhaustively cover all of the different cases, we will focus on some of the most common administrative tasks that we will have to perform, and how to do them.

How to perform maintenance on replica sets

If we have some maintenance tasks that we have to perform in every member in a replica set, we always start with the secondaries. We perform maintenance by performing the following steps:

1. First, we connect to one of the secondaries via the mongo shell. Then, we stop that secondary:

   ```
   > use admin
   > db.shutdownServer()
   ```

2. Then, using the same user that was connected to the mongo shell in the previous step, we restart the mongo server as a standalone server in a different port:

   ```
   > mongod --port 95658 --dbpath <wherever our mongoDB data resides
   in this host>
   ```

3. The next step is to connect to this `mongod` server (which is using `dbpath`):

   ```
   > mongo --port 37017
   ```

4. At this point, we can safely perform all of the administrative tasks on our standalone server without affecting our replica set operations. When we are done, we shut down the standalone server in the same way that we did in the first step.

5. We can then restart our server in the replica set by using the command line or the configuration script that we normally use. The final step is to verify that everything works fine by connecting to the replica set server and getting its replica set `status`:

   ```
   > rs.status()
   ```

The server should initially be in `state: RECOVERING`, and, once it has caught up with the secondary, it should be back in `state: SECONDARY`, like it was before starting the maintenance.

We will repeat the same process for every secondary server. In the end, we have to perform maintenance on the primary. The only difference in the process for the primary is that we will start by stepping down our primary server into a secondary server before every other step:

```
> rs.stepDown(600)
```

By using the above argument, we prevent our secondary from being elected as a master for 10 minutes. This should be enough time to shut down the server and continue with our maintenance, like we did with the secondaries.

Re-syncing a member of a replica set

Secondaries sync up with the primary by replaying the contents of the oplog. If our oplog is not large enough, or if we encounter network issues (partitioning, an underperforming network, or just an outage of the secondary server) for a period of time larger than the oplog, then MongoDB cannot use the oplog to catch up to the primary anymore.

At this point, we have two options:

- The more straightforward option is to delete our `dbpath` directory and restart the `mongod` process. In this case, MongoDB will start an initial sync from scratch. This option has the downside of putting a strain on our replica set, and our network, as well.
- The more complicated (from an operational standpoint) option is to copy data files from another well-behaving member of the replica set. This goes back to the contents of `Chapter 8`, *Monitoring, Backup, and Security*. The important thing to keep in mind is that a simple file copy will probably not suffice, as data files will have changed from the time that we started copying to the time that the copying ended.

Thus, we need to be able to take a snapshot copy of the filesystem under our `data` directory.

Another point of consideration is that by the time we start our secondary server with the newly copied files, our MongoDB secondary server will try to sync up to the primary using the oplog again. So, if our oplog has fallen so far behind the primary that it can't find the entry on our primary server, this method will fail, too.

 Keep a sufficiently sized oplog. Don't let data grow out of hand in any replica set member. Design, test, and deploy sharding early on.

Changing the oplog's size

Hand in hand with the previous operational tip, we may need to rethink and resize our oplog as our data grows. Operations become more complicated and time-consuming as our data grows, and we need to adjust our oplog size to accommodate for it. The steps for changing the oplog's size are as follows:

1. The first step is to restart our MongoDB secondary server as a standalone server, an operation that was described in the *How to perform maintenance on replica sets* section.

2. We then make a backup of our existing oplog:

   ```
   > mongodump --db local --collection 'oplog.rs' --port 37017
   ```

3. We keep a copy of this data, just in case. We then connect to our standalone database:

   ```
   > use local
   > db = db.getSiblingDB('local')
   > db.temp.drop()
   ```

   Up until now, we have connected to the `local` database and deleted the `temp` collection, just in case it had any leftover documents.

4. The next step is to get the last entry of our current oplog and save it in the `temp` collection:

   ```
   > db.temp.save( db.oplog.rs.find( { }, { ts: 1, h: 1 } ).sort(
   {$natural : -1} ).limit(1).next() )
   ```

6. This entry will be used when we restart our secondary server, in order to track where it has reached in the oplog replication:

```
> db = db.getSiblingDB('local')
> db.oplog.rs.drop()
```

7. Now, we delete our existing oplog, and in the next step, we will create a new oplog of 4 GB in `size`:

```
> db.runCommand( { create: "oplog.rs", capped: true, size: (4 *
1024 * 1024 * 1024) } )
```

8. The next step is to copy the one entry from our `temp` collection back to our oplog:

```
> db.oplog.rs.save( db.temp.findOne() )
```

9. Finally, we cleanly shut down our server from the `admin` database, using the `db.shutdownServer()` command, and we restart our secondary as a member of the replica set.

10. We repeat this process for all secondary servers, and as a last step, we repeat the procedure for our primary member, which is done after we step the primary down by using the following command:

```
> rs.stepDown(600)
```

Reconfiguring a replica set when we have lost the majority of our servers

This is only intended as an interim solution and a last resort when we are faced with downtime and disrupted cluster operations. When we lose the majority of our servers and we still have enough servers to start a replica set (maybe including some quickly spawned arbiters), we can force a reconfiguration with only the surviving members.

First, we get the replica set configuration document:

```
> cfg = rs.conf()
```

Using `printjson(cfg)`, we identify the members that are still operational. Let's say that these are 1, 2, and 3:

```
> cfg.members = [cfg.members[1] , cfg.members[2] , cfg.members[3]]
> rs.reconfig(cfg, {force : true})
```

By using `force : true`, we are forcing this reconfiguration to happen. Of course, we need to have at least three surviving members in our replica set for this to work.

> It's important to remove the failing servers as soon as possible, by killing the processes and/or taking them out of the network, avoid unintended consequences; these servers may believe that they are still a part of a cluster that doesn't acknowledge them anymore.

Chained replication

Replication in MongoDB usually happens from the primary to the secondaries. In some cases, we may want to replicate from another secondary, instead of the primary. Chained replication helps to alleviate the primary from read load, but at the same time, it increases the average replication lag for the secondary that chooses to replicate from a secondary. This makes sense, as replication has to go from the primary to the secondary (1), and then from this server to another secondary (2).

Chained replication can be enabled (and disabled, respectively) with the following `cfg` command:

```
> cfg.settings.chainingAllowed = true
```

In cases where `printjson(cfg)` doesn't reveal a settings sub-document, we need to create an empty one first:

```
> cfg.settings = { }
```

> If there is already a `settings` document, the preceding command will result in deleting its settings, leading to potential data loss.

Cloud options for a replica set

We can set up and operate a replica set from our own servers, but we can reduce our operational overhead by using a **Database as a Service** (**DBaaS**) provider to do so. The two most widely used MongoDB cloud providers are mLab (formerly MongoLab) and MongoDB Atlas, the native offering from MongoDB, Inc.

In this section, we will go over these options and how they fare in comparison to using our own hardware and data centers.

mLab

mLab is one of the most popular cloud DBaaS providers for MongoDB. It has been offered since 2011 and it is considered a stable and mature provider.

After signing up, we can easily deploy a replica set cluster in a set of cloud servers without any operational overhead. Configuration options include AWS, Microsoft Azure, or Google Cloud as the underlying server provider.

There are multiple sizing options for the latest MongoDB version. There was no support at the time of writing this book for the MMAPv1 storage engine. There are multiple regions for each provider (US, Europe, and Asia). Most notably, the regions that are missing are the AWS China, AWS US Gov, and AWS Germany regions.

MongoDB Atlas

MongoDB Atlas is a newer offering from MongoDB, Inc., and was launched in summer 2016. Similar to mLab, it offers the deployment of single-server, replica set, or sharded clusters, through a web interface.

It offers the latest MongoDB version. The only storage option is WiredTiger. There are multiple regions for each provider (US, Europe, and Asia).

Most notably, the regions that are missing are the AWS China and AWS US Gov regions.

 In both (and most of the other) providers, we can't have a cross-region replica set. This is prohibitive if we want to deploy a truly global service, serving users from multiple data centers around the globe, with our MongoDB servers being as close to the application servers as possible.

The running costs for cloud-hosted services can be significantly higher than setting them up in our own servers. What we gain in convenience and time to market may have to be paid in operational costs.

Replica set limitations

A replica set is great when we understand why we need it and what it cannot do. The different limitations for a replica set are as follows:

- It will not scale horizontally; we need sharding for it
- We will introduce replication issues if our network is flaky
- We will make debugging issues more complex if we use secondaries for reads, and these have fallen behind our primary server

On the flip side, as we explained in previous sections in this chapter, a replica set can be a great choice for replication, data redundancy, conforming with data privacy, backups, and even recovery from errors caused by humans, or otherwise.

Summary

In this chapter, we discussed replica sets and how to administer them. Starting with an architectural overview of replica sets and replica set internals involving elections, we dove into setting up and configuring a replica set.

You learned how to perform various administrative tasks with replica sets, and you learned about the main options for outsourcing operations to a cloud DBaaS provider. Finally, we identified some of the limitations that replica sets in MongoDB currently have.

In the next chapter, we will move on to one of the most interesting concepts in MongoDB (which helps it to achieve horizontal scaling): sharding.

13
Sharding

Sharding is the ability to horizontally scale out our database by partitioning our datasets across different servers—the shards. It has been a feature of MongoDB since version 1.6 was released in August, 2010. Foursquare and Bitly are two of MongoDB's most famous early customers, and have used the sharding feature from its inception all the way to its general release.

In this chapter, we will learn the following topics:

- How to design a sharding cluster and how to make the single most important decision concerning its use—choosing the shard key
- Different sharding techniques and how to monitor and administrate sharded clusters
- The `mongos` router and how it is used to route our queries across different shards
- How we can recover from errors in our shard

Why do we use sharding?

In database systems and computing systems in general, we have two ways to improve performance. The first one is to simply replace our servers with more powerful ones, keeping the same network topology and systems architecture. This is called **vertical scaling**.

An advantage of vertical scaling is that it is simple, from an operational standpoint, especially with cloud providers such as Amazon making it a matter of a few clicks to replace an **m2.medium** with an **m2.extralarge** server instance. Another advantage is that we don't need to make any code changes, and so there is little to no risk of something going catastrophically wrong.

The main disadvantage of vertical scaling is that there is a limit to it; we can only get servers that are as powerful as those that our cloud provider can give to us.

A related disadvantage is that getting more powerful servers generally comes with an increase in cost that is not linear but exponential. So, even if our cloud provider offers more powerful instances, we will hit the cost effectiveness barrier before we hit the limit of our department's credit card.

The second way to improve performance is by using the same servers with the same capacity and increase their number. This is called **horizontal scaling**.

Horizontal scaling offers the advantage of theoretically being able to scale exponentially while remaining practical enough for real-world applications. The main disadvantage is that it can be operationally more complex and requires code changes and the careful design of the system upfront. Horizontal scaling is also more complex when it comes to the system because it requires communication between the different servers over network links that are not as reliable as inter-process communication on a single server. The following diagram shows the difference between horizontal and vertical scaling:

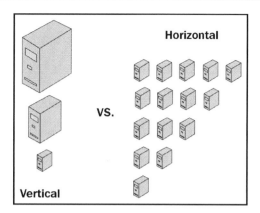

To understand scaling, it's important to understand the limitations of single-server systems. A server is typically bound by one or more of the following characteristics:

- **CPU**: A CPU-bound system is one that is limited by our CPU's speed. A task such as the multiplication of matrices that can fit in RAM will be CPU bound because there is a specific number of steps that have to be performed in the CPU without any disk or memory access needed for the task to complete. In this case, CPU usage is the metric that we need to keep track of.

- **I/O**: Input-output bound systems are similarly limited by the speed of our storage system (HDD or SSD). A task such as reading large files from a disk to load into memory will be I/O bound as there is little to do in terms of CPU processing; the great majority of the time is spent reading the files from the disk. The important metrics to keep track of are all the metrics related to disk access, the reads per second, and the writes per second, compared to the practical limit of our storage system.

- **Memory and cache**: Memory-bound and cache-bound systems are restricted by the amount of available RAM memory and/or the cache size that we have assigned to them. A task that multiplies matrices larger than our RAM size will be memory bound, as it will need to page in/out data from the disk to perform the multiplication. The important metric to keep track of is the memory used. This may be misleading in MongoDB MMAPv1, as the storage engine will allocate as much memory as possible through the filesystem cache.

In the WiredTiger storage engine, on the other hand, if we don't allocate enough memory for the core MongoDB process, out-of-memory errors may kill it, and this is something that we want to avoid at all costs.

Monitoring memory usage has to be done both directly through the operating system and indirectly by keeping a track of page in/out data. An increasing memory paging number is often an indication that we are running short of memory and the operating system is using virtual address space to keep up.

 MongoDB, being a database system, is generally memory and I/O bound. Investing in SSD and more memory for our nodes is almost always a good investment. Most systems are a combination of one or more of the preceding limitations. Once we add more memory, our system may become CPU bound, as complex operations are almost always a combination of CPU, I/O, and memory usage.

MongoDB's sharding is simple enough to set up and operate, and this has contributed to its huge success over the years as it provides the advantages of horizontal scaling without requiring a large commitment of engineering and operations resources.

That being said, it's really important to get sharding right from the beginning, as it is extremely difficult from an operational standpoint to change the configuration once it has been set up. Sharding should not be an afterthought, but rather a key architectural design decision from an early point in the design process.

Architectural overview

A sharded cluster is comprised of the following elements:

- Two or more shards. Each shard must be a replica set.
- One or more query routers (`mongos`). A `mongos` provides an interface between our application and the database.
- A replica set of config servers. Config servers store metadata and configuration settings for the entire cluster.

The relationships between these elements is shown in the following diagram:

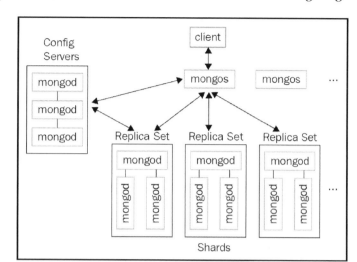

 As of MongoDB 3.6, shards must be implemented as replica sets.

Development, continuous deployment, and staging environments

In preproduction environments, it may be overkill to use the full set of servers. For efficiency reasons, we may opt to use a more simplified architecture.

The simplest possible configuration that we can deploy for sharding is the following:

- One mongos router
- One sharded replica set with one MongoDB server and two arbiters
- One replica set of config servers with one MongoDB server and two arbiters

This should be strictly used for development and testing as this architecture defies most of the advantages that a replica set provides, such as high availability, scalability, and replication of data.

Staging is strongly recommended to mirror our production environment in terms of its servers, configuration, and (if possible) dataset requirements too, in order to avoid surprises at deployment time.

Planning ahead with sharding

As we will see in the next sections, sharding is complicated and expensive, operation wise. It is important to plan ahead and make sure that we start the sharding process long before we hit our system's limits.

Some rough guidelines on when you need to start sharding are as follows:

- When you have a CPU utilization of less than 70% on average
- When I/O (and especially write) capacity is less than 80%
- When memory utilization is less than 70% on average

As sharding helps with write performance, it's important to keep an eye on our I/O write capacity and the requirements of our application.

Don't wait until the last minute to start sharding in an already busy-up-to-the-neck MongoDB system, as it can have unintended consequences.

Sharding setup

Sharding is performed at the collection level. We can have collections that we don't want or need to shard for several reasons. We can leave these collections unsharded.

These collections will be stored in the primary shard. The primary shard is different for each database in MongoDB. The primary shard is automatically selected by MongoDB when we create a new database in a sharded environment. MongoDB will pick the shard that has the least data stored at the moment of creation.

If we want to change the primary shard at any other point, we can issue the following command:

```
> db.runCommand( { movePrimary : "mongo_books", to : "UK_based" } )
```

With this, we move the database named mongo_books to the shard named UK_based.

Choosing the shard key

Choosing our shard key is the most important decision we need to make: once we shard our data and deploy our cluster, it becomes very difficult to change the shard key. First, we will go through the process of changing the shard key.

Changing the shard key

There is no command or simple procedure to change the shard key in MongoDB. The only way to change the shard key involves backing up and restoring all of our data, something that may range from being extremely difficult to impossible in high-load production environments.

The following are the steps that we need to go through in order to change the shard key:

1. Export all data from MongoDB
2. Drop the original sharded collection
3. Configure sharding with the new key
4. Presplit the new shard key range
5. Restore our data back into MongoDB

Of these steps, step 4 is the one that needs further explanation.

MongoDB uses chunks to split data in a sharded collection. If we bootstrap a MongoDB sharded cluster from scratch, chunks will be calculated automatically by MongoDB. MongoDB will then distribute the chunks across different shards to ensure that there are an equal number of chunks in each shard.

The only time when we cannot really do this is when we want to load data into a newly sharded collection.

The reasons for this are threefold:

- MongoDB creates splits only after an `insert` operation.
- Chunk migration will copy all of the data in that chunk from one shard to another.
- The `floor(n/2)` chunk migrations can happen at any given time, where n is the number of shards we have. Even with three shards, this is only a `floor(1.5)=1` chunk migration at a time.

These three limitations mean that letting MongoDB figure it out on its own will definitely take much longer, and may result in an eventual failure. This is why we want to presplit our data and give MongoDB some guidance on where our chunks should go.

In our example of the `mongo_books` database and the `books` collection, this would be as follows:

```
> db.runCommand( { split : "mongo_books.books", middle : { id : 50 } } )
```

The `middle` command parameter will split our key space in documents that have `id` less than or equal to `50` and documents that have `id` greater than `50`. There is no need for a document to exist in our collection with `id` that is equal to `50` as this will only serve as the guidance value for our partitions.

In this example, we chose `50`, as we assume that our keys follow a uniform distribution (that is, there is the same count of keys for each value) in the range of values from `0` to `100`.

> We should aim to create at least 20-30 chunks to grant MongoDB flexibility in potential migrations. We can also use `bounds` and `find` instead of `middle` if we want to manually define the partition key, but both parameters need data to exist in our collection before applying them.

Choosing the correct shard key

After the previous section, it's now self-evident that we need to take the choice of our shard key into consideration as it is a decision that we have to stick with.

A great shard key has three characteristics:

- High cardinality
- Low frequency
- Nonmonotonic changes in value

We will go over the definitions of these three properties first to understand what they mean:

- **High cardinality**: It means that the shard key must have as many distinct values as possible. A Boolean can take only the values of `true`/`false`, and so it is a bad shard key choice. A 64-bit long value field that can take any value from $-(2^{63})$ to $2^{63}-1$ is a good shard key choice, in terms of cardinality.

- **Low frequency**: It directly relates to the argument about high cardinality. A low-frequency shard key will have a distribution of values as close to a perfectly random/uniform distribution. Using the example of our 64-bit long value, it is of little use to us if we have a field that can take values ranging from $-(2^{63})$ to $2^{63}-1$ if we end up observing the values of zero and one all the time. In fact, it is as bad as using a Boolean field, which can also take only two values. If we have a shard key with high-frequency values, we will end up with chunks that are indivisible. These chunks cannot be further divided and will grow in size, negatively affecting the performance of the shard that contains them.

- **Nonmonotonically changing values**: It mean that our shard key should not be, for example, an integer that always increases with every new insert. If we choose a monotonically increasing value as our shard key, this will result in all writes ending up in the last of all of our shards, limiting our write performance.

> If we want to use a monotonically changing value as the shard key, we should consider using hash-based sharding.

In the next section, we will describe different sharding strategies, including their advantages and disadvantages.

Range-based sharding

The default and most widely used sharding strategy is range-based sharding. This strategy will split our collection's data into chunks, grouping documents with nearby values in the same shard.

For our example database and collection, `mongo_books` and `books` respectively, we have the following:

```
> sh.shardCollection("mongo_books.books", { id: 1 } )
```

This creates a range-based shard key on `id` with an ascending direction. The direction of our shard key will determine which documents will end up in the first shard and which ones in the subsequent ones.

This is a good strategy if we plan to have range-based queries, as these will be directed to the shard that holds the result set instead of having to query all shards.

Hash-based sharding

If we don't have a shard key (or can't create one) that achieves the three goals mentioned previously, we can use the alternative strategy of using hash-based sharding. In this case, we are trading data distribution with query isolation.

Hash-based sharding will take the values of our shard key and hash them in a way that guarantees close to uniform distribution. This way, we can be sure that our data will be evenly distributed across the shards. The downside is that only exact match queries will get routed to the exact shard that holds the value. Any range query will have to go out and fetch data from all the shards.

For our example database and collection (`mongo_books` and `books` respectively), we have the following:

```
> sh.shardCollection("mongo_books.books", { id: "hashed" } )
```

Similar to the preceding example, we are now using the `id` field as our hashed shard key.

 Suppose we use fields with float values for hash-based sharding. Then we will end up with collisions if the precision of our floats is more than 2^53. These fields should be avoided where possible.

Coming up with our own key

Range-based sharding does not need to be confined to a single key. In fact, in most cases, we would like to combine multiple keys to achieve high cardinality and low frequency.

A common pattern is to combine a low-cardinality first part (but still with a number of distinct values more than two times the number of shards that we have) with a high-cardinality key as its second field. This achieves both read and write distribution from the first part of the sharding key and then cardinality and read-locality from the second part.

On the other hand, if we don't have range queries, then we can get away with using hash-based sharding on a primary key, as this will exactly target the shard and document that we are going after.

To make things more complicated, these considerations may change depending on our workload. A workload that consists almost exclusively (say 99.5%) of reads won't care about write distribution. We can use the built-in `_id` field as our shard key, and this will only add 0.5% load to the last shard. Our reads will still be distributed across shards. Unfortunately, in most cases, this is not simple.

Location-based data

Because of government regulations and the desire to have our data as close to our users as possible, there is often a constraint and need to limit data in a specific data center. By placing different shards at different data centers, we can satisfy this requirement.

 Every shard is essentially a replica set. We can connect to it as we would connect to a replica set for administrative and maintenance operations. We can query one shard's data directly, but the results will only be a subset of the full sharded result set.

Sharding administration and monitoring

Sharded MongoDB environments have some unique challenges and limitations compared to single-server or replica set deployments. In this section, we will explore how MongoDB balances our data across shards using chunks and how we can tweak them if we need to. Together, we will explore some of sharding's design limitations.

Balancing data – how to track and keep our data balanced

One of the advantages of sharding in MongoDB is that it is mostly transparent to the application and requires minimal administration and operational effort.

One of the core tasks that MongoDB needs to perform continuously is balancing data between shards. No matter whether we implement range-based or hash-based sharding, MongoDB will need to calculate bounds for the hashed field to be able to figure out which shard to direct every new document insert or update toward. As our data grows, these bounds may need to get readjusted to avoid having a hot shard that ends up with the majority of our data.

For the sake of this example, let's assume that there is a data type named `extra_tiny_int` with integer values from [-12, 12). If we enable sharding on this `extra_tiny_int` field, then the initial bounds of our data will be the whole range of values denoted by `$minKey: -12` and `$maxKey: 11`.

After we insert some initial data, MongoDB will generate chunks and recalculate the bounds of each chunk to try and balance our data.

By default, the initial number of chunks created by MongoDB is 2 × *number of shards.*

In our case of two shards and four initial chunks, the initial bounds will be calculated as follows:

Chunk1: [-12..-6)

Chunk2: [-6..0)

Chunk3: [0..6)

Chunk4: [6,12) where *'['* is inclusive and *')'* is not inclusive

The following diagram illustrates the preceding explanation:

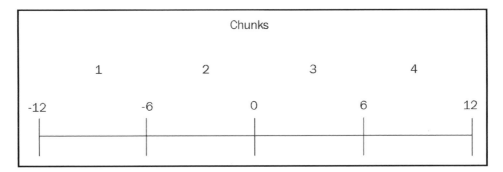

After we insert some data, our chunks will look as follows:

- *ShardA:*
    - *Chunk1: -12,-8,-7*
    - *Chunk2: -6*
- *ShardB:*
    - *Chunk3: 0, 2*
    - *Chunk4: 7,8,9,10,11,11,11,11*

The following diagram illustrates the preceding explanation:

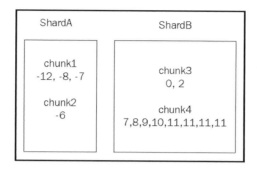

In this case, we observe that *chunk4* has more items than any other chunk. MongoDB will first split *chunk4* into two new chunks, attempting to keep the size of each chunk under a certain threshold (64 MB, by default).

Now, instead of *chunk4*, we have *chunk4A: 7,8,9,10* and *chunk4B: 11,11,11,11*.

The following diagram illustrates the preceding explanation:

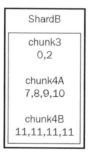

The new bounds of this are as follows:

- *chunk4A: [6,11)*
- *chunk4B: [11,12)*

Note that *chunk4B* can only hold one value. This is now an indivisible chunk—a chunk that cannot be broken down into smaller ones anymore—and will grow in size unbounded, causing potential performance issues down the line.

This clarifies why we need to use a high-cardinality field as our shard key and why something like a Boolean, which only has `true`/`false` values, is a bad choice for a shard key.

In our case, we now have two chunks in *ShardA* and three chunks in *ShardB*. Let's look at the following table:

Number of chunks	Migration threshold
≤19	2
20-79	4
≥80	8

We have not reached our migration threshold yet, since *3-2 = 1*.

The migration threshold is calculated as the number of chunks in the shard with the highest count of chunks and the number of chunks in the shard with the lowest count of chunks, as follows:

- *Shard1 -> 85 chunks*
- *Shard2 -> 86 chunks*
- *Shard3 -> 92 chunks*

In the preceding example, balancing will not occur until *Shard3* (or *Shard2*) reaches *93* chunks because the migration threshold is *8* for ≥80 chunks and the difference between *Shard1* and *Shard3* is still *7* chunks (*92-85*).

If we continue adding data in *chunk4A*, it will eventually be split into *chunk4A1* and *chunk4A2*.

Now we have four chunks in *ShardB* (*chunk3, chunk4A1, chunk4A2,* and *chunk4B*) and two chunks in *ShardA* (*chunk1* and *chunk2*).

The following diagram illustrates the relationships of the chunks to the shards:

The MongoDB balancer will now migrate one chunk from *ShardB* to *ShardA* as 4-2 = 2, reaching the migration threshold for fewer than *20* chunks. The balancer will adjust the boundaries between the two shards in order to be able to query more effectively (targeted queries). The following diagram illustrates the preceding explanation:

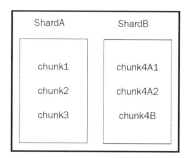

As you can see from the preceding diagram, MongoDB will try to split *>64* MB chunks in half in terms of size. The bounds between the two resulting chunks may be completely uneven if our data distribution is uneven to begin with. MongoDB can split chunks into smaller ones, but cannot merge them automatically. We need to manually merge chunks, a delicate and operationally expensive procedure.

Chunk administration

Most of the time, we should leave chunk administration to MongoDB. We should manually manage chunks at the start, upon receiving the initial load of data, when we change our configuration from a replica set to sharding.

Moving chunks

To move a chunk manually, we need to issue the following command after connecting to mongos and the admin database:

```
> db.runCommand( { moveChunk : 'mongo_books.books' ,
            find : {id: 50},
            to : 'shard1.packtdb.com' } )
```

Using the preceding command, we move the chunk containing the document with id: 50 (this has to be the shard key) from the books collection of the mongo_books database to the new shard named shard1.packtdb.com.

We can also more explicitly define the bounds of the chunk that we want to move. Now the syntax is as follows:

```
> db.runCommand( { moveChunk : 'mongo_books.books' ,
                bounds :[ { id : <minValue> } ,
    { id : <maxValue> } ],
                to : 'shard1.packtdb.com' } )
```

Here, `minValue` and `maxValue` are the values that we get from `db.printShardingStatus()`.

In the example used previously, for *chunk2*, `minValue` would be -6 and `maxValue` would be 0.

Do not use `find` in hash-based sharding. Use `bounds` instead.

Changing the default chunk size

To change the default chunk size, we need to connect to a `mongos` router and, consequently, to the `config` database.

Then we issue the following command to change our global `chunksize` to 16 MB:

```
> db.settings.save( { _id:"chunksize", value: 16 } )
```

The main reasoning behind changing `chunksize` comes from cases where the default `chunksize` of 64 MB can cause more I/O than our hardware can handle. In this case, defining a smaller `chunksize` will result in more frequent but less data-intensive migrations.

Changing the default chunk size has the following drawbacks:

- Creating more splits by defining a smaller chunk size cannot be undone automatically.
- Increasing the chunk size will not force any chunk migration; instead, chunks will grow through inserts and updates until they reach the new size.
- Lowering the chunk size may take quite some time to complete.

- Automatic splitting to comply with the new chunk size if it is lower will only happen upon an insert or update. We may have chunks that don't get any write operations, and thus will not be changed in size.

The chunk size can be 1 to 1024 MB.

Jumbo chunks

In rare cases, we may end up with jumbo chunks, chunks that are larger than the chunk size and cannot be split by MongoDB. We may also run into the same situation if the number of documents in our chunk exceeds the maximum document limit.

These chunks will have the `jumbo` flag enabled. Ideally, MongoDB will keep track of whether it can split the chunk, and, as soon as it can, it will get split; however, we may decide that we want to manually trigger the split before MongoDB does.

The way to do this is as follows:

1. Connect via shell to your `mongos` router and run the following:

   ```
   > sh.status(true)
   ```

2. Identify the chunk that has `jumbo` in its description using the following code:

   ```
   databases:
   ...
   mongo_books.books
   . . .
   chunks:
   ...
               shardB   2
               shardA   2
           { "id" : 7 } -->> { "id" : 9 } on : shardA Timestamp(2, 2)
       jumbo
   ```

3. Invoke `splitAt()` or `splitFind()` manually to split the chunk on the `books` collection of the `mongo_books` database at the `id` that is equal to 8 using the following code:

   ```
   > sh.splitAt( "mongo_books.books", { id: 8 })
   ```

    The `splitAt()` function will split based on the split point we define. The two new splits may or may not be balanced.

Alternatively, if we want to leave it to MongoDB to find where to split our chunk, we can use splitFind, as follows:

```
> sh.splitFind("mongo_books.books", {id: 7})
```

The splitFind phrase will try to find the chunk that the id: 7 query belongs to and automatically define the new bounds for the split chunks so that they are roughly balanced.

In both cases, MongoDB will try to split the chunk, and if successful, it will remove the jumbo flag from it.

4. If the preceding operation is unsuccessful, then, and only then, should we try stopping the balancer first, while also verifying the output and waiting for any pending migrations to finish first, as shown in the following code:

```
> sh.stopBalancer()
> sh.getBalancerState()
> use config
while( sh.isBalancerRunning() ) {
        print("waiting...");
        sleep(1000);
}
```

This should return false

5. Wait for any waiting... messages to stop printing, and then find the jumbo flagged chunk in the same way as before.

6. Then update the chunks collection in your config database of the mongos router, like this:

```
> db.getSiblingDB("config").chunks.update(
  { ns: "mongo_books.books", min: { id: 7 }, jumbo: true },
  { $unset: { jumbo: "" } }
)
```

The preceding command is a regular update() command, with the first argument being the find() part to find out which document to update and the second argument being the operation to apply to it ($unset: jumbo flag).

7. After all this is done, we re-enable the balancer, as follows:

```
> sh.setBalancerState(true)
```

8. Then, we connect to the `admin` database to flush the new configuration to all nodes, as follows:

```
> db.adminCommand({ flushRouterConfig: 1 } )
```

Always back up the `config` database before modifying any state manually.

Merging chunks

As we have seen previously, usually MongoDB will adjust the bounds for each chunk in our shard to make sure that our data is equally distributed. This may not work in some cases—especially when we define the chunks manually—if our data distribution is surprisingly unbalanced, or if we have many `delete` operations in our shard.

Having empty chunks will invoke unnecessary chunk migrations and give MongoDB a false impression of which chunk needs to be migrated. As we have explained before, the threshold for chunk migration is dependent on the number of chunks that each shard holds. Having empty chunks may or may not trigger the balancer when it's needed.

Chunk merging can only happen when at least one of the chunks is empty, and only between adjacent chunks.

To find empty chunks, we need to connect to the database that we want to inspect (in our case, `mongo_books`) and use `runCommand` with `dataSize` set as follows:

```
> use mongo_books
> db.runCommand({
    "dataSize": "mongo_books.books",
    "keyPattern": { id: 1 },
    "min": { "id": -6 },
    "max": { "id": 0 }
})
```

The `dataSize` phrase follows the `database_name.collection_name` pattern, whereas `keyPattern` is the shard key that we have defined for this collection.

The `min` and `max` values should be calculated by the chunks that we have in this collection. In our case, we have entered *chunkB's* details from the example earlier in this chapter.

If the bounds of our query (which, in our case, are the bounds of *chunkB*) return no documents, the result will resemble the following:

```
{ "size" : 0, "numObjects" : 0, "millis" : 0, "ok" : 1 }
```

Now that we know that *chunkB* has no data, we can merge it with another chunk (in our case, this could only be *chunkA*) like this:

```
> db.runCommand( { mergeChunks: "mongo_books.books",
            bounds: [ { "id": -12 },
                      { id: 0 } ]
        } )
```

On a success, this will return MongoDB's default `ok` status message, as shown in the following code:

```
{ "ok" : 1 }
```

We can then verify that we only have one chunk on *ShardA* by invoking `sh.status()` again.

Adding and removing shards

Adding a new shard to our cluster is as easy as connecting to `mongos`, connecting to the `admin` database, and invoking `runCommand` with the following:

```
> db.runCommand( {
addShard: "mongo_books_replica_set/rs01.packtdb.com:27017", maxSize: 18000,
name: "packt_mongo_shard_UK"
} )
```

This adds a new shard from the replica set named `mongo_books_replica_set` from the `rs01.packtdb.com` host running on port `27017`. We also define the `maxSize` of data for this shard as `18000` MB (or we can set it to `0` to give it no limit) and the name of the new shard as `packt_mongo_shard_UK`.

 This operation will take quite some time to complete as chunks will have to be rebalanced and migrated to the new shard.

Removing a shard, on the other hand, requires more involvement since we have to make sure that we won't lose any data on the way. We do this as follows:

1. First, we need to make sure that the balancer is enabled using `sh.getBalancerState()`. Then, after identifying the shard we want to remove using any one of the `sh.status()`, `db.printShardingStatus()`, or `listShards admin` commands, we connect to the `admin` database and invoke `removeShard` as follows:

   ```
   > use admin
   > db.runCommand( { removeShard: "packt_mongo_shard_UK" } )
   ```

   The output should contain the following:

   ```
   . . .
      "msg" : "draining started successfully",
      "state" : "started",
   . . .
   ```

2. Then, if we invoke the same command again, we get the following:

   ```
   > db.runCommand( { removeShard: "packt_mongo_shard_UK" } )
   ...
   "msg" : "draining ongoing",
      "state" : "ongoing",
      "remaining" : {
         "chunks" : NumberLong(2),
         "dbs" : NumberLong(3)
      },
   ...
   ```

   The remaining document in the result contains the number of `chunks` and `dbs` that are still being transferred. In our case, it's 2 and 3 respectively.

All the commands need to be executed in the `admin` database.

An extra complication in removing a shard can arise if the shard we want to remove serves as the primary shard for one or more of the databases that it contains. The primary shard is allocated by MongoDB when we initiate sharding, so when we remove the shard, we need to manually move these databases to a new shard.

3. We will know whether we need to perform this operation by looking at the following section of the result from `removeShard()`:

```
...
"note" : "you need to drop or movePrimary these databases",
   "dbsToMove" : [
      "mongo_books"
   ],
...
```

We need to drop or `movePrimary` our `mongo_books` database. The way to do this is to first make sure that we are connected to the `admin` database.

We need to wait for all of the chunks to finish migrating before running this command.

4. Make sure that the result contains the following before proceeding:

```
..."remaining" : {
"chunks" : NumberLong(0) }...
```

5. Only after we have made sure that the chunks to be moved are down to zero can we safely run the following command:

```
> db.runCommand( { movePrimary: "mongo_books", to:
"packt_mongo_shard_EU" })
```

6. This command will invoke a blocking operation, and, when it returns, it should have the following result:

```
{ "primary" : "packt_mongo_shard_EU", "ok" : 1 }
```

7. Invoking the same `removeShard()` command after we are all done should return the following result:

```
> db.runCommand( { removeShard: "packt_mongo_shard_UK" } )

... "msg" : "removeshard completed successfully",
   "state" : "completed",
   "shard" : "packt_mongo_shard_UK"
   "ok" : 1
...
```

8. Once we get to `state` as `completed` and `ok` as 1, it is safe to remove our `packt_mongo_shard_UK` shard.

Removing a shard is naturally more complicated than adding one. We need to allow some time, hope for the best, and plan for the worst when performing potentially destructive operations on our live cluster.

Sharding limitations

Sharding comes with great flexibility. Unfortunately, there are a few limitations in the way that we perform some of the operations.

We will highlight the most important ones in the following list:

- The `group()` database command does not work. The `group()` command should not be used anyway; use `aggregate()` and the aggregation framework instead, or `mapreduce()`.
- The `db.eval()` command does not work and should be disabled in most cases for security reasons.
- The `$isolated` option for updates does not work. This is a functionality that is missing in sharded environments. The `$isolated` option for `update()` provides the guarantee that, if we update multiple documents at once, other readers and writers will not see some of the documents updated with the new value, and the others will still have the old value. The way this is implemented in unsharded environments is by holding a global write lock and/or serializing operations to a single thread to make sure that every request for the documents affected by `update()` will not be accessed by other threads/operations. This implementation means that it is not performant and does not support any concurrency, which makes it prohibitive to allow the `$isolated` operator in a sharded environment.
- The `$snapshot` operator for queries is not supported.
  The `$snapshot` operator in the `find()` cursor prevents documents from appearing more than once in the results, as a result of being moved to a different location on the disk after an update. The `$snapshot` operator is operationally expensive and often not a hard requirement. The way to substitute it is by using an index for our queries on a field whose keys will not change for the duration of the query.

- The indexes cannot cover our queries if our queries do not contain the shard key. Results in sharded environments will come from the disk and not exclusively from the index. The only exception is if we query only on the built-in _id field and return only the _id field, in which case, MongoDB can still cover the query using built-in indexes.
- The update() and remove() operations work differently. All update() and remove() operations in a sharded environment must include either the _id of the documents that are to be affected or the shard key; otherwise, the mongos router will have to do a full table scan across all collections, databases, and shards, which would be operationally very expensive.
- Unique indexes across shards need to contain the shard key as a prefix of the index. In other words, to achieve uniqueness of documents across shards, we need to follow the data distribution that MongoDB follows for the shards.
- The shard key has to be up to 512 bytes in size. The shard key index has to be in ascending order on the key field that gets sharded and optionally other fields as well, or a hashed index on it.

The shard key value in a document is also immutable. If our shard key for our User collection is email, then we cannot update the email value for any user after we set it.

Querying sharded data

Querying our data using a MongoDB shard is different than a single-server deployment or a replica set. Instead of connecting to the single server or the primary of the replica set, we connect to the mongos router that decides which shard to ask for our data. In this section, we will explore how the query router operates and use Ruby to illustrate how similar to a replica set this is for the developer .

The query router

The query router, also known as the mongos process, acts as the interface and entry point to our MongoDB cluster. Applications connect to it instead of connecting to the underlying shards and replica sets; mongos executes queries, gathers results and passes them to our application.

The mongos process doesn't hold any persistent state and is typically low on system resources.

The `mongos` process is typically hosted in the same instance as the application server.

It acts as a proxy for requests. When a query comes in, `mongos` will examine and decide which shards need to execute the query and establish a cursor in each one of them.

Find

If our query includes the shard key or a prefix of the shard key, `mongos` will perform a targeted operation, only querying the shards that hold the keys that we are looking for.

For example, with a composite shard key of `{_id, email, address}` on our `User` collection, we can have a targeted operation with any of the following queries:

```
> db.User.find({_id: 1})
> db.User.find({_id: 1, email: 'alex@packt.com'})
> db.User.find({_id: 1, email: 'janluc@packt.com', address: 'Linwood
Dunn'})
```

These queries consist of either a prefix (as is the case with the first two) or the complete shard key.

On the other hand, a query on `{email, address}` or `{address}` will not be able to target the right shards, resulting in a broadcast operation. A broadcast operation is any operation that doesn't include the shard key or a prefix of the shard key, and they result in `mongos` querying every shard and gathering results from them. They are also known as **scatter-and-gather operations** or **fan out queries**.

This behavior is a direct result of the way indexes are organized, and is similar to the behavior that we identified in the chapter about indexing.

Sort/limit/skip

If we want to sort our results, we have the following two options:

- If we are using the shard key in our sort criteria, then `mongos` can determine the order in which it has to query the shard or shards. This results in an efficient and, again, targeted operation.

- If we are not using the shard key in our sort criteria, then, as is the case with a query without any sort criteria, it's going to be a fan out query. To sort the results when we are not using the shard key, the primary shard executes a distributed merge sort locally before passing on the sorted result set to mongos.

A limit on the queries is enforced on each individual shard and then again at the mongos level, as there may be results from multiple shards. A skip operator, on the other hand, cannot be passed on to individual shards, and will be applied by mongos after retrieving all the results locally.

If we combine the skip and limit operators, mongos will optimize the query by passing both values to individual shards. This is particularly useful in cases such as pagination. If we query without sort and the results are coming from more than one shard, mongos will round robin across shards for the results.

Update/remove

In document modifier operations, such as update and remove, we have a similar situation to the one we saw with find. If we have the shard key in the find section of the modifier, then mongos can direct the query to the relevant shard.

If we don't have the shard key in the find section, then it will again be a fanout operation.

The UpdateOne, replaceOne, and removeOne operations must have the shard key or the _id value.

The following table sums up the operations that we can use with sharding:

Type of operation	Query topology
Insert	Must have the shard key
Update	Can have the shard key
Query with shard key	Targeted operation
Query without shard key	Scatter-and-gather operation/fan out query
Indexed, sorted query with shard key	Targeted operation
Indexed, sorted query without shard key	Distributed sort merge

Querying using Ruby

Connecting to a sharded cluster using Ruby is no different than connecting to a replica set. Using the official Ruby driver, we have to configure the `client` object to define the set of `mongos` servers, as shown in the following code:

```
client = Mongo::Client.new('mongodb://key:password@mongos-server1-
host:mongos-server1-port,mongos-server2-host:mongos-server2-
port/admin?ssl=true&authSource=admin')
```

The `mongo-ruby-driver` will then return a `client` object, which is no different than connecting to a replica set from the Mongo Ruby client. We can then use the `client` object as we did in previous chapters, with all the caveats around how sharding behaves differently than a standalone server or a replica set with regards to querying and performance.

Performance comparison with replica sets

Developers and architects are always looking out for ways to compare performance between replica sets and sharded configurations.

The way MongoDB implements sharding is based on top of replica sets. Every shard in production should be a replica set. The main difference in performance comes from fan out queries. When we are querying without the shard key, MongoDB's execution time is limited by the worst performing replica set. In addition, when using sorting without the shard key, the primary server has to implement the distributed merge sort on the entire dataset. This means that it has to collect all data from different shards, merge sort them, and pass them as sorted to `mongos`. In both cases, network latency and limitations in bandwidth can slow down operations, which they wouldn't do with a replica set.

On the flip side, by having three shards, we can distribute our working set requirements across different nodes, thereby serving results from RAM instead of reaching out to the underlying storage, HDD or SSD.

On the other hand, writes can be sped up significantly since we are no longer bound by a single node's I/O capacity, and we can have writes in as many nodes as there are shards. Summing up, in most cases, and especially for the cases where we are using the shard key, both queries and modification operations will be significantly sped up by sharding.

> The shard key is the single most important decision in sharding, and should reflect and apply to our most common application use cases.

Sharding recovery

In this section, we will explore different failure types and how we can recover in a sharded environment. Failure in a distributed system can take multiple forms and shapes. In this section we will cover all the possible cases, from the simplest case of a stateless component like mongos failing to an entire shard going down.

mongos

The mongos process is a relatively lightweight process that holds no state. In the case that the process fails, we can just restart it or spin up a new process in a different server. It's recommended that mongos processes are located in the same server as our application, and so it makes sense to connect from our application using the set of mongos servers that we have colocated in our application servers to ensure a high availability of mongos processes.

mongod

A mongod process failing in a sharded environment is no different than it failing in a replica set. If it is a secondary, the primary and the other secondary (assuming three-node replica sets) will continue as usual.

If it is a mongod process acting as a primary, then an election round will start to elect a new primary in this shard (which is really a replica set).

In both cases, we should actively monitor and try to repair the node as soon as possible, as our availability can be impacted.

Config server

Starting from MongoDB 3.4, config servers are also configured as a replica set. A config server failing is no different than a regular mongod process failing. We should monitor, log, and repair the process.

A shard goes down

Losing an entire shard is pretty rare, and in many cases can be attributed to network partitioning rather than failing processes. When a shard goes down, all operations that would go to this shard will fail. We can (and should) implement fault tolerance in our application level, allowing our application to resume for the operations that can be completed.

Choosing a shard key that can easily map on our operational side can also help; for example, if our shard key is based on location, we may lose the EU shard, but will still be able to write and read data regarding US-based customers through our US shard.

The entire cluster goes down

If we lose the entire cluster, we can't do anything other than get it back up and running as soon as possible. It's important to have monitoring, and to put a proper process in place to understand what needs to be done, when, and by whom, should this ever happen.

Recovering when the entire cluster goes down essentially involves restoring from backups and setting up new shards, which is complicated and will take time. Dry testing this in a staging environment is also advisable, as is investing in regular backups via MongoDB Ops Manager or any other backup solution.

A member of each shard's replica set could be in a different location for disaster-recovery purposes.

Further reading

The following sources are recommended for you to study sharding in depth:

- *Scaling MongoDB* by Kristina Chodorow
- *MongoDB: The Definitive Guide* by Kristina Chodorow and Michael Dirolf
- `https://docs.mongodb.com/manual/sharding/`
- `https://www.mongodb.com/blog/post/mongodb-16-released`
- `https://github.com/mongodb/mongo/blob/r3.4.2-rc0/src/mongo/s/commands/cluster_shard_collection_cmd.cpp#L469`

- https://www.mongodb.com/blog/post/sharding-pitfalls-part-iii-chunk-balancing-and
- http://plusnconsulting.com/post/mongodb-sharding-and-chunks/
- https://github.com/mongodb/mongo/wiki/Sharding-Internals
- http://learnmongodbthehardway.com/schema/sharding
- http://learnmongodbthehardway.com/schema/sharding/
- https://www.infoq.com/news/2010/08/MongoDB-1.6
- http://www.pc-freak.net/images/horizontal-vs-vertical-scaling-vertical-and-horizontal-scaling-explained-diagram.png

Summary

In this chapter, we explored sharding, one of the most interesting features of MongoDB. We started with an architectural overview of sharding and moved on to how we can design a shard and choose the right shard key.

We learned about monitoring, administration, and the limitations that come with sharding. We also learned about mongos, the MongoDB sharding router that directs our queries to the correct shard. Finally, we discussed recovery from common failure types in a MongoDB sharded environment.

The next chapter on fault tolerance and high availability will offer some useful tips and tricks that have not been covered in the 11 other chapters.

14
Fault Tolerance and High Availability

In this chapter, we will try to fit in the information that we didn't manage to discuss in the previous chapters, and we will place emphasis on some other topics. Throughout the previous 13 chapters, we have gone all the way from the basic concepts to effective querying, to administration and data management, to scaling and high availability concepts.

In this chapter, we will cover the following topics:

- We will discuss how our application design should be accommodating and proactive with regard to our database needs.
- Day-to-day operations are another area that we will discuss, including tips and best practices that can help us to avoid nasty surprises down the line.
- In light of recent attempts by ransomware to infect and hold MongoDB servers hostage, we will offer more tips on security.
- Finally, we will try to sum up the advice that's been given in a series of checklists that should be followed to ensure that the best practices are properly set up and followed.

Application design

In this section, we will describe some useful tips for application design that we did not cover or emphasize enough in the previous chapters.

Schema-less doesn't mean schema design-less

A big part of MongoDB's success can be attributed to the increased popularity of ORM/ODMs. Especially with languages like JavaScript and the MEAN stack, the developer can use JavaScript from the frontend (Angular/Express) to the backend (Node.js) to the database (MongoDB). This is frequently coupled with an ODM that abstracts away the internals of the database, mapping collections to Node.js models.

The major advantage is that developers don't need to fiddle with the database schema design, as this is automatically provided by the ODM. The downside is that database collections and schema designs are left up to the ODM, which does not have the business domain knowledge of different fields and access patterns.

In the case of MongoDB and other NoSQL-based databases, this boils down to making architectural decisions based not only on immediate needs, but also on what needs to be done down the line. On an architectural level, this may mean that instead of a monolithic approach, we can combine different database technologies for our diverse and evolving needs by using a graph database for graph-related querying, a relational database for hierarchical, unbounded data, and MongoDB for JSON retrieval, processing, and storage.

In fact, many of MongoDB's successful use cases come from the fact that it's not being used as a one-size-fits-all solution, but only for the use cases that make sense.

Read performance optimization

In this section, we will discuss some tips for optimizing read performance. Read performance is directly correlated to the number of queries and their complexity. Performing fewer queries in a schema without complex nested data structures and arrays will generally result in better read performance. However, many times, optimizing for read performance can mean that the write performance will degrade. This is something to keep in mind and continuously measure when we are making performance optimizations in MongoDB.

Consolidating read querying

We should aim to have as few queries as possible. This can be achieved by embedding information into sub-documents instead of having separate entities. This can lead to an increased write load, as we have to keep the same data points in multiple documents and maintain their values everywhere when they change in one place.

The design considerations here are as follows:

- The read performance benefits from data duplication/denormalization.
- The data integrity benefits from data references (DBRef or in-application code, using an attribute as a foreign key).

We should denormalize, especially if our read/write ratio is too high (our data rarely changes values, but it gets accessed several times in between) if our data can afford to be inconsistent for brief periods of time, and, most importantly, if we absolutely need our reads to be as fast as possible and are willing to pay the price in consistency/write performance.

The most obvious candidates for fields that we should denormalize (embed) are dependent fields. If we have an attribute or a document structure that we don't plan to query on its own, but only as part of a contained attribute/document, then it makes sense to embed it, rather than have it in a separate document/collection.

Using our MongoDB books example, a book can have a related data structure that refers to a review from a reader of the book. If our most common use case is showing a book along with its associated reviews, then we can embed reviews into the book document.

The downside to this design is that when we want to find all of the book reviews by a user, this will be costly, as we will have to iterate all of the books for the associated reviews. Denormalizing users and embedding their reviews can be a solution to this problem.

A counterexample is data that can grow unbounded. In our example, embedding reviews along with heavy metadata can lead to an issue if we hit the 16 MB document size limit. A solution is to distinguish between data structures that we expect to grow rapidly and those that we don't, and to keep an eye on their sizes through monitoring processes that query our live dataset at off-peak times and reporting on attributes that may pose a risk down the line.

 Don't embed data that can grow unbounded.

When we embed attributes, we have to decide whether we will use a sub-document or an enclosing array.

When we have a unique identifier to access the sub-document, we should embed it as a sub-document. If we don't know exactly how to access it or we need the flexibility to be able to query for an attribute's values, then we should embed it in an array.

For example, with our `books` collection, if we decide to embed reviews into each book document, we have the following two design options:

- A book document with an array:

```
{
Isbn: '1001',
Title: 'Mastering MongoDB',
Reviews: [
{ 'user_id': 1, text: 'great book', rating: 5 },
{ 'user_id': 2, text: 'not so bad book', rating: 3 },
]
}
```

- A book with an embedded document:

```
{
Isbn: '1001',
Title: 'Mastering MongoDB',
Reviews:
{ 'user_id': 1, text: 'great book', rating: 5 },
{ 'user_id': 2, text: 'not so bad book', rating: 3 },
}
```

The array structure has the advantage that we can directly query MongoDB for all of the reviews with a `rating` greater than 4 through the embedded array reviews.

Using the embedded document structure, on the other hand, we can retrieve all of the reviews the same way that we would using the array, but if we want to filter them, it has to be done on the application side, rather than on the database side.

Defensive coding

More of a generic principle, **defensive coding** refers to a set of practices and software designs that ensures the continuing functionality of a piece of software under unforeseen circumstances.

It prioritizes code quality, readability, and predictability. Readability was best explained by John F. Woods in his *comp.lang.c++* post, on September 24, 1991:

> *"Always code as if the guy who ends up maintaining your code will be a violent psychopath who knows where you live. Code for readability."*

Our code should be readable and understandable by humans, as well as by machines. With code quality metrics, as derived by static analysis tools, code reviews, and bugs reported/resolved, we can estimate the quality of our code base and aim for a certain threshold at each sprint, or when we are ready to release. Code predictability, on the other hand, means we should always expect results in unexpected input and program states.

These principles apply to every software system. In the context of system programming using MongoDB, there are some extra steps that we must take to ensure that code predictability and, subsequently, quality are measured by the number of resulting bugs.

MongoDB limitations that will result in a loss of database functionality should be monitored and evaluated on a periodic basis, as follows:

- **Document size limit**: We should keep an eye on the collections in which we expect to have documents growing the most, running a background script to examine document sizes and alert us if we have documents approaching the limit (16 MB), or if the average size has grown significantly since the last check.
- **Data integrity checks**: If we are using denormalization for read optimization, then it's a good practice to check for data integrity. Through a software bug or a database error, we may end up with inconsistent duplicate data among collections.
- **Schema checks**: If we don't want to use the document validation feature of MongoDB, but rather we want a lax document schema, it's still a good idea to periodically run scripts to identify fields that are present in our documents, and their frequencies. Then, along with relative access patterns, we can identify whether these fields can be identified and consolidated. This is mostly useful if we are ingesting data from another system wherein data input changes over time, which may result in a wildly varying document structure on our end.
- **Data storage checks**: This mostly applies when using MMAPv1, where document padding optimization can help performance. By keeping an eye on document size relative to its padding, we can make sure that our size-modifying updates won't incur a move of the document in physical storage.

These are the basic checks that we should implement when defensively coding for our MongoDB application. On top of this, we need to defensively code our application-level code to make sure that when failures occur in MongoDB, our application will continue operating—perhaps with degraded performance, but still operational.

An example of this is replica set failover and failback. When our replica set master fails, there is a brief period to detect this failure and the new master is elected, promoted, and operational. During this brief period, we should make sure that our application continues to operate in read-only mode, instead of throwing **500** errors. In most cases, electing a new primary is done in seconds, but in some cases we may end up in the minority end of a network partition and unable to contact a master for a long period of time. Similarly, some secondaries may end up in a recovering state (for example, if they fall way behind the master in replication); our application should be able to pick a different secondary in this case.

Designing for secondary access is one of the most useful examples of defensive coding. Our application should weigh between fields that can only be accessed by the primary to ensure data consistency and fields that are okay to be updated in near real-time, instead of in real time, in which case we can read these from secondary servers. By keeping track of replication lag for our secondaries by using automated scripts, we can have a view of our cluster's load and how safe it is to enable this functionality.

Another defensive coding practice is to always perform writes with journaling on. Journaling helps to recover from server crashes and power failures.

Finally, we should aim to use replica sets as early as possible. Other than the performance and workload improvements, they help us to recover from server failures.

Monitoring integrations

All of this adds up to a greater adoption of monitoring tools and services. As much as we can script some of them, integrating with cloud and on-premise monitoring tools can help us to achieve more in a smaller amount of time.

The metrics that we keep a track of should do one of the following:

- **Detect failures**: Failure detection is a reactive process, where we should have clear protocols in place for what happens when each of the failure detection flags goes off. For example, what should the recovery steps be if we lose a server, a replica set, or a shard?
- **Prevent failures**: Failure prevention, on the other hand, is a proactive process, designed to help us catch problems before they become a potential source of failure in the future. For example, CPU/storage/memory usage should be actively monitored with yellow and red thresholds, and clear processes should be put in place as to what we should do in the event that we reach either threshold.

Operations

When connecting to our production MongoDB servers, we want to make sure that our operations are as lightweight as possible (and are certainly non-destructive) and do not alter the database state in any sense.

The two useful utilities that we can chain to our queries are as follows:

```
> db.collection.find(query).maxTimeMS(999)
```

Our `query` will only take up to 999 ms, and will then return an exceeded time limit error:

```
> db.collection.find(query).maxScan(1000)
```

Our `query` will examine 1000 documents at the most, in order to find results and then return (no error raised).

Whenever we can, we should bind our queries by time or document result size to avoid running unexpectedly long queries that may affect our production database. A common reason for accessing our production database is troubleshooting degraded cluster performance. This can be investigated via cloud monitoring tools, as we described in previous chapters.

The `db.currentOp()` command, through the MongoDB shell, will give us a list of all of the current operations. We can then isolate the ones that have large `.secs_running` values and identify them through the `.query` field.

If we want to kill an in-progress operation that takes a long time, we need to note the value of the `.opid` field and pass it on `db.killOp(<opid>)`.

Finally, it's important to recognize (from an operational standpoint) that everything may go wrong. We must have a backup strategy in place that is implemented consistently. Most importantly, we should practice restoring from backup to make sure that it works as intended.

Security

After the recent waves of ransomware that were locking down unsecured MongoDB servers, asking for ransom payments in cryptocurrency from the administrators to unlock the MongoDB servers, many developers have become more security-conscious. Security is one of the items on a checklist that we, as developers, may not prioritize highly enough, due to the optimistic belief that it won't happen to us. The truth is, in the modern internet landscape, everyone can be a target of automated or directed attacks, so security should always be taken into account, from the early stages of the design to after production deployment.

Enabling security by default

Every database (other than local development servers, perhaps) should be set up with the following in the `mongod.conf` file:

```
auth = true
```

 SSL should always be enabled, as we described in the relevant Chapter 8, *Monitoring, Backup, and Security*.

REST and HTTP status interfaces should be disabled by adding the following lines to `mongod.conf`:

```
nohttpinterface = true
rest = false
```

Access should be restricted to only communication between application servers and MongoDB servers, and only in the interfaces that are required. Using `bind_ip`, we can force MongoDB to listen to specific interfaces, instead of the default binding to every interface-available behavior:

```
bind_ip = 10.10.0.10,10.10.0.20
```

Isolating our servers

We should secure our infrastructure perimeter with AWS VPC or the equivalent from the cloud provider of our choice. As an extra layer of security, we should isolate our servers in a cloud of their own, only allowing external connections to reach our application servers and never allowing them to directly connect to our MongoDB servers:

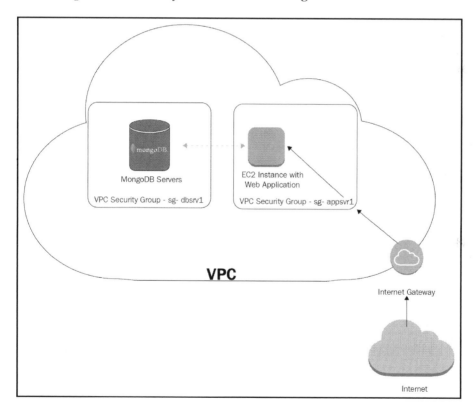

We should invest in role-based authorization. Security lies not only in protecting against data leaks caused by external actors, but also in making sure that internal actors have the appropriate levels of access to our data. Using role-based authorization at the MongoDB level, we can make sure that our users have the appropriate levels of access.

Consider Enterprise Edition for large deployments. Enterprise Edition offers some convenient features concerning security, more integrations with well-known tools, and should be evaluated for large deployments, with an eye for changing needs as we transition from a single replica set to an enterprise-complex architecture.

Checklists

Operations require the completion of many tasks and complexity. A good practice is to keep a set of checklists with all of the tasks that need to be performed and their order of significance. This will ensure that we don't let something slip through. A deployment and security checklist, for example, could be as follows:

- **Hardware**:
  - **Storage**: How much disk space is needed per node? What is the growth rate?
  - **Storage technology**: Do we need SSD versus HDD? What is the throughput of our storage?
  - **RAM**: What is the expected working set? Can we fit it in the RAM? If not, are we going to be okay with SSD instead of HDD? What is the growth rate?
  - **CPU**: This usually isn't a concern for MongoDB, but it could be if we planned to run CPU-intensive jobs in our cluster (for example, aggregation or `MapReduce`).
  - **Network**: What are the network links between servers? This is usually trivial if we are using a single data center, but it can get complicated if we have multiple data centers and/or offsite servers for disaster recovery.

- **Security**:
    - Enable auth.
    - Enable SSL.
    - Disable REST/HTTP interfaces.
    - Isolate our servers (for example, VPC).
    - Authorization is enabled. With great power comes great responsibility. Make sure that the powerful users are the ones that you trust. Don't give potentially destructive powers to inexperienced users.

A monitoring and operations checklist could be as follows:

- **Monitoring**:
    - Usage of hardware (CPU, memory, storage, and network).
    - Health checks, using Pingdom or an equivalent service to make sure that we get a notification when one of our servers fails.
    - Client performance monitoring: Integrating periodic mystery shopper tests using service as a customer in a manual or automated way, from an end-to-end perspective, in order to find out if it behaves as expected. We don't want to learn about application performance issues from our customers.
    - Use MongoDB Cloud Manager monitoring; it has a free tier, it can provide useful metrics, and it is the tool that MongoDB engineers can take a look at if we run into issues and need their help, especially as a part of support contracts.

- **Disaster recovery**:
    - **Evaluate the risk**: What is the risk, from a business perspective, of losing MongoDB data? Can we recreate this dataset? If yes, how costly is it in terms of time and effort?
    - **Devise a plan**: Have a plan for each failure scenario, with the exact steps that we need to take in case something happens.
    - **Test the plan**: Having a dry run of every recovery strategy is as important as having one. Many things can go wrong in disaster recovery, and having an incomplete plan (or one that fails in each purpose) is something that we shouldn't allow to happen under any circumstance.

- **Have an alternative to the plan**: No matter how well we devise a plan and test it, anything can go wrong during planning, testing, or execution. We need to have a backup plan for our plan, in case we can't recover our data using plan A. This is also called plan B, or the last resort plan. It doesn't have to be efficient, but it should alleviate any business reputation risks.
- **Load test**: We should make sure that we load test our application end to end before deployment, with a realistic workload. This is the only way to ensure that our application will behave as expected.

Further reading

You can refer to the following links for further information:

- `http://mo.github.io/2017/01/22/mongo-db-tips-and-tricks.html`
- `https://studio3t.com/whats-new/tips-for-sql-users-new-to-mongodb/`
- `https://www.hostreview.com/blog/170327-top-7-mongodb-performance-tips-must-know`
- `https://groups.google.com/forum/#!msg/comp.lang.c++/rYCO5yn4lXw/oITtSkZOtoUJ`

Summary

In this chapter, we covered some topics that were not detailed in previous chapters. It is important to apply the best practices according to our workload requirements. Read performance is usually what we want to optimize for; that is why we discussed consolidating queries and the denormalization of our data.

Operations are also important when we go from deployment to ensuring the continuous performance and availability of our cluster. Security is something that we often don't think about until it affects us. That's why we should invest the time beforehand to plan and make sure that we have the measures in place to be sufficiently secure.

Finally, we introduced the concept of checklists to keep track of our tasks and to make sure that we complete all of them before major operational events (deployment, cluster upgrades, moving to sharding from replica sets, and so on).

Other Books You May Enjoy

If you enjoyed this book, you may be interested in these other books by Packt:

MongoDB 4 Quick Start Guide
Doug Bierer

ISBN: 9781789343533

- Get a standard MongoDB database up and running quickly
- Perform simple CRUD operations on the database using the MongoDB command shell
- Set up a simple aggregation pipeline to return subsets of data grouped, sorted, and filtered
- Safeguard your data via replication and handle massive amounts of data via sharding
- Publish data from a web form to the database using a program language driver
- Explore the basic CRUD operations performed using the PHP MongoDB driver

MongoDB Administrator's Guide

Cyrus Dasadia

ISBN: 9781787126480

- Install and deploy MongoDB in production
- Manage and implement optimal indexes
- Optimize monitoring in MongoDB
- Fine-tune the performance of your queries
- Debug and diagnose your database's performance
- Optimize database backups and recovery and ensure high availability
- Make your MongoDB instance scalable
- Implement security and user authentication features in MongoDB
- Master optimal cloud deployment strategies

Leave a review - let other readers know what you think

Please share your thoughts on this book with others by leaving a review on the site that you bought it from. If you purchased the book from Amazon, please leave us an honest review on this book's Amazon page. This is vital so that other potential readers can see and use your unbiased opinion to make purchasing decisions, we can understand what our customers think about our products, and our authors can see your feedback on the title that they have worked with Packt to create. It will only take a few minutes of your time, but is valuable to other potential customers, our authors, and Packt. Thank you!

Index

Printed in Great Britain
by Amazon